Developmentally Appropriate Practice

in Early Childhood Programs

REVISED EDITION

Sue Bredekamp and Carol Copple, Editors

National Association for the Education of Young Children

Washington, D.C.

First edition 1986. Expanded edition 1987. Revised edition 1997. Second printing 1997. Third printing 1998.

National Association for the Education of Young Children
1509 16th Street, NW
Washington, DC 20036-1426
202-232-8777 or 800-424-2460
Website: http://www.naeyc.org

The National Association for the Education of Young Children (NAEYC) attempts through its publications program to provide a forum for discussion of major issues and ideas in our field. We hope to provoke thought and promote professional growth. Part 1 is an official position of NAEYC, adopted July 1996. NAEYC wishes to thank the editors and all who donated their time to the development of this book as a contribution to our profession.

Photographs copyright © by:
C.W. Shields/page 1 top
Renaud Thomas/1 bottom, 22, 53 top left & top right
Harvey Phillips/5
Dr. Vme Edom Smith/12, 42, 145
Francis Wardle/18, 31, 37, 49, 111, 150, 153, 158
BmPorter/Don Franklin/35, 45, 46, 154
Michael Siluk/39, 40, 67, 157
CLEO Photography/50, 139 top right
Robert Settles/53 bottom right
Hildegard Adler/57, 63, 53 bottom left, 95 bottom right, 179
Robert Hill/61, 143
Marilyn Nolt/69, 118, 139 top left & bottom right
Betty C. Ford/95 top right
Marti McDonald/95 top left
Cris Kelly/95 bottom left
Bettina Bairley/100
Eva Anthony/106
Marietta Lynch/114
Nancy P. Alexander/121, 136
Tyroler & Cooper/139 bottom left
Dena Bawinkel/146
Barbara Comnes/149

Library of Congress Catalog Number: 96-71189

ISBN Catalog Number: 0-935989-79-X

NAEYC #234

Book design/production: Jack Zibulsky; *Copyediting:* Millie Riley; *Editorial assistance:* Sandi Collins, Anika Trahan, and Roma White.

Printed in the United States of America.

Contents

Preface

The National Association for the Education of Young Children (NAEYC), the nation's largest professional organization of early childhood educators, published position statements on developmentally appropriate practice in 1986 and 1987 (Bredekamp 1987). The documents were developed in response to specific, identified needs within a historical context (Bredekamp 1991). The primary purpose of the position statements was to provide guidance to program personnel seeking accreditation by NAEYC's National Academy of Early Childhood Programs. The accreditation criteria call for "developmentally appropriate" activities, materials, and expectations (Bredekamp 1984; NAEYC 1991). A second, more widely applicable purpose for the guidelines was to respond to a growing trend toward more formal, academic instruction of young children—a trend characterized by downward escalation of public school curriculum (Shepard & Smith 1988).

At the time, many early childhood programs were placing undue emphasis on rote learning and whole-group instruction of narrowly defined academic skills at the expense of more active learning approaches based on a broader interpretation of children's educational needs and abilities. Testing, placement, and retention practices also raised serious concerns (NAEYC 1988; Bredekamp & Shepard 1989). As a result of readiness and screening practices that reflected many of the same narrowly defined academic goals that characterized primary-grade curricula, an increasing proportion of children were being identified as unready for kindergarten or first grade and were being assigned to transition classes, retained in grade, or denied enrollment.

These trends were especially evident in kindergartens and primary grades where next-grade expectations were imposed on earlier grades regardless of children's current interests, needs, and competencies. However, concern about appropriate practices also applied across the early childhood age span. Increasing numbers of infants and toddlers were being served in group-care settings where expectations and practices more appropriate for older children were too often imposed on them.

On the basis of these concerns, NAEYC assumed a leadership role in adopting guidelines for developmentally appropriate practice. The primary position was that programs designed *for* young children be based on what is known *about* young children. The guidelines also reflected a clear commitment regarding the rights of young children to respectful and supportive learning environments and to an education that would prepare them for participation in a free and democratic society.

Since their publication, the guidelines have served an important function for the early childhood field, nationally and internationally. That the guidelines met a need in the profession is clear, given that more than half a million copies of the book's position statement and several million brochures have been distributed. The guidelines' usefulness in contributing to policy and program evaluation decisions is reflected in their adoption by numerous state departments of education in this country (e.g., Maine 1987; California 1988, 1993; Connecticut 1988, 1990; Maryland 1989, 1992; Missouri 1989; Minnesota 1990; Stark County [Ohio] 1991; Nebraska/Iowa 1993; Colorado 1994; Texas 1994), and in several other countries (British Columbia 1990a & b, 1991; Australia 1993; New Zealand 1996). Similarly, other national education organizations took positions on early childhood education that are congruent with NAEYC's statement (e.g., NAECS/SDE 1987; NASBE 1988; IRA 1989; NAESP 1990; SREB 1995).

Like all NAEYC position statements, the documents reflected current understandings, values, and goals at the time of their publication. This knowledge base is derived from reviewing the literature as well as review by many experienced, knowledgeable early childhood educators. As is true in any profession, such bases for decisionmaking are expected to be dynamic and changing in response to new knowledge as well as to benefit from the shared experiences of and interactions among professionals. Given this expectation of change, the Association reviews and revises all position statements periodically to ensure their currency and accuracy; NAEYC anticipates the review process for this document will occur regularly (at least every seven years with a revised document every 10 years).

Perhaps the most important contribution of the 1987 developmentally appropriate practice position statements was that they created an opportunity for increased conversation within and outside our field about our early childhood practice. As a result, the 1987 edition itself established a new context in which early childhood programs operate. Thus, as numerous programs used the guidelines to improve practices, a great deal was learned that expanded our knowledge. In addition, there was also widespread misinterpretation (and, at times, misrepresentation) of the concept of developmentally appropriate practice (Bredekamp 1991; Bredekamp & Rosegrant 1992; Kostelnik 1992). Also observed was a trend to co-opt the concept (with commercially prepared curriculum and even tests labeled as "DAP"). Thus, another purpose of the regular revision process is to more clearly address ideas that are easily susceptible to misunderstanding.

The revision process also enables the Association to respond in a thoughtful fashion to critiques that challenge the premises, processes, and effects of the position statement. Thus, the current review process has been even more extensive than the original, including a review of current research and theory, written critiques of the positions (e.g., Bloch 1991; Kessler 1991; Spodek 1991; Swadener & Kessler 1991; McGill-Franzen 1993; Reifel 1993; Mallory & New 1994; Fleer 1995), and the solicitation of input from NAEYC members through articles in *Young Children* and other journals, as well as through open hearings held throughout the country and during NAEYC annual conferences and at meetings of other professional groups.

Experts serving on NAEYC's Panel on Revisions to Developmentally Appropriate Practice worked for more than two years advising on the proposed revisions to the position statement. NAEYC is very grateful for their significant contributions of wisdom and time to this important project. Panel members were Barbara Bowman, Victoria Fu, Lilian Katz, Rebecca New, Carol Brunson Phillips, Teresa Rosegrant, and Deborah Ziegler; Sue Bredekamp served as staff to the Panel. One goal for the revised position statement is that it will stimulate the kind of serious debate and dialogue that characterized the work of the Panel.

Among the most frequent themes of the Panel's discussions was the need to move beyond the *either/or* polarizing debates in the early childhood field (a trend toward which NAEYC's 1987 document, contrasting appropriate and inappropriate practice, inadvertently contributed) to more *both/and* thinking that better reflects the complexity of the decisions inherent in the work of early childhood education. The revised position statement continues "to take a position" on issues of controversy in the field and also emphasizes that some practices are inappropriate and even harmful to children. Nevertheless, the document acknowledges that there are many ways for practices to be developmentally appropri-

ate, just as there is more than one way to err in decisions about how to support children's development.

As a result of this review and revision process, this updated edition represents NAEYC's current best understanding of theory and research regarding how children learn as well as shared beliefs about what practices are most supportive and respectful of children's healthy development. The guidelines for developmentally appropriate practice described here vary from the 1987 document not only in currency but also in increased attention to issues of appropriate curriculum content and assessment, issues that are addressed more thoroughly in a separate position statement of NAEYC and NAECS/SDE (1992; Bredekamp & Rosegrant 1992, 1995).

This document is intended for use by teachers, administrators, curriculum developers, parents, policymakers, and others involved with programs serving young children, birth through age 8, in schools, centers, and homes. As with so many NAEYC projects, it represents the thoughtful suggestions and careful review of hundreds of early childhood professionals. In addition, the position statement following on pages 3–30 was officially approved by NAEYC's Governing Board in July 1996.

This revised edition builds on the fundamental principles articulated in the previous edition and expands them to better reflect the

1. critical role of the teacher in supporting children's development and learning;

2. concept of classrooms or groups of children as communities of learners in which relationships among adults and groups of children support development and learning;

3. role of culture in the processes of development and learning and the fact that all development and learning occur in and are influenced by sociocultural contexts;

4. significant role of families in early childhood education;

5. applicability of the principles to children with disabilities and other special learning and developmental needs;

6. importance of meaningful and contextually relevant curriculum;

7. necessity of assessment practices that are authentic and meaningful for children and families; and

8. importance of an infrastructure of policy and adequate resources to support delivery of high-quality, developmentally appropriate programs for all children.

Overview of the book

NAEYC's revised "Position Statement on Developmentally Appropriate Practice in Early Childhood Programs Serving Children from Birth through Age 8" appears as Part 1 of this book. Adopted by the NAEYC Governing Board in July 1996, the position statement defines developmentally appropriate practice as the outcome of a process of teacher decisionmaking that draws on at least three critical, interrelated bodies of knowledge: (1) what teachers know about how children develop and learn; (2) what teachers know about the individual children in their group; and (3) knowledge of the social and cultural context in which those children live and learn. The other parts of this book provide elaboration and examples to help teachers think about applying the principles and guidelines contained in the position statement. Only Part 1 is an official position of the Association.

In Part 2, Sue Bredekamp describes and illustrates the teacher decisionmaking process inherent in developmentally appropriate practice. This section is based on experiences over the last several years, during which time an NAEYC Panel of experts (listed earlier) thoroughly debated the issues and controversies related to the concept of developmentally appropriate practice. Members of the Panel held sessions or open hearings at various meetings throughout the United States and in several other countries, receiving input from thousands of early childhood professionals. The Panel's work was marked by informed and respectful dialogue that included many strong differences of opinion. The process of engaging in serious reflection about early childhood practice, learning from one another, expanding our personal perspectives, and working toward resolution of our disagreements was not only professionally rewarding for all of us but also mirrored the kind of decisionmaking process that early childhood professionals engage in every day. This process is described in more detail in Part 2 in the hope that the publication of NAEYC's revised position statement will encourage other early childhood professionals to engage in serious reflection about their practice.

Making informed decisions about teaching young children requires that teachers have knowledge on which to base their practices. In subsequent parts of this book, we provide more specific descriptions and examples to inform this decisionmaking process for teachers working with children in each of three age groups: infants and toddlers (Part 3); preschoolers and kindergartners, 3- through 5-year-olds (Part 4); and primary-grade children, ages 6 through 8 (Part 5). Each part provides a sketch of characteristics and widely held expectations of children at this period of the life span, with considerations for practices that are consistent or inconsistent, in our view, with the principles and guidelines of the position statement—that is, that are appropriate or inappropriate.

Subdividing the early childhood age span into parts is always arbitrary because of children's individual differences. In fact, NAEYC believes that all early childhood professionals should be knowledgeable about working with children from birth through age 8 (NAEYC, DEC/CEC, & NBPTS 1996). With many early childhood programs using multiage or family grouping (as is common practice in family child care) and more teachers staying with the same children over several years, the need increases for teachers to understand the full age span.

This revised edition continues to include charts that contrast appropriate and inappropriate practices. The decision to include these charts was not made lightly. Panel members were concerned that in the 1987 edition such charts at times contributed to misunderstanding and oversimplification of the concepts of developmentally appropriate practice. Nevertheless, we also heard from many early childhood professionals that the charts were important tools for education and advocacy. Therefore, we have revised the charts to achieve several goals. We hope to maintain their power to help people understand developmentally appropriate practices by visualizing both positive and negative exemplars of the concepts. We encourage early childhood professionals to use these charts not as prescriptions but to stimulate reflection, debate, and discussion of their practice. We expanded the charts to include more examples of both appropriate and inappropriate practices (practices that are more or less congruent with the principles and guidelines of NAEYC's position statement). And finally, we clearly identify these charts as examples, not official position statements.

The knowledge base informing early childhood practice has greatly increased in the last decade, building on the rich contributions of scholars and practitioners of the past. The challenge for early childhood teachers and teacher educators is to remain lifelong learners in this growing and changing profession—a challenge that, as developmentalists, we embrace.

References

Australia National Childcare Accreditation Council. 1993. *Putting children first: Quality improvement and accreditation system.* Sydney: Author.

Bloch, M. 1991. Critical science and the history of child development's influence on early education research. *Early Education and Development* 2 (2): 95–108.

Bredekamp, S., ed. 1984. *Accreditation criteria & procedures of the National Academy of Early Childhood Programs.* Washington, DC: NAEYC.

Bredekamp, S., ed. 1987. *Developmentally appropriate practice in early childhood programs serving children from birth through age 8.* Exp. ed. Washington, DC: NAEYC.

Bredekamp, S. 1991. Redeveloping early childhood education: A response to Kessler. *Early Childhood Research Quarterly* 6 (2): 199–209.

Bredekamp, S., & T. Rosegrant, eds. 1992. *Reaching potentials: Appropriate curriculum and assessment for young children, volume 1.* Washington, DC: NAEYC.

Bredekamp, S., & T. Rosegrant, eds. 1995. *Reaching potentials: Transforming early childhood curriculum and assessment, volume 2.* Washington, DC: NAEYC.

Bredekamp, S., & L. Shepard. 1989. How best to protect children from inappropriate school expectations, practices, and policies. *Young Children* 44 (3): 14–24.

British Columbia Ministry of Education. 1990a. *Primary program foundation document.* Victoria, BC, Canada: Author.

British Columbia Ministry of Education. 1990b. *Primary program resource document.* Victoria, BC, Canada: Author.

British Columbia Ministry of Education. 1991. *Supporting learning: Understanding and assessing the progress of children in the primary grades. A resource for parents and teachers.* Victoria, BC, Canada: Author.

California Kindergarten Association. 1993. *Exemplary programs criteria: A process guide for improvement through collaboration.* San Mateo: Author.

California State Department of Education. 1988. *Here they come: Ready or not—Report of the School Readiness Task Force.* Sacramento: Author.

Colorado State Department of Education. 1994. *Quality standards for early childhood care and education services.* Denver: Author.

Connecticut State Department of Education. 1988. *Guide to program development for kindergarten.* Hartford: Author.

Connecticut State Department of Education. 1990. *The teacher's ongoing role in creating a developmentally appropriate early childhood program: A self-study process for teachers of children ages 5–8.* Hartford: Author.

Fleer, M., ed. 1995. *DAPcentrism: Challenging developmentally appropriate practice.* Watson ACT: Australian Early Childhood Association.

IRA (International Reading Association). 1989. *Literacy development and prefirst grade.* Newark, DE: Author.

Kessler, S. 1991. Alternative perspectives on early childhood education. *Early Childhood Research Quarterly* 7 (2): 183–97.

Kostelnik, M. 1992. Myths associated with developmentally appropriate programs. *Young Children* 47 (4): 17–23.

Maine Department of Educational and Cultural Services. 1987. *A framework for curriculum design: People, process, and product.* Augusta: Author.

Mallory, B., & R. New. 1994. *Diversity and developmentally appropriate practices: Challenges for early childhood education.* New York: Teachers College Press.

Maryland Commission on the Early Learning Years. 1992. *Laying the foundation for school success: Recommendations for improving early learning programs.* Baltimore: Maryland State Department of Education.

Maryland State Department of Education. 1989. *Standards for implementing quality prekindergarten education.* ERIC, ED 238 525. Baltimore: Maryland State Department of Education, Division of Instruction, Language, and Supplementary Programs.

McGill-Franzen, A. 1993. *Shaping the preschool agenda: Early literacy, public policy, and professional beliefs.* Albany: State University of New York Press.

Minnesota State Department of Education. 1990. *Model learner outcomes for early childhood education programs, birth to 9 years.* St. Paul: Author.

Missouri Department of Elementary and Secondary Education. 1989. *Project Construct: Curriculum and assessment specifications.* St. Louis: Author.

NAECS/SDE (National Association of Early Childhood Specialists in State Departments of Education). 1987. Unacceptable trends in kindergarten entry and placement. Unpublished paper.

NAESP (National Association of Elementary School Principals). 1990. *Standards for quality programs for young children: Early childhood education and the elementary school principal.* Alexandria, VA: Author.

NAEYC. 1988. Position statement on standardized testing of young children 3 through 8 years of age. *Young Children* 43 (3): 42–47.

NAEYC. 1991. *Accreditation criteria and procedures of the National Academy of Early Childhood Programs.* Rev. ed. Washington, DC: Author.

NAEYC & NAECS/SDE (National Association of Early Childhood Specialists in State Departments of Education). 1992. Guidelines for appropriate curriculum content and assessment in programs serving children ages 3 through 8. In *Reaching potentials: Appropriate curriculum and assessment for young children, volume 1,* eds. S. Bredekamp & T. Rosegrant, 9–27. Washington, DC: NAEYC.

NAEYC, DED/CEC, & NBPTS (Division for Early Childhood/Council for Exceptional Children & National Board for Professional Teaching Standards). 1996. *Guidelines for preparation of early childhood professionals.* Washington, DC: NAEYC.

NASBE (National Association of State Boards of Education). 1988. *Right from the start.* Alexandria, VA: Author.

Nebraska and Iowa State Departments of Education. 1993. *The primary program: Growing and learning in the heartland. A joint project of Nebraska Department of Education, Iowa Department of Education, Iowa Area Education Agencies, & Head Start/State Collaboration Project.* Lincoln, NE: Author.

New Zealand Ministry of Education. 1996. *Te Whariki: Early childhood curriculum.* Wellington: Author.

Reifel, S., ed. 1993. Introduction. In *Perspectives on developmentally appropriate practice,* vol. 5 of *Advances in early education and day care,* ix. Greenwich, CT: JAI Press.

Shepard, L., & M. Smith. 1988. Escalating academic demand in kindergarten: Some nonsolutions. *Elementary School Journal* 89 (2): 135–46.

Spodek, B. 1991. Early childhood curriculum and cultural definitions of knowledge. In *Issues in early childhood curriculum,* eds. B. Spodek & O. Saracho, 1–20. New York: Teachers College Press.

SREB (Southern Regional Educational Board). 1995. *Getting schools ready for children: The other side of the readiness goal.* Atlanta, GA: Author.

Stark County Department of Education. 1991. *The Ohio early childhood curriculum guide.* Canton: Author.

Swadener, B., & S. Kessler, eds. 1991. *Reconceptualizing early childhood education.* Special issue of *Early Education and Development* 2 (2).

Texas Education Agency. 1994. *First impressions, Primeras impesiones. Report of the Task Force on Early Childhood and Elementary Education.* Austin: Author.

Acknowledgments

This book represents the expertise and experience of literally thousands of early childhood professionals who have worked over the years to interpret and implement developmentally appropriate practice in programs for young children. We are especially grateful to all those who read the 1987 edition of this book and gave us their feedback as well as to the many directors and teachers in programs that have participated in NAEYC accreditation. While we cannot acknowledge all of the contributions, we must mention several key groups and individuals:

NAEYC's Panel on Revisions to Developmentally Appropriate Practice (1993–96), whose members gave tirelessly of their time and wisdom to the conceptualization of this document: Barbara Bowman, Victoria Fu, Lilian Katz, Rebecca New, Carol Brunson Phillips, Teresa Rosegrant, and Deborah Ziegler

Members of NAEYC's 1985 Commission on Appropriate Education for 4- and 5-Year-Olds and, specifically, its chair Bernard Spodek, who provided early leadership and continued challenge

Staff and representatives of ZERO TO THREE/National Center for Infants, Toddlers, and Families, including Abbey Griffin, Emily Fenichel, J. Ronald Lally, Marilyn Segal, Eleanor Szanton, Bernice Weissbourd, and the late Sally Provence, and many other colleagues, particularly Magda Gerber, for their work on developmentally appropriate practice for infants and toddlers

Staff and representatives of the Division for Early Childhood of the Council for Exceptional Children, especially Barbara Smith, Don Bailey, Bruce Mallory, Phil Strain, Mark Wolery, Deborah Ziegler, and many other colleagues, for their work on developmentally appropriate, inclusive practice for all children

Representatives of the Early Childhood Interest Group of the National Association for Bilingual Education, including Antonia Lopez, Amie Beckett, Mary Contee, Eugene Garcia, Alice Paul, and Lourdes Diaz Soto, for their work on addressing issues of language and culture in developmentally appropriate practice

Staff and representatives of the National Black Child Development Institute, including Evelyn Moore, Carol Brunson Phillips, Barbara Bowman, Ruby Burgess, Dwayne Crompton, Janice Hale, Barbara Richardson, and many other colleagues, for their work on developmentally appropriate practice for African American children

Leaders of the National Association of Early Childhood Specialists in State Departments of Education, especially Susan Andersen, Harriet Egertson, and Tynette Hills

The late Loris Malaguzzi and our colleagues in Reggio Emilia, Italy, including Carlina Rinaldi, Tiziana Filippini, Vea Vecchi, Sergio Spaggiari, Amelia Gambetti, and Lella Gandini, who inspired and challenged us, and the many Americans, including Carolyn Edwards, George Forman, Lilian Katz, Rebecca New, Brenda Fyfe, and Maurice Sykes, who are working to build bridges between the Reggio approach and practice in the United States

The individuals who have come to be known as "reconceptualizers," for critically reviewing our work and challenging us on many different fronts (we have not always agreed with their points, but we have been changed as a result of considering their views)

Key individuals who helped frame the 1987 edition on which this edition builds—Polly Greenberg, Jan Brown McCracken, and the late Bess-Gene Holt, whose contributions to our field and NAEYC continue to be felt every day

Teresa Rosegrant, for her deep knowledge of child development and wisdom from years of teaching young children and for her enormous generosity in sharing her time and expertise with the NAEYC staff

Members of the NAEYC Governing Board, especially reviewers Jerlean Daniel, Richard Clifford, Marjorie Kostelnik, Margaret King, Susan Andersen, Diane Turner, Ed Greene, and Larry Schweinhart, for leadership and guidance through the revision process

Carol Seefeldt, Jenni Klein, Barbara Willer, Marilyn Smith, and J.D. Andrews, for personal guidance, mentoring, and support

Patty Smith Hill, Lois Meek Stolz, and Rose Alschuler, for their vision, courage, leadership, and commitment in forming an organization that would one day become NAEYC and for framing as its mission the achievement of developmentally appropriate practice in programs for young children

—*Sue Bredekamp and Carol Copple, editors*

Developmentally Appropriate Practice in Early Childhood Programs
Serving Children from Birth through Age 8

Adopted July 1996

This statement defines and describes principles of developmentally appropriate practice in early childhood programs for administrators, teachers, parents, policymakers, and others who make decisions about the care and education of young children. An early childhood program is any group program in a center, school, or other facility that serves children from birth through age 8. Early childhood programs include child care centers, family child care homes, private and public preschools, kindergartens, and primary-grade schools.

The early childhood profession is responsible for establishing and promoting standards of high-quality, professional practice in early childhood programs. These standards must reflect current knowledge and shared beliefs about what constitutes high-quality, developmentally appropriate early childhood education in the context within which services are delivered.

This position paper is organized into several components, which include the following:

1. a description of the current context in which early childhood programs operate;

2. a description of the rationale and need for NAEYC's position statement;

3. a statement of NAEYC's commitment to children;

4. the statement of the position and definition of *developmentally appropriate practice*;

5. a summary of the principles of child development and learning and the theoretical perspectives that inform decisions about early childhood practice;

6. guidelines for making decisions about developmentally appropriate practices that address the following integrated components of early childhood practice: creating a caring community of learners, teaching to enhance children's learning and development, constructing appropriate curriculum, assessing children's learning and development, and establishing reciprocal relationships with families;

7. a challenge to the field to move from *either/ or* to *both/and* thinking; and

8. recommendations for policies necessary to ensure developmentally appropriate practices for all children.

This statement is designed to be used in conjunction with NAEYC's "Criteria for High Quality Early Childhood Programs," the standards for accreditation by the National Academy of Early Childhood Programs (NAEYC 1991), and with "Guidelines for Appropriate Curriculum Content and Assessment in Programs Serving Children Ages 3 through 8" (NAEYC & NAECS/ SDE 1992; Bredekamp & Rosegrant 1992, 1995).

The current context of early childhood programs

The early childhood knowledge base has expanded considerably in recent years, affirming some of the profession's cherished beliefs about good practice and challenging others. In addition to gaining new knowledge, early childhood programs have experienced several important changes in recent years. The number of programs continues to increase not only in response to the growing demand for out-of-home child care but also in recognition of the critical importance of educational experiences during the early years (Willer et al. 1991; NCES 1993). For example, in the late 1980s Head Start embarked on the largest expansion in its history, continuing this expansion into the 1990s with significant new services for families with infants and toddlers. The National Education Goals Panel established as an objective of Goal 1 that by the year 2000 all children will have access to high-quality, developmentally appropriate preschool programs (NEGP 1991). Welfare reform portends a greatly increased demand for child care services for even the youngest children from very low-income families.

Some characteristics of early childhood programs have also changed in recent years. Increasingly, programs serve children and families from diverse cultural and linguistic backgrounds, requiring that all programs demonstrate understanding of and responsiveness to cultural and linguistic diversity. Because culture and language are critical components of children's development, practices cannot be developmentally appropriate unless they are responsive to cultural and linguistic diversity.

The Americans with Disabilities Act and the Individuals with Disabilities Education Act now require that all early childhood programs make reasonable accommodations to provide access for children with disabilities or developmental delays (DEC/CEC & NAEYC 1993). This legal right reflects the growing consensus that young children with disabilities are best served in the same community settings where their typically developing peers are found (DEC/CEC 1994).

The trend toward full inclusion of children with disabilities must be reflected in descriptions of recommended practices, and considerable work has been done toward merging the perspectives of early childhood and early childhood special education (Carta et al. 1991; Mallory 1992, 1994; Wolery, Strain, & Bailey 1992; Bredekamp 1993b; DEC Task Force 1993; Mallory & New 1994b; Wolery & Wilbers 1994).

Other important program characteristics include age of children and length of program day. Children are now enrolled in programs at younger ages, many from infancy. The length of the program day for all ages of children has been extended in response to the need for extended hours of care for employed families. Similarly, program sponsorship has become more diverse. The public schools in the majority of states now provide prekindergarten programs, some for children as young as 3, and many offer before- and after-school child care (Mitchell, Seligson, & Marx 1989; Seppanen, Kaplan deVries, & Seligson 1993; Adams & Sandfort 1994).

Corporate America has become a more visible sponsor of child care programs, with several key corporations leading the way in promoting high quality (for example, IBM, AT&T, and the American Business Collaboration). Family child care homes have become an increasingly visible sector of the child care community, with greater emphasis on professional development and the National Association for Family Child Care taking the lead in establishing an accreditation system for high-quality family child care (Hollestelle 1993; Cohen & Modigliani 1994; Galinsky et al. 1994). Many different settings in this country provide services to young children, and it is legitimate—even beneficial—for these settings to vary in certain ways. However, since it is vital to meet children's learning and developmental needs wherever they are served, high standards of quality should apply to all settings.

The context in which early childhood programs operate today is also characterized by ongoing debates about how best to teach young children and discussions about what sort of practice is most likely to contribute to their development and learning. Perhaps the most important contribution of NAEYC's 1987 position statement on developmentally appropriate practice (Bredekamp 1987) was that it created an opportunity for increased conversation within and outside the early childhood field about practices. In revising the position statement, NAEYC's goal is not only to improve the quality of current early childhood practice but also to continue to encourage the kind of questioning and debate among early childhood professionals that are necessary for the continued growth of professional knowledge in the field. A related goal is to express NAEYC's position more clearly so that energy is not wasted in unproductive debate about apparent rather than real differences of opinion.

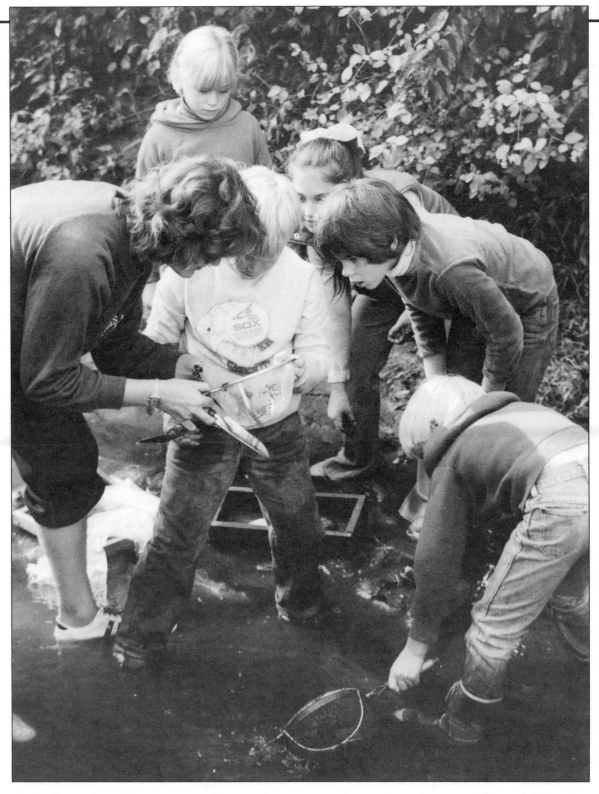

Educational practices are most effective when they are attuned to the way children develop and learn—that is, when they are developmentally appropriate.

Rationale for the position statement

The increased demand for early childhood education services is partly due to the increased recognition of the crucial importance of experiences during the earliest years of life. Children's experiences during early childhood not only influence their later functioning in school but also can have effects throughout life. For example, current research demonstrates the early and lasting effects of children's environments and experiences on brain development and cognition (Chugani, Phelps, & Mazziotta 1987; Caine & Caine 1991; Kuhl 1994). Studies show that, "From infancy through about age 10, brain cells not only form most of the connections they will maintain throughout life but during this time they retain their greatest malleability" (Dana Alliance for Brain Initiatives 1996, 7).

Positive, supportive relationships, important during the earliest years of life, appear essential not only for cognitive development but also for healthy emotional development and social attachment (Bowlby 1969; Stern 1985). The preschool years are an optimum time for development of fundamental motor skills (Gallahue 1993), language development (Dyson & Genishi 1993), and other key foundational aspects of development that have lifelong implications.

Recognition of the importance of the early years has heightened interest and support for early childhood education programs. A number of studies demonstrating long-term, positive consequences of participation in high-quality early childhood programs for children from low-income families influenced the expansion of Head Start and public school prekindergarten (Lazar & Darlington 1982; Lee, Brooks-Gunn, & Schuur 1988; Schweinhart, Barnes, & Weikart 1993; Campbell & Ramey 1995). Several decades of research clearly demonstrate that high-quality, developmentally appropriate early childhood programs produce short- and long-term positive effects on children's cognitive and social development (Barnett 1995).

From a thorough review of the research on the long-term effects of early childhood education programs, Barnett concludes that "across all studies, the findings were relatively uniform and constitute overwhelming evidence that early childhood care and education can produce sizeable improvements in school success" (1995, 40). Children from low-income families who participated in high-quality preschool programs were significantly less likely to have been assigned to special education, retained in grade, engaged in crime, or to have dropped out of school. The longitudinal studies, in general, suggest positive consequences for programs that used an approach consistent with principles of developmentally appropriate practice (Lazar & Darlington 1982; Berreuta-Clement et al. 1984; Miller & Bizzell 1984; Schweinhart, Weikart, & Larner 1986; Schweinhart, Barnes, & Weikart 1993; Frede 1995; Schweinhart & Weikart 1996).

Research on the long-term effects of early childhood programs indicates that children who attend good-quality child care programs, even at very young ages, demonstrate positive outcomes, and children who attend poor-quality programs show negative effects (Vandell & Powers 1983; Phillips, McCartney, & Scarr 1987; Fields et al. 1988; Vandell, Henderson, & Wilson 1988; Arnett 1989; Vandell & Corasanti 1990; Burchinal et al. 1996). Specifically, children who experience high-quality, stable child care engage in more complex play, demonstrate more secure attachments to adults and other children, and score higher on measures of thinking ability and language development. High-quality child care can predict academic success, adjustment to school, and reduced behavioral problems for children in first grade (Howes 1988).

While the potential positive effects of high-quality child care are well documented, several large-scale evaluations of child care find that high-quality experiences are not the norm (Whitebook, Howes, & Phillips 1989; Howes, Phillips, & Whitebook 1992; Layzer, Goodson, & Moss 1993; Galinsky et al. 1994; Cost, Quality, & Child Outcomes Study Team 1995). Each of these studies, which included observations of child care and preschool quality in several states, found that good quality that supports children's health and social and cognitive development is being provided in only about 15% of programs.

Of even greater concern was the large percentage of classrooms and family child care homes that were rated "barely adequate" or "inadequate" for quality. From 12 to 20% of the children were in settings that were considered dangerous to their health and safety and harmful to their social and cognitive development. An alarming number of infants and toddlers (35 to 40%) were found to be in unsafe settings (Cost, Quality, & Child Outcomes Study Team 1995).

Experiences during the earliest years of formal schooling are also formative. Studies demonstrate that children's success or failure during the first years of school often predicts the course of later schooling (Alexander & Entwisle 1988; Slavin, Karweit, & Madden 1989). A growing body of research indicates that more developmentally appropriate teaching in preschool and kindergarten predicts greater success in the early grades (Frede & Barnett 1992; Marcon 1992; Charlesworth et al. 1993).

As with preschool and child care, the observed quality of children's early schooling is uneven (Durkin 1987, 1990; Hiebert & Papierz 1990; Bryant, Clifford, & Peisner 1991; Carnegie Task Force 1996). For instance, in a statewide observational study of kindergarten classrooms, Durkin (1987) found that despite assessment results indicating considerable individual variation in children's literacy skills, which would call for various teaching strategies as well as individual and small-group work, teachers relied on one instructional strategy—whole-group, phonics instruction—and judged children who did not learn well with this one method as unready for first grade. Currently, too many children—especially children from low-income families and some minority groups—experience school failure, are retained in grade, get assigned to special education, and eventually drop out of school (Natriello, McDill, & Pallas 1990; Legters & Slavin 1992).

Results such as these indicate that while early childhood programs have the potential for producing positive and lasting effects on children, this potential will not be achieved unless more attention is paid to ensuring that all programs meet the highest standards of quality. As the number and type of early childhood programs increase, the need increases for a shared vision and agreed-upon standards of professional practice.

NAEYC's commitment to children

It is important to acknowledge at the outset the core values that undergird all of NAEYC's work. As stated in NAEYC's *Code of Ethical Conduct*, standards of professional practice in early childhood programs are based on commitment to certain fundamental values that are deeply rooted in the history of the early childhood field:

- appreciating childhood as a unique and valuable stage of the human life cycle [and valuing the quality of children's lives in the present, not just as preparation for the future];

- basing our work with children on knowledge of child development [and learning];

- appreciating and supporting the close ties between the child and family;

- recognizing that children are best understood in the context of family, culture, and society;

- respecting the dignity, worth, and uniqueness of each individual (child, family member, and colleague); and

- helping children and adults achieve their full potential in the context of relationships that are based on trust, respect, and positive regard. (Feeney & Kipnis 1992, 3)

Taken together, these core values define NAEYC's basic commitment to children and underlie its position on developmentally appropriate practice.

Statement of the position

Based on an enduring commitment to act on behalf of children, NAEYC's mission is to promote high-quality, developmentally appropriate programs for all children and their families. Because we define developmentally appropriate programs as programs that contribute to children's development, we must articulate our goals for children's development. The principles of practice advocated in this position statement are based on a set of goals for children: what we want for them, both in their present lives and as they develop to adulthood, and what personal characteristics should be fostered because they contribute to a peaceful, prosperous, and democratic society.

As we approach the 21st century, enormous changes are taking place in daily life and work. At the same time, certain human capacities will undoubtedly remain important elements in individual and societal well-being—no matter what economic or technological changes take place. With a recognition of both the continuities in human existence and the rapid changes in our world, broad agreement is emerging (e.g., Resnick 1996) that when today's children become adults they will need the ability to

- communicate well, respect others and engage with them to work through differences of opinion, and function well as members of a team;

- analyze situations, make reasoned judgments, and solve new problems as they emerge;

- access information through various modes, including spoken and written language, and intelligently employ complex tools and technologies as they are developed; and

- continue to learn new approaches, skills, and knowledge as conditions and needs change.

Clearly, people in the decades ahead will need, more than ever, fully developed literacy and numeracy skills, and these abilities are key goals of the educational process. In science, social studies (which includes history and geography), music and the visual arts, physical education and health, children need to acquire a body of knowledge and skills, as identified by those in the various disciplines (e.g., Bredekamp & Rosegrant 1995).

Besides acquiring a body of knowledge and skills, children must develop positive dispositions and attitudes. They need to understand that effort is necessary for achievement, for example, and they need to have curiosity and confidence in themselves as learners. Moreover, to live in a highly pluralistic society and world, young people need to develop a positive self-identity and a tolerance for others whose perspective and experience may be different from their own.

Beyond the shared goals of the early childhood field, every program for young children should establish its own goals in collaboration with families. All early childhood programs will not have identical goals; priorities may vary in some respects because programs serve a diversity of children and families. Such differences notwithstanding, NAEYC believes that all high-quality, developmentally appropriate programs will have certain attributes in common. A high-quality early childhood program is one that provides a safe and nurturing environment that promotes the physical, social, emotional, aesthetic, intellectual, and language development of each child while being sensitive to the needs and preferences of families.

Many factors influence the quality of an early childhood program, including (but not limited to) the extent to which knowledge about how children develop and learn is applied in program practices. Developmentally appropriate programs are based on what is known about how children develop and learn; such programs promote the development and enhance the learning of each individual child served.

Developmentally appropriate practices result from the process of professionals making decisions about the well-being and education of children based on at least three important kinds of information or knowledge:

1. *what is known about child development and learning*—knowledge of age-related human characteristics that permits general predictions within an age range about what activities, materials, interactions, or experiences will be safe, healthy, interesting, achievable, and also challenging to children;

2. *what is known about the strengths, interests, and needs of each individual child in the group* to be able to adapt for and be responsive to inevitable individual variation; and

3. *knowledge of the social and cultural contexts in which children live* to ensure that learning experiences are meaningful, relevant, and respectful for the participating children and their families.

Furthermore, each of these dimensions of knowledge—human development and learning, individual characteristics and experiences, and social and cultural contexts—is dynamic and changing, requiring that early childhood teachers remain learners throughout their careers.

An example illustrates the interrelatedness of these three dimensions of the decisionmaking process. Children all over the world acquire language at approximately the same period of the life span and in similar ways (Fernald 1992). But tremendous individual variation exists in the rate and pattern of language acquisition (Fenson et al. 1994). Also, children acquire the language or languages of the culture in which they live (Kuhl 1994). Thus, to adequately support a developmental task such as language acquisition, the teacher must draw on at least all three interrelated dimensions of knowledge to determine a developmentally appropriate strategy or intervention.

Principles of child development and learning that inform developmentally appropriate practice

Developmentally appropriate practice is based on knowledge about how children develop and learn. As Katz states, "In a developmental approach to curriculum design, . . . [decisions] about what should be learned and how it would best be learned depend on what we know of the learner's developmental status and our understanding of the relationships between early experience and subsequent development" (1995, 109). To guide their decisions about practice, all early childhood teachers need to understand the developmental changes that typically occur in the years from birth through age 8 and beyond, variations in development that may occur, and how best to support children's learning and development during these years.

A complete discussion of the knowledge base that informs early childhood practice is beyond the scope of this document (see, for example, Seefeldt 1992; Sroufe, Cooper, & DeHart 1992; Kostelnik, Soderman, & Whiren 1993; Spodek 1993; Berk 1996). Because development and learning are so complex, no one theory is sufficient to explain these phenomena. However, a broad-based review of the literature on early childhood education generates a set of principles to inform early childhood practice. *Principles* are generalizations that are sufficiently reliable that they should be taken into account when making decisions (Katz & Chard 1989; Katz 1995). Following is a list of empirically based principles of child development and learning that inform and guide decisions about developmentally appropriate practice.

1. **Domains of children's development—physical, social, emotional, and cognitive—are closely related. Development in one domain influences and is influenced by development in other domains.**

Development in one domain can limit or facilitate development in others (Sroufe, Cooper, & DeHart 1992; Kostelnik, Soderman, & Whiren 1993). For example, when babies begin to crawl or walk, their ability to explore the world expands, and their mobility, in turn, affects their cognitive development. Likewise, children's language skill affects their ability to establish social relationships with adults and other children, just as their skill in social interaction can support or impede their language development.

Because developmental domains are interrelated, educators should be aware of and use these interrelationships to organize children's learning experiences in ways that help children develop optimally in all areas and that make meaningful connections across domains.

Recognition of the connections across developmental domains is also useful for curriculum planning with the various age groups represented in the early childhood period. Curriculum with infants and toddlers is almost solely driven by the need to support their healthy development in all domains. During the primary grades, curriculum planning attempts to help children develop conceptual understandings that apply across related subject-matter disciplines.

2. **Development occurs in a relatively orderly sequence, with later abilities, skills, and knowledge building on those already acquired.**

Human development research indicates that relatively stable, predictable sequences of growth and change occur in children during the first nine years of life (Piaget 1952; Erikson 1963; Dyson & Genishi 1993; Gallahue 1993; Case & Okamoto 1996). Predictable changes occur in all domains of development—physical, emotional, social, language, and cognitive—although the ways that these changes are manifest and the meaning attached to them may vary in different cultural contexts. Knowledge of typical development of children within the age span served by the program provides a general framework to guide how teachers prepare the learning environment and plan realistic curriculum goals and objectives and appropriate experiences.

3. **Development proceeds at varying rates from child to child as well as unevenly within different areas of each child's functioning.**

Individual variation has at least two dimensions: the inevitable variability around the average or normative course of development and the uniqueness of each person as an individual (Sroufe, Cooper, & DeHart 1992). Each child is a unique person with an individual pattern and timing of growth, as well as individual personality, temperament, learning style, and experiential and family background. All children have their own strengths, needs, and interests; for some children, special learning and developmental needs or abilities are identified. Given the enormous variation among children of the same chronological age, a child's age must be recognized as only a crude index of developmental maturity.

Recognition that individual variation is not only to be expected but also valued requires that decisions about curriculum and adults' interactions with children be as individualized as possible. Emphasis on individual appropriateness is not the same as "individualism." Rather, this recognition requires that children be considered not solely as members of an age group, expected to perform to a predetermined norm and without adaptation to individual variation of any kind. Having high expectations for all children is important, but rigid expectations of group norms do not reflect what is known about real differences in individual development and learning during the early years. Group-norm expectancy can be especially harmful for children with special learning and developmental needs (NEGP 1991; Mallory 1992; Wolery, Strain, & Bailey 1992).

4. **Early experiences have both cumulative and delayed effects on individual children's development. Optimal periods exist for certain types of development and learning.**

Children's early experiences, either positive or negative, are cumulative in the sense that if an experience occurs occasionally, it may have minimal effects. If positive or negative experiences occur frequently, however, they can have powerful, lasting, even "snowballing," effects (Katz & Chard 1989; Kostelnik, Soderman, & Whiren 1993; Wieder & Greenspan 1993). For example, a child's social experiences with other children in the preschool years help him develop social skills and confidence that enable him to make friends in the early school years, and these experiences further enhance the child's social competence. Conversely, children who fail to develop minimal social competence and are neglected or rejected by peers are at significant risk to drop out of school, become delinquent, and experience mental health problems in adulthood (Asher, Hymel, & Renshaw 1984; Parker & Asher 1987).

Similar patterns can be observed in babies whose cries and other attempts at communication are regularly responded to, thus enhancing their own sense of efficacy and increasing communicative competence. Likewise, when children have or do not have early literacy experiences, such as being read to regularly, their later success in learning to read is affected accordingly. Perhaps most convincing is the growing body of research demonstrating that social and sensorimotor experiences during the first three years directly affect neurological development of the brain, with important and lasting implications for children's capacity to learn (Dana Alliance for Brain Initiatives 1996).

Early experiences can also have delayed effects, either positive or negative, on subsequent development. For instance, some evidence suggests that reliance on extrinsic rewards (such as candy or money) to shape children's behavior, a strategy that can be very effective in the short term, under certain circumstances lessens children's intrinsic motivation to engage in the rewarded behavior in the long term (Dweck 1986; Kohn 1993). For example, paying children to read books may over time undermine their desire to read for their own enjoyment and edification.

At certain points in the life span, some kinds of learning and development occur most efficiently. For example, the first three years of life appear to be an optimal period for verbal language development (Kuhl 1994). Although delays in language development due to physical or environmental deficits can be amelio-

rated later on, such intervention usually requires considerable effort. Similarly, the preschool years appear to be optimum for fundamental motor development (that is, fundamental motor skills are more easily and efficiently acquired at this age) (Gallahue 1995). Children who have many opportunities and adult support to practice large-motor skills (running, jumping, hopping, skipping) during this period have the cumulative benefit of being better able to acquire more sophisticated, complex motor skills (balancing on a beam or riding a two-wheel bike) in subsequent years. On the other hand, children whose early motor experiences are severely limited may struggle to acquire physical competence and may also experience delayed effects when attempting to participate in sports or personal fitness activities later in life.

5. Development proceeds in predictable directions toward greater complexity, organization, and internalization.

Learning during early childhood proceeds from behavioral knowledge to symbolic or representational knowledge (Bruner 1983). For example, children learn to navigate their homes and other familiar settings long before they can understand the words *left* and *right* or read a map of the house. Developmentally appropriate programs provide opportunities for children to broaden and deepen their behavioral knowledge by providing a variety of firsthand experiences and by helping children acquire symbolic knowledge through representing their experiences in a variety of media, such as drawing, painting, construction of models, dramatic play, verbal and written descriptions (Katz 1995).

Even very young children are able to use various media to represent their understanding of concepts. Furthermore, through representation of their knowledge, the knowledge itself is enhanced (Edwards, Gandini, & Forman 1993; Malaguzzi 1993; Forman 1994). Representational modes and media also vary with the age of the child. For instance, most learning for infants and toddlers is sensory and motoric, but by age 2 children use one object to stand for another in play (a block for a phone or a spoon for a guitar).

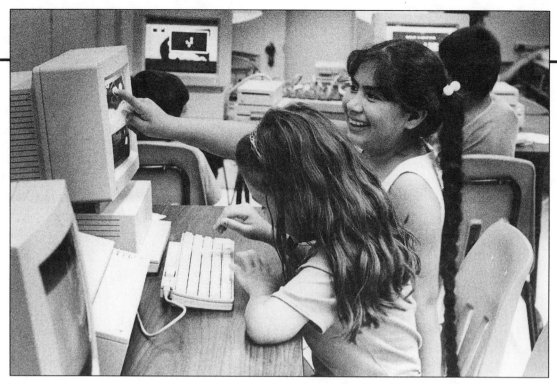

The goal is that all children learn to function well in the society as a whole and move comfortably among groups of people from both similar and dissimilar backgrounds.

6. Development and learning occur in and are influenced by multiple social and cultural contexts.

Bronfenbrenner (1979, 1989, 1993) provides an ecological model for understanding human development. He explains that children's development is best understood within the sociocultural context of the family, educational setting, community, and broader society. These various contexts are interrelated, and all have an impact on the developing child. For example, even a child in a loving, supportive family within a strong, healthy community is affected by the biases of the larger society, such as racism or sexism, and may show the effects of negative stereotyping and discrimination.

We define *culture* as the customary beliefs and patterns of and for behavior, both explicit and implicit, that are passed on to future generations by the society they live in and/or by a social, religious, or ethnic group within it. Because culture is often discussed in the context of diversity or multiculturalism, people fail to recognize the powerful role that culture plays in influencing the development of *all* children. Every culture structures and interprets children's behavior and development (Edwards & Gandini 1989; Tobin, Wu, & Davidson 1989; Rogoff et al. 1993). As Bowman states, "Rules of development are the same for all children,

but social contexts shape children's development into different configurations" (1994, 220). Early childhood teachers need to understand the influence of sociocultural contexts on learning, recognize children's developing competence, and accept a variety of ways for children to express their developmental achievements (Vygotsky 1978; Wertsch 1985; Forman, Minick, & Stone 1993; New 1993, 1994; Bowman & Stott 1994; Mallory & New 1994a; Phillips 1994; Bruner 1996; Wardle 1996).

Teachers should learn about the culture of the majority of the children they serve if that culture differs from their own. However, recognizing that development and learning are influenced by social and cultural contexts does not require teachers to understand all the nuances of every cultural group they may encounter in their practice; this would be an impossible task. Rather, this fundamental recognition sensitizes teachers to the need to acknowledge how their own cultural experience shapes their perspective and to realize that multiple perspectives, in addition to their own, must be considered in decisions about children's development and learning.

Children are capable of learning to function in more than one cultural context simultaneously. However, if teachers set low expectations for children based on their home culture and language, children cannot develop and learn optimally. Education should be an additive process. For example, children whose primary language is not English should be able to learn English without being forced to give up their home language (NAEYC 1996a). Likewise, children who speak only English benefit from learning another language. The goal is that all children learn to function well in the society as a whole and move comfortably among groups of people who come from both similar and dissimilar backgrounds.

7. Children are active learners, drawing on direct physical and social experience as well as culturally transmitted knowledge to construct their own understandings of the world around them.

Children contribute to their own development and learning as they strive to make meaning out of their daily experiences in the home, the early childhood program, and the community. Principles of developmentally appropriate practice are based on several prominent theories that view intellectual development from a constructivist, interactive perspective (Montessori 1909/1964; Dewey 1916; Piaget 1952; Vygotsky 1978; DeVries & Kohlberg 1990; Rogoff 1990; Gardner 1991; Kamii & Ewing 1996).

From birth, children are actively engaged in constructing their own understandings from their experiences, and these understandings are mediated by and clearly linked to the sociocultural context. Young children actively learn from observing and participating with other children and adults, including parents and teachers. Children need to form their own hypotheses and keep trying them out through social interaction, physical manipulation, and their own thought processes—observing what happens, reflecting on their findings, asking questions, and formulating answers. When objects, events, and other people challenge the working model that the child has mentally constructed, the child is forced to adjust the model or alter the mental structures to account for the new information. Throughout early childhood, the child in processing new experiences continually reshapes, expands, and reorganizes mental structures (Piaget 1952; Vygotsky 1978; Case & Okamoto 1996). When teachers and other adults use various strategies to encourage children to reflect on their experiences by planning beforehand and "revisiting" afterward, the knowledge and understanding gained from the experience is deepened (Copple, Sigel, & Saunders 1984; Edwards, Gandini, & Forman 1993; Stremmel & Fu 1993; Hohmann & Weikart 1995).

In the statement of this principle, the term "physical and social experience" is used in the broadest sense to include children's exposure to physical knowledge, learned through firsthand experience of using objects (observing that a ball thrown in the air falls down), and social knowledge, including the vast body of culturally acquired and transmitted knowledge that children need to function in the world. For example, children progressively construct their own understanding of various symbols, but the symbols they use (such as the alphabet or numerical system) are the ones used within their culture and transmitted to them by adults.

In recent years, discussions of cognitive development have at times become polarized (see Seifert 1993). Piaget's theory stressed that development of certain cognitive structures was a necessary prerequisite to learning (i.e., development precedes learning), while other research has demonstrated that instruction in specific concepts or strategies can facilitate development of more mature cognitive structures (learning precedes development) (Vygotsky 1978; Gelman & Baillargeon 1983). Current attempts to resolve this apparent dichotomy (Seifert 1993; Sameroff & McDonough 1994; Case & Okamoto 1996) acknowledge that essentially both theoretical perspectives are correct in explaining aspects of cognitive development during early childhood. Strategic teaching, of course, can enhance children's learning. Yet direct instruction may be totally ineffective; it fails when it is not attuned to the cognitive capacities and knowledge of the child at that point in development.

8. Development and learning result from interaction of biological maturation and the environment, which includes both the physical and social worlds that children live in.

The simplest way to express this principle is to say that human beings are products of both heredity and environment and these forces are interrelated. Behaviorists focus on the environmental influences that determine learning, while maturationists emphasize the unfolding of predetermined, hereditary characteristics. Each perspective is true to some extent, and yet neither perspective is sufficient to explain learning or development. More often today, development is viewed as the result of an interactive, transactional process between the growing, changing individual and his or her experiences in the social and physical worlds (Scarr & McCartney 1983; Plomin 1994a, b). For example, a child's genetic makeup may predict healthy growth, but inadequate nutrition in the early years of life may keep this potential from being fulfilled. Or a severe disability, whether inherited or environmentally caused, may be ameliorated through systematic, appropriate intervention. Likewise, a child's inherited temperament—whether a predisposition to be wary or outgoing—shapes and is shaped by how other children and adults communicate with that child.

9. Play is an important vehicle for children's social, emotional, and cognitive development, as well as a reflection of their development.

Understanding that children are active constructors of knowledge and that development and learning are the result of interactive processes, early childhood teachers recognize that children's play is a highly supportive context for these developing processes (Piaget 1952; Fein 1981; Bergen 1988; Smilansky & Shefatya 1990; Fromberg 1992; Berk & Winsler 1995). Play gives children opportunities to understand the world, interact with others in social ways, express and control emotions, and develop their symbolic capabilities. Children's play gives adults insights into children's development and opportunities to support the development of new strategies. Vygotsky (1978) believed that play leads development, with written language growing out of oral language through the vehicle of symbolic play that promotes the development of symbolic representation abilities. Play provides a context for children to practice newly acquired skills and also to function on the edge of their developing capacities to take on new social roles, attempt novel or challenging tasks, and solve complex problems that they would not (or could not) otherwise do (Mallory & New 1994b).

Research demonstrates the importance of sociodramatic play as a tool for learning curriculum content with 3- through 6-year-old children. When teachers provide a thematic organization for play; offer appropriate props, space, and time; and become involved in the play by extending and elaborating on children's ideas, children's language and literacy skills can be enhanced (Levy, Schaefer, & Phelps 1986; Schrader 1989, 1990; Morrow 1990; Pramling 1991; Levy, Wolfgang, & Koorland 1992).

In addition to supporting cognitive development, play serves important functions in children's physical, emotional, and social development (Herron & Sutton-Smith 1971). Children express and represent their ideas, thoughts, and feelings when engaged in symbolic play. During play a child can learn to deal with emotions, to interact with others, to resolve conflicts, and to gain a sense of competence—all in the safety that only play affords. Through play, children also can develop their imaginations and creativity. Therefore, child-initiated, teacher-supported play is an essential component of developmentally appropriate practice (Fein & Rivkin 1986).

10. Development advances when children have opportunities to practice newly acquired skills as well as when they experience a challenge just beyond the level of their present mastery.

Research demonstrates that children need to be able to successfully negotiate learning tasks most of the time if they are to maintain motivation and persistence (Lary 1990; Brophy 1992). Confronted by repeated failure, most children will simply stop trying. So most of the time, teachers should give young children tasks that with effort they can accomplish and present them with content that is accessible at their level of understanding. At the same time, children continually gravitate to situations and stimuli that give them the chance to work at their "growing edge" (Berk & Winsler 1995; Bodrova & Leong 1996). Moreover, in a task just beyond the child's independent reach, the adult and more-competent peers contribute significantly to development by providing the supportive "scaffolding" that allows the child to take the next step.

Development and learning are dynamic processes requiring that adults understand the continuum, observe children closely to match curriculum and teaching to children's emerging competencies, needs, and interests, and then help children move forward by targeting educational experiences to the edge of children's changing capacities so as to challenge but not frustrate them. Human beings, especially children, are highly motivated to understand what they almost, but not quite, comprehend and to master what they can almost, but not quite, do (White 1965; Vygotsky 1978). The principle of learning is that children can do things first in a supportive context and then later independently and in a variety of contexts. Rogoff (1990) describes the process of adult-assisted learning as "guided participation" to emphasize that children actively collaborate with others to move to more complex levels of understanding and skill.

11. Children demonstrate different modes of knowing and learning and different ways of representing what they know.

For some time, learning theorists and developmental psychologists have recognized that human beings come to understand the world in many ways and that individuals tend to have preferred or stronger modes of learning. Studies of differences in learning modalities have contrasted visual, auditory, or tactile learners. Other work has identified learners as field-dependent or independent (Witkin 1962). Gardner (1983) expanded on this concept by theorizing that human beings possess at least seven "intelligences." In addition to having the ones traditionally emphasized in schools, linguistic and logical-mathematical, individuals are more or less proficient in at least these other areas: musical, spatial, bodily-kinesthetic, intrapersonal, and interpersonal.

Malaguzzi (1993) used the metaphor of "100 languages" to describe the diverse modalities through which children come to understand the world and represent their knowledge. The processes of representing their understanding can with the assistance of teachers help children deepen, improve, and expand their understanding (Copple, Sigel, & Saunders 1984; Forman 1994; Katz 1995). The prin-

ciple of diverse modalities implies that teachers should provide not only opportunities for individual children to use their preferred modes of learning to capitalize on their strengths (Hale-Benson 1986) but also opportunities to help children develop in the modes or intelligences in which they may not be as strong.

12. Children develop and learn best in the context of a community where they are safe and valued, their physical needs are met, and they feel psychologically secure.

Maslow (1954) conceptualized a hierarchy of needs in which learning was not considered possible unless physical and psychological needs for safety and security were first met. Because children's physical health and safety too often are threatened today, programs for young children must not only provide adequate health, safety, and nutrition but may also need to ensure more comprehensive services, such as physical, dental, and mental health and social services (NASBE 1991; U.S. Department of Health & Human Services 1996). In addition, children's development in all areas is influenced by their ability to establish and maintain a limited number of positive, consistent primary relationships with adults and other children (Bowlby 1969; Stern 1985; Garbarino et al. 1992). These primary relationships begin in the family but extend over time to include children's teachers and members of the community; therefore, practices that are developmentally appropriate address children's physical, social, and emotional needs as well as their intellectual development.

*   *   *

A linear listing of principles of child development and learning, such as the above, cannot do justice to the complexity of the phenomena that it attempts to describe and explain. Just as all domains of development and learning are interrelated, so, too, there are relationships among the principles. Similarly, the following guidelines for practice do not match up one-to-one with the principles. Instead, early childhood professionals draw on all these fundamental ideas (as well as many others) when making decisions about their practice.

Guidelines for decisions about developmentally appropriate practice

An understanding of the nature of development and learning during the early childhood years, from birth through age 8, generates guidelines that inform the practices of early childhood educators. Developmentally appropriate practice requires that teachers integrate the many dimensions of their knowledge base. They must know about child development and the implications of this knowledge for how to teach, the content of the curriculum—what to teach and when—how to assess what children have learned, and how to adapt curriculum and instruction to children's individual strengths, needs, and interests. Further, they must know the particular children they teach and their families and be knowledgeable as well about the social and cultural context.

The following guidelines address five interrelated dimensions of early childhood professional practice: creating a caring community of learners, teaching to enhance development and learning, constructing appropriate curriculum, assessing children's development and learning, and establishing reciprocal relationships with families. (The word *teacher* is used to refer to any adult responsible for a group of children in any early childhood program, including infant/toddler caregivers, family child care providers, and specialists in other disciplines who fulfill the role of teacher.)

Examples of appropriate and inappropriate practice in relation to each of these dimensions are given for infants and toddlers (Part 3, pp. 72–90), children 3 through 5 (Part 4, pp. 123–35), and children 6 through 8 (Part 5, pp. 161–79). In the references at the end of each part, readers will be able to find fuller discussion of the points summarized here and strategies for implementation.

1. Creating a caring community of learners

Developmentally appropriate practices occur within a context that supports the development of relationships between adults and children, among children, among teachers, and between teachers and families. Such a community reflects what is known about the social construction of knowledge and the importance of establishing a caring, inclusive community in which all children can develop and learn.

A. The early childhood setting functions as a community of learners in which all participants consider and contribute to each other's well-being and learning.

B. Consistent, positive relationships with a limited number of adults and other children are a fundamental determinant of healthy human development and provide the context for children to learn about themselves and their world and also how to develop positive, constructive relationships with other people. The early childhood classroom is a community in which each child is valued. Children learn to respect and acknowledge differences in abilities and talents and to value each person for his or her strengths.

C. Social relationships are an important context for learning. Each child has strengths or interests that contribute to the overall functioning of the group. When children have opportunities to play together, work on projects in small groups, and talk with other children and adults, their own development and learning are enhanced. Interacting with other children in small groups provides a context for children to operate on the edge of their developing capacities. The learning environment enables children to construct understanding through interactions with adults and other children.

D. The learning environment is designed to protect children's health and safety and is supportive of children's physiological needs for activity, sensory stimulation, fresh air, rest, and nourishment. The program provides a balance of rest and active movement for children throughout the program day. Outdoor experiences are provided for children of all ages. The program protects children's psychological safety; that is, children feel secure, relaxed, and comfortable rather than disengaged, frightened, worried, or stressed.

E. Children experience an organized environment and an orderly routine that provides an overall structure in which learning takes place; the environment is dynamic and changing but predictable and comprehensible from a child's point of view. The learning environment provides a variety of materials and opportunities for children to have firsthand, meaningful experiences.

2. Teaching to enhance development and learning

Adults are responsible for ensuring children's healthy development and learning. From birth, relationships with adults are critical determinants of children's healthy social and emotional development and serve as well as mediators of language and intellectual development. At the same time, children are active constructors of their own understanding, who benefit from initiating and regulating their own learning activities and interacting with peers. Therefore, early childhood teachers strive to achieve an optimal balance between children's self-initiated learning and adult guidance or support.

Teachers accept responsibility for actively supporting children's development and provide occasions for children to acquire important knowledge and skills. Teachers use their knowledge of child development and learning to identify the range of activities, materials, and learning experiences that are appropriate for a group or individual child. This knowledge is used in conjunction with knowledge of the context and understanding about individual children's growth patterns, strengths, needs, interests, and experiences to design the curriculum and learning environment and guide teachers' interactions with children. The following guidelines describe aspects of the teachers' role in making decisions about practice:

A. Teachers respect, value, and accept children and treat them with dignity at all times.

B. Teachers make it a priority to know each child well.

(1) Teachers establish positive, personal relationships with children to foster the child's development and keep informed about the child's needs and potentials. Teachers listen to children and adapt their responses to children's differing needs, interests, styles, and abilities.

(2) Teachers continually observe children's spontaneous play and interaction with the physical environment and with other children to learn about their interests, abilities, and developmental progress. On the basis of this information, teachers plan experiences that enhance children's learning and development.

(3) Understanding that children develop and learn in the context of their families and communities, teachers establish relationships with families that increase their knowledge of children's lives outside the classroom and their awareness of the perspectives and priorities of those individuals most significant in the child's life.

(4) Teachers are alert to signs of undue stress and traumatic events in children's lives and aware of effective strategies to reduce stress and support the development of resilience.

(5) Teachers are responsible at all times for all children under their supervision and plan for children's increasing development of self-regulation abilities.

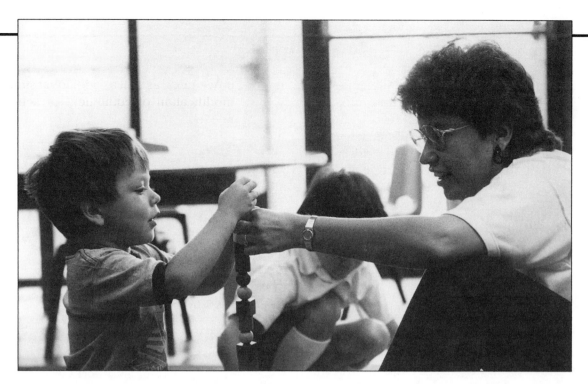

Teachers calibrate the complexity and challenge of activities to suit children's level of skill and knowledge, increasing the challenge as children gain competence and understanding.

C. Teachers create an intellectually engaging, responsive environment to promote each child's learning and development.

(1) Teachers use their knowledge about children in general and the particular children in the group as well as their familiarity with what children need to learn and develop in each curriculum area to organize the environment and plan curriculum and teaching strategies.

(2) Teachers provide children with a rich variety of experiences, projects, materials, problems, and ideas to explore and investigate, ensuring that these are worthy of children's attention.

(3) Teachers provide children with opportunities to make meaningful choices and time to explore through active involvement. Teachers offer children the choice to participate in a small-group or a solitary activity, assist and guide children who are not yet able to use and enjoy child-choice activity periods, and provide opportunities for practice of skills as a self-chosen activity.

(4) Teachers organize the daily and weekly schedule and allocate time so as to provide children with extended blocks of time in which to engage in play, projects, and/or study in integrated curriculum.

D. Teachers make plans to enable children to attain key curriculum goals across various disciplines, such as language arts, mathematics, social studies, science, art, music, physical education, and health (see "Constructing appropriate curriculum," pp. 20–21).

(1) Teachers incorporate a wide variety of experiences, materials and equipment, and teaching strategies in constructing curriculum to accommodate a broad range of children's individual differences in prior experiences, maturation rates, styles of learning, needs, and interests.

(2) Teachers bring each child's home culture and language into the shared culture of the school so that the unique contributions of each group are recognized and valued by others.

(3) Teachers are prepared to meet identified special needs of individual children, including children with disabilities and those who exhibit unusual interests and skills. Teachers use all the strategies identified here, consult with appropriate specialists, and see that the child gets the specialized services he or she requires.

E. Teachers foster children's collaboration with peers on interesting, important enterprises.

(1) Teachers promote children's productive collaboration without taking over to the extent that children lose interest.

(2) Teachers use a variety of ways of flexibly grouping children for the purposes of instruction, supporting collaboration among children, and building a sense of community. At various times, children have opportunities to work individually, in small groups, and with the whole group.

F. Teachers develop, refine, and use a wide repertoire of teaching strategies to enhance children's learning and development.

(1) To help children develop their initiative, teachers encourage them to choose and plan their own learning activities.

(2) Teachers pose problems, ask questions, and make comments and suggestions that stimulate children's thinking and extend their learning.

(3) Teachers extend the range of children's interests and the scope of their thought through presenting novel experiences and introducing stimulating ideas, problems, experiences, or hypotheses.

(4) To sustain an individual child's effort or engagement in purposeful activities, teachers select from a range of strategies, including but not limited to modeling, demonstrating specific skills, and providing information, focused attention, physical proximity, verbal encouragement, reinforcement and other behavioral

procedures, as well as additional structure and modification of equipment or schedules as needed.

(5) Teachers coach and/or directly guide children in the acquisition of specific skills as needed.

(6) Teachers calibrate the complexity and challenge of activities to suit children's level of skill and knowledge, increasing the challenge as children gain competence and understanding.

(7) Teachers provide cues and other forms of "scaffolding" that enable the child to succeed in a task that is just beyond his or her ability to complete alone.

(8) To strengthen children's sense of competence and confidence as learners, motivation to persist, and willingness to take risks, teachers provide experiences for children to be genuinely successful and to be challenged.

(9) To enhance children's conceptual understanding, teachers use various strategies that encourage children to reflect on and "revisit" their learning experiences.

G. Teachers facilitate the development of responsibility and self-regulation in children.

(1) Teachers set clear, consistent, and fair limits for children's behavior and hold children accountable to standards of acceptable behavior. To the extent that children are able, teachers engage them in developing rules and procedures for behavior of class members.

(2) Teachers redirect children to more acceptable behavior or activity or use children's mistakes as learning opportunities, patiently reminding children of rules and their rationale as needed.

(3) Teachers listen and acknowledge children's feelings and frustrations, respond with respect, guide children to resolve conflicts, and model skills that help children to solve their own problems.

3. Constructing appropriate curriculum

The content of the early childhood curriculum is determined by many factors, including the subject matter of the disciplines, social or cultural values, and parental input. In developmentally appropriate programs, decisions about curriculum content also take into consideration the age and experience of the learners. Achieving success for all children depends, among other essentials, on providing a challenging, interesting, developmentally appropriate curriculum. NAEYC does not endorse specific curricula. However, one purpose of these guidelines is as a framework for making decisions about developing curriculum or selecting a curriculum model. Teachers who use a validated curriculum model benefit from the evidence of its effectiveness and the accumulated wisdom and experience of others.

In some respects, the curriculum strategies of many teachers today do not demand enough of children and in other ways demand too much of the wrong thing. On the one hand, narrowing the curriculum to those basic skills that can be easily measured on multiple-choice tests diminishes the intellectual challenge for many children. Such intellectually impoverished curriculum underestimates the true competence of children, which has been demonstrated to be much higher than is often assumed (Gelman & Baillargeon 1983; Gelman & Meck 1983; Edwards, Gandini, & Forman 1993; Resnick 1996). Watered-down, oversimplified curriculum leaves many children unchallenged, bored, uninterested, or unmotivated. In such situations, children's experiences are marked by a great many missed opportunities for learning.

On the other hand, curriculum expectations in the early years of schooling sometimes are not appropriate for the age groups served. When next-grade expectations of mastery of basic skills are routinely pushed down to the previous grade and whole-group and teacher-led instruction is the dominant teaching strategy, children who cannot sit still and attend to teacher lectures or who are bored and unchallenged or frustrated by doing workbook pages for long periods of time are mislabeled as immature, disruptive, or unready for school (Shepard & Smith 1988).

Constructing appropriate curriculum requires attention to at least the following guidelines for practice:

A. Developmentally appropriate curriculum provides for all areas of a child's development: physical, emotional, social, linguistic, aesthetic, and cognitive.

B. Curriculum includes a broad range of content across disciplines that is socially relevant, intellectually engaging, and personally meaningful to children.

C. Curriculum builds upon what children already know and are able to do (activating prior knowledge) to consolidate their learning and to foster their acquisition of new concepts and skills.

D. Effective curriculum plans frequently integrate across traditional subject-matter divisions to help children make meaningful connections and provide opportunities for rich conceptual development; focusing on one subject is also a valid strategy at times.

E. Curriculum promotes the development of knowledge and understanding, processes and skills, as well as the dispositions to use and apply skills and to go on learning.

F. Curriculum content has intellectual integrity, reflecting the key concepts and tools of inquiry of recognized disciplines in ways that are accessible and achievable for young children, ages 3 through 8 (e.g., Bredekamp & Rosegrant 1992, 1995). Children directly participate in study of the disciplines, for instance, by conducting scientific experiments, writing, performing, solving mathematical problems, collecting and analyzing data, collecting oral history, and performing other roles of experts in the disciplines.

G. Curriculum provides opportunities to support children's home culture and language while also developing all children's abilities to participate in the shared culture of the program and the community.

H. Curriculum goals are realistic and attainable for most children in the designated age range for which they are designed.

I. When used, technology is physically and philosophically integrated in the classroom curriculum and teaching. (See "NAEYC Position Statement: Technology and Young Children—Ages Three through Eight" [NAEYC 1996b].)

4. Assessing children's learning and development

Assessment of individual children's development and learning is essential for planning and implementing appropriate curriculum. In developmentally appropriate programs, assessment and curriculum are integrated, with teachers continually engaging in observational assessment for the purpose of improving teaching and learning.

Accurate assessment of young children is difficult because their development and learning are rapid, uneven, episodic, and embedded within specific cultural and linguistic contexts. Too often, inaccurate and inappropriate assessment measures have been used to label, track, or otherwise harm young children. Developmentally appropriate assessment practices are based on the following guidelines:

A. Assessment of young children's progress and achievements is ongoing, strategic, and purposeful. The results of assessment are used to benefit children—in adapting curriculum and teaching to meet the developmental and learning needs of children, communicating with the child's family, and evaluating the program's effectiveness for the purpose of improving the program.

B. The content of assessments reflects progress toward important learning and developmental goals. The program has a systematic plan for collecting and using assessment information that is integrated with curriculum planning.

C. The methods of assessment are appropriate to the age and experiences of young children. Therefore, assessment of young children relies heavily on the results of observations of children's development, descriptive data, collections of representative work by children, and demonstrated performance during authentic, not contrived, activities. Input from families as well as children's evaluations of their own work are part of the overall assessment strategy.

D. Assessments are tailored to a specific purpose and used only for the purpose for which they have been demonstrated to produce reliable, valid information.

E. Decisions that have a major impact on children, such as enrollment or placement, are never made on the basis of a single developmental assessment or screening device but are based on multiple sources of relevant information, particularly observations by teachers and parents.

F. To identify children who have special learning or developmental needs and to plan appropriate curriculum and teaching for them, developmental assessments and observations are used.

G. Assessment recognizes individual variation in learners and allows for differences in styles and rates of learning. Assessment takes into consideration such factors as the child's facility in English, stage of language acquisition, and whether the child has had the time and opportunity to develop proficiency in his or her home language as well as in English.

H. Assessment legitimately addresses not only what children can do independently but also what they can do with assistance from other children or adults. Teachers study children as individuals as well as in relationship to groups by documenting group projects and other collaborative work.

(For a more complete discussion of principles of appropriate assessment, see the position statement "Guidelines for Appropriate Curriculum Content and Assessment in Programs Serving Children Ages 3 through 8" [NAEYC & NAECS/SDE 1992]; see also Shepard 1994.)

5. Establishing reciprocal relationships with families

Developmentally appropriate practices derive from deep knowledge of individual children and the context within which they develop and learn. The younger the child, the more necessary it is for professionals to acquire this knowledge through relationships with children's families. The traditional approach to families has been a parent education orientation in which the professionals see themselves as knowing what is best for children and view parents as needing to be educated. There is also the limited view of parent involvement that sees PTA membership as the primary goal. These approaches do not adequately convey the complexity of the partnership between teachers and parents that is a fundamental element of good practice (Powell 1994).

When the parent education approach is criticized in favor of a more family-centered approach, this shift may be misunderstood to mean that parents dictate all program content and professionals abdicate responsibility, doing whatever parents want regardless of whether professionals agree that it is in children's best interest. Either of these extremes oversimplifies the importance of relationships with families and fails to provide the kind of environment in which parents and professionals work together to achieve shared goals for children. Such programs with this shared focus are characterized by at least the following guidelines for practice:

A. Reciprocal relationships between teachers and families require mutual respect, cooperation, shared responsibility, and negotiation of conflicts toward achievement of shared goals.

B. Early childhood teachers work in collaborative partnerships with families, establishing and maintaining regular, frequent two-way communication with children's parents.

C. Parents are welcome in the program and participate in decisions about their children's care and education. Parents observe and participate and serve in decisionmaking roles in the program.

D. Teachers acknowledge parents' choices and goals for children and respond with sensitivity and respect to parents' preferences and concerns without abdicating professional responsibility to children.

E. Teachers and parents share their knowledge of the child and understanding of children's development and learning as part of day-to-day communication and planned conferences. Teachers support families in ways that maximally promote family decisionmaking capabilities and competence.

F. To ensure more accurate and complete information, the program involves families in assessing and planning for individual children.

G. The program links families with a range of services, based on identified resources, priorities, and concerns.

H. Teachers, parents, programs, social service and health agencies, and consultants who may have educational responsibility for the child at different times should, with family participation, share developmental information about children as they pass from one level or program to another.

Teachers and parents share their knowledge of the child and understanding of children's development and learning.

Moving from either/or to both/and thinking in early childhood practice

Some critical reactions to NAEYC's (1987) position statement on developmentally appropriate practice reflect a recurring tendency in the American discourse on education: the polarizing into *either/or* choices of many questions that are more fruitfully seen as *both/and*. For example, heated debates have broken out about whether children in the early grades should receive whole-language or phonics instruction, when, in fact, the two approaches are quite compatible and most effective in combination.

It is true that there are practices clearly inappropriate for early childhood professionals—use of physical punishment or disparaging verbal comments about children, discriminating against children or their families, and many other examples that could be cited (see Parts 3, 4, and 5 for examples relevant to different age groups). However, most questions about practice require more complex responses. It is not that children need food **or** water; they need both.

To illustrate the many ways that early childhood practice draws on *both/and* thinking and to convey some of the complexity and interrelationship among the principles that guide our practice, we offer the following statements as **examples**:

- Children construct their own understanding of concepts, **and** they benefit from instruction by more competent peers and adults.

- Children benefit from opportunities to see connections across disciplines through integration of curriculum **and** from opportunities to engage in in-depth study within a content area.

- Children benefit from predictable structure and orderly routine in the learning environment **and** from the teacher's flexibility and spontaneity in responding to their emerging ideas, needs, and interests.

- Children benefit from opportunities to make meaningful choices about what they will do and learn **and** from having a clear understanding of the boundaries within which choices are permissible.

- Children benefit from situations that challenge them to work at the edge of their developing capacities **and** from ample opportunities to practice newly acquired skills and to acquire the disposition to persist.

- Children benefit from opportunities to collaborate with their peers and acquire a sense of being part of a community **and** from being treated as individuals with their own strengths, interests, and needs.

- Children need to develop a positive sense of their own self-identity **and** a respect for other people whose perspectives and experiences may be different from their own.

- Children have enormous capacities to learn and almost boundless curiosity about the world, **and** they have recognized, age-related limits on their cognitive and linguistic capacities.

- Children benefit from engaging in self-initiated, spontaneous play **and** from teacher-planned and -structured activities, projects, and experiences.

The above list is not exhaustive. Many more examples could be cited to convey the interrelationships among the principles of child development and learning or among the guidelines for early childhood practice.

Policies essential for achieving developmentally appropriate early childhood programs

Early childhood professionals working in diverse situations with varying levels of funding and resources are responsible for implementing practices that are developmentally appropriate for the children they serve. Regardless of the resources available, professionals have an ethical responsibility to practice, to the best of their ability, according to the standards of their profession. Nevertheless, the kinds of practices advocated in this position statement are more likely to be implemented within an infrastructure of supportive policies and resources. NAEYC strongly recommends that policymaking groups at the state and local levels consider the following when implementing early childhood programs:

1. A comprehensive professional preparation and development system is in place to ensure that early childhood programs are staffed with qualified personnel (NAEYC 1994).

- A system exists for early childhood professionals to acquire the knowledge and practical skills needed to practice through college-level specialized preparation in early childhood education/child development.

- Teachers in early childhood programs are encouraged and supported to obtain and maintain, through study and participation in inservice training, current knowledge of child development and learning and its application to early childhood practice.

- Specialists in early childhood special education are available to provide assistance and consultation in meeting the individual needs of children in the program.

- In addition to management and supervision skills, administrators of early childhood programs have appropriate professional qualifications, including training specific to the education and development of young children, and they provide teachers time and opportunities to work collaboratively with colleagues and parents.

2. Funding is provided to ensure adequate staffing of early childhood programs and fair staff compensation that promotes continuity of relationships among adults and children (Willer 1990).

- Funding is adequate to limit the size of the groups and provide sufficient numbers of adults to ensure individualized and appropriate care and education. Even the most well-qualified teacher cannot individualize instruction and adequately supervise too large a group of young children. An acceptable adult-child ratio for 4- and 5-year-olds is two adults with no more than 20 children (Ruopp et al. 1979; Francis & Self 1982; Howes 1983; Taylor & Taylor 1989; Howes, Phillips, & Whitebook 1992; Cost, Quality, & Child Outcomes Study Team 1995; Howes, Smith, & Galinsky 1995). Younger children require much smaller groups. Group size and ratio of children to adults should increase gradually through the primary grades, but one teacher with no more than 18 children or two adults with no more than 25 children is optimum (Nye et al. 1992; Nye, Boyd-Zaharias, & Fulton 1994). Inclusion of children with disabilities may necessitate additional adults or smaller group size to ensure that all children's needs are met.

- Programs offer staff salaries and benefits commensurate with the skills and qualifications required for specific roles to ensure the provision of quality services and the effective recruitment and retention of qualified, competent staff. (See *Compensation Guidelines for Early Childhood Professionals* [NAEYC 1993].)

- Decisions related to how programs are staffed and how children are grouped result in increased opportunities for children to experience continuity of relationships with teachers and other children. Such strategies include but are not limited to multiage grouping and multiyear teacher-child relationships (Katz, Evangelou, & Hartman 1990; Zero to Three 1995; Burke 1996).

3. Resources and expertise are available to provide safe, stimulating learning environments with a sufficient number and variety of appropriate materials and equipment for the age group served (Bronson 1995; Kendrick, Kaufmann, & Messenger 1995).

4. Adequate systems for regulating and monitoring the quality of early childhood programs are in place (see position on licensing [NAEYC 1987]; accreditation criteria and procedures [NAEYC 1991]).

5. Community resources are available and used to support the comprehensive needs of children and families (Kagan 1991; NASBE 1991; Kagan et al. 1995; NCSL 1995).

6. When individual children do not make expected learning progress, neither grade retention nor social promotion are used; instead, initiatives such as more focused time, individualized instruction, tutoring, or other individual strategies are used to accelerate children's learning (Shepard & Smith 1989; Ross et al. 1995).

7. Early childhood programs use multiple indicators of progress in all development domains to evaluate the effect of the program on children's development and learning and regularly report children's progress to parents. Group-administered, standardized, multiple-choice achievement tests are not used before third grade, preferably before fourth grade. When such tests are used to demonstrate public accountability, a sampling method is used (see Shepard 1994).

References

Adams, G., & J. Sandfort. 1994. *First steps, promising futures: State prekindergarten initiatives in the early 1990s*. Washington, DC: Children's Defense Fund.

Alexander, K.L., & D.R. Entwisle. 1988. *Achievement in the first 2 years of school: Patterns and processes*. Monographs of the Society for Research in Child Development, vol. 53, no. 2, serial no. 218. Ann Arbor: University of Michigan.

Arnett, J. 1989. Caregivers in day-care centers: Does training matter? *Journal of Applied Developmental Psychology* 10 (4): 541–52.

Asher, S., S. Hymel, & P. Renshaw. 1984. Loneliness in children. *Child Development* 55: 1456–64.

Barnett, W.S. 1995. Long-term effects of early childhood programs on cognitive and school outcomes. *The Future of Children* 5 (3): 25–50.

Bergen, D. 1988. *Play as a medium for learning and development*. Portsmouth, NH: Heinemann.

Berk, L.E. 1996. *Infants and children: Prenatal through middle childhood*. 2d ed. Needham Heights, MA: Allyn & Bacon.

Berk, L., & A. Winsler. 1995. *Scaffolding children's learning: Vygotsky and early childhood education*. Washington, DC: NAEYC.

Berruetta-Clement, J.R., L.J. Schweinhart, W.S. Barnett, A.S. Epstein, & D.P. Weikart. 1984. *Changed lives: The effects of the Perry Preschool Program on youths through age 19*. Monographs of the High/Scope Educational Research Foundation, no. 8. Ypsilanti, MI: High/Scope Press.

Bodrova, E., & D. Leong. 1996. *Tools of the mind: The Vygotskian approach to early childhood education*. Englewood Cliffs, NJ: Merrill/Prentice Hall.

Bowlby, J. 1969. *Attachment and and loss: Vol. 1. Attachment*. New York: Basic.

Bowman, B. 1994. The challenge of diversity. *Phi Delta Kappan* 76 (3): 218–25.

Bowman, B., & F. Stott. 1994. Understanding development in a cultural context: The challenge for teachers. In *Diversity and developmentally appropriate practices: Challenges for early childhood education*, eds. B. Mallory & R. New, 119–34. New York: Teachers College Press.

Bredekamp, S., ed. 1987. *Developmentally appropriate practice in early childhood programs serving children from birth through age 8*. Exp. ed. Washington, DC: NAEYC.

Bredekamp, S. 1993a. Reflections on Reggio Emilia. *Young Children* 49 (1): 13–17.

Bredekamp, S. 1993b. The relationship between early childhood education and early childhood special education: Healthy marriage or family feud? *Topics in Early Childhood Special Education* 13 (3): 258–73.

Bredekamp, S., & T. Rosegrant, eds. 1992. *Reaching potentials: Appropriate curriculum and assessment for young children, volume 1*. Washington, DC: NAEYC.

Bredekamp, S., & T. Rosegrant, eds. 1995. *Reaching potentials: Transforming early childhood curriculum and assessment, volume 2*. Washington, DC: NAEYC.

Bronfenbrenner, U. 1979. *The ecology of human development: Experiments by nature and design.* Cambridge, MA: Harvard University Press.

Bronfenbrenner, U. 1989. Ecological systems theory. In *Annals of child development,* vol. 6, ed. R. Vasta, 187–251. Greenwich, CT: JAI Press.

Bronfenbrenner, U. 1993. The ecology of cognitive development: Research models and fugitive findings. In *Development in context,* eds. R.H. Wozniak & K.W. Fischer, 3–44. Hillsdale, NJ: Erlbaum.

Bronson, M.B. 1995. *The right stuff for children birth to 8: Selecting play materials to support development.* Washington, DC: NAEYC.

Brophy, J. 1992. Probing the subtleties of subject matter teaching. *Educational Leadership* 49 (7): 4–8.

Bruner, J.S. 1983. *Child's talk: Learning to use language.* New York: Norton.

Bruner, J.S. 1996. *The culture of education.* Cambridge, MA: Harvard University Press.

Bryant, D.M., R. Clifford, & E.S. Peisner. 1991. Best practices for beginners: Developmental appropriateness in kindergarten. *American Educational Research Journal* 28 (4): 783–803.

Burchinal, M., J. Robert, L. Nabo, & D. Bryant. 1996. Quality of center child care and infant cognitive and language development. *Child Development* 67 (2): 606–20.

Burke, D. 1996. Multi-year teacher/student relationships are a long-overdue arrangement. *Phi Delta Kappan* 77 (5): 360–61.

Caine, R., & G. Caine. 1991. *Making connections: Teaching and the human brain.* New York: Addison-Wesley.

Campbell, F., & C. Ramey. 1995. Cognitive and school outcomes for high-risk African-American students at middle adolescence: Positive effects of early intervention. *American Educational Research Journal* 32 (4): 743–72.

Carnegie Task Force on Learning in the Primary Grades. 1996. *Years of promise: A comprehensive learning strategy for America's children.* New York: Carnegie Corporation of New York.

Carta, J., I. Schwartz, J. Atwater, & S. McConnell. 1991. Developmentally appropriate practice: Appraising its usefulness for young children with disabilities. *Topics in Early Childhood Special Education* 11 (1): 1–20.

Case, R., & Y. Okamoto. 1996. *The role of central conceptual structures in the development of children's thought.* Monographs of the Society of Research in Child Development, vol. 61, no. 2, serial no. 246. Chicago: University of Chicago Press.

Charlesworth, R., C.H. Hart, D.C. Burts, & M. DeWolf. 1993. The LSU studies: Building a research base for developmentally appropriate practice. In *Perspectives on developmentally appropriate practice,* vol. 5 of *Advances in early education and day care,* ed. S. Reifel, 3–28. Greenwich, CT: JAI Press.

Chugani, H., M.E. Phelps, & J.C. Mazziotta. 1987. Positron emission tomography study of human brain functional development. *Annals of Neurology* 22 (4): 495.

Cohen, N., & K. Modigliani. 1994. The family-to-family project: Developing family child care providers. In *The early childhood career lattice: Perspectives on professional development,* eds. J. Johnson & J.B. McCracken, 106–10. Washington, DC: NAEYC.

Copple, C., I.E. Sigel, & R. Saunders. 1984. *Educating the young thinker: Classroom strategies for cognitive growth.* Hillsdale, NJ: Erlbaum.

Cost, Quality, & Child Outcomes Study Team. 1995. *Cost, quality, and child outcomes in child care centers, public report.* 2d ed. Denver: Economics Department, University of Colorado at Denver.

Dana Alliance for Brain Initiatives. 1996. *Delivering results: A progress report on brain research.* Washington, DC: Author.

DEC/CEC (Division for Early Childhood of the Council for Exceptional Children). 1994. Position on inclusion. *Young Children* 49 (5): 78.

DEC (Division for Early Childhood) Task Force on Recommended Practices. 1993. *DEC recommended practices: Indicators of quality in programs for infants and young children with special needs and their families.* Reston, VA: Council for Exceptional Children.

DEC/CEC & NAEYC (Division for Early Childhood of the Council for Exceptional Children & the National Association for the Education of Young Children). 1993. *Understanding the ADA—The Americans with Disabilities Act: Information for early childhood programs.* Pittsburgh, PA, & Washington, DC: Authors.

DeVries, R., & W. Kohlberg. 1990. *Constructivist early education: Overview and comparison with other programs.* Washington, DC: NAEYC.

Dewey, J. 1916. *Democracy and education: An introduction to the philosophy of education.* New York: Macmillan.

Durkin, D. 1987. A classroom-observation study of reading instruction in kindergarten. *Early Childhood Research Quarterly* 2 (3): 275–300.

Durkin, D. 1990. Reading instruction in kindergarten: A look at some issues through the lens of new basal reader materials. *Early Children Research Quarterly* 5 (3): 299–316.

Dweck, C. 1986. Motivational processes affecting learning. *American Psychologist* 41: 1030–48.

Dyson, A.H., & C. Genishi. 1993. Visions of children as language users: Language and language education in early childhood. In *Handbook of research on the education of young children,* ed. B. Spodek, 122–36. New York: Macmillan.

Edwards, C.P., & L. Gandini. 1989. Teachers' expectations about the timing of developmental skills: A cross-cultural study. *Young Children* 44 (4): 15–19.

Edwards, C., L. Gandini, & G. Forman, eds. 1993. *The hundred languages of children: The Reggio Emilia approach to early childhood education.* Norwood, NJ: Ablex.

Erikson, E. 1963. *Childhood and society.* New York: Norton.

Feeney, S., & K. Kipnis. 1992. *Code of ethical conduct & statement of commitment.* Washington, DC: NAEYC.

Fein, G. 1981. Pretend play: An integrative review. *Child Development* 52: 1095–118.

Fein, G., & M. Rivkin, eds. 1986. *The young child at play: Reviews of research.* Washington, DC: NAEYC.

Fenson, L., P. Dale, J.S. Reznick, E. Bates, D. Thal, & S. Pethick. 1994. *Variability in early communicative development.* Monographs of the Society for Research in Child Development, vol. 59, no. 2, serial no. 242. Chicago: University of Chicago Press.

Fernald, A. 1992. Human maternal vocalizations to infants as biologically relevant signals: An evolutionary perspective. In *The adapted mind: Evolutionary psychology and the generation of culture,* eds. J.H. Barkow, L. Cosmides, & J. Tooby, 391–428. New York: Oxford University Press.

Fields, T., W. Masi, S. Goldstein, S. Perry, & S. Parl. 1988. Infant day care facilitates preschool social behavior. *Early Childhood Research Quarterly* 3 (4): 341–59.

Forman, G. 1994. Different media, different languages. In *Reflections on the Reggio Emilia approach,* eds. L. Katz & B. Cesarone, 37–46. Urbana, IL: ERIC Clearinghouse on Elementary and Early Childhood Education.

Forman, E.A., N. Minick, & C.A. Stone. 1993. *Contexts for learning: Sociocultural dynamics in children's development.* New York: Oxford University Press.

Francis, P., & P. Self. 1982. Imitative responsiveness of young children in day care and home settings: The importance of the child to caregiver ratio. *Child Study Journal* 12: 119–26.

Frede, E. 1995. The role of program quality in producing early childhood program benefits. *The Future of Children* 5 (3): 115–132.

Frede, E., & W.S. Barnett. 1992. Developmentally appropriate public school preschool: A study of implementation of the High/Scope curriculum and its effects on disadvantaged children's skills at first grade. *Early Childhood Research Quarterly* 7 (4): 483–99.

Fromberg, D. 1992. Play. In *The early childhood curriculum: A review of current research,* 2d ed., ed. C. Seefeldt, 35–74. New York: Teachers College Press.

Galinsky, E., C. Howes, S. Kontos, & M. Shinn. 1994. *The study of children in family child care and relative care: Highlights of findings.* New York: Families and Work Institute.

Gallahue, D. 1993. Motor development and movement skill acquisition in early childhood education. In *Handbook of research on the education of young children,* ed. B. Spodek, 24–41. New York: Macmillan.

Gallahue, D. 1995. Transforming physical education curriculum. In *Reaching potentials: Transforming early childhood curriculum and assessment, volume 2,* eds. S. Bredekamp & T. Rosegrant, 125–44. Washington, DC: NAEYC.

Garbarino, J., N. Dubrow, K. Kostelny, & C. Pardo. 1992. *Children in danger: Coping with the consequences of community violence.* San Francisco: Jossey-Bass.

Gardner, H. 1983. *Frames of mind: The theory of multiple intelligences.* New York: Basic.

Gardner, H. 1991. *The unschooled mind: How children think and how schools should teach.* New York: Basic.

Gelman, R., & R. Baillargeon. 1983. A review of some Piagetian concepts. In *Handbook of child psychology,* vol. 3, ed. P.H. Mussen, 167–230. New York: Wiley.

Gelman, R., & E. Meck. 1983. Preschoolers' counting: Principles before skill. *Cognition* 13: 343–59.

Hale-Benson, J. 1986. *Black children: Their roots, cultures, and learning styles.* Rev. ed. Baltimore: Johns Hopkins University Press.

Herron, R., & B. Sutton-Smith. 1971. *Child's play.* New York: Wiley.

Hiebert, E.H., & J.M. Papierz. 1990. The emergent literacy construct and kindergarten and readiness books of basal reading series. *Early Childhood Research Quarterly* 5 (3): 317–34.

Hohmann, M., & D. Weikart. 1995. *Educating young children: Active learning practices for preschool and child care programs.* Ypsilanti, MI: High/Scope Educational Research Foundation.

Hollestelle, K. 1993. At the core: Entrepreneurial skills for family child care providers. In *The early childhood career lattice: Perspectives on professional development,* eds. J. Johnson & J.B. McCracken, 63–65. Washington, DC: NAEYC.

Howes, C. 1983. Caregiver behavior in center and family day care. *Journal of Applied Developmental Psychology* 4: 96–107.

Howes, C. 1988. Relations between early child care and schooling. *Developmental Psychology* 24 (1): 53–57.

Howes, C., D.A. Phillips, & M. Whitebook. 1992. Thresholds of quality: Implications for the social development of children in center-based child care. *Child Development* 63 (2): 449–60.

Howes, C., E. Smith, & E. Galinsky. 1995. *The Florida child care quality improvement study.* New York: Families and Work Institute.

Kagan, S.L. 1991. *United we stand: Collaboration for child care and early educaion services.* New York: Teachers College Press.

Kagan, S., S. Goffin, S. Golub, & E. Pritchard. 1995. *Toward systematic reform: Service integration for young children and their families.* Falls Church, VA: National Center for Service Integration.

Kamii, C., & J.K. Ewing. 1996. Basing teaching on Piaget's constructivism. *Childhood Education* 72 (5): 260–64.

Katz, L. 1995. *Talks with teachers of young children: A collection.* Norwood, NJ: Ablex.

Katz, L., & S. Chard. 1989. *Engaging children minds: The project approach.* Norwood, NJ: Ablex.

Katz, L., D. Evangelou, & J. Hartman. 1990. *The case for mixed-age grouping in early education.* Washington, DC: NAEYC.

Kendrick, A., R. Kaufmann, & K. Messenger, eds. 1995. *Healthy young children: A manual for programs.* Washington, DC: NAEYC.

Kohn, A. 1993. *Punished by rewards.* Boston: Houghton Mifflin.

Kostelnik, M., A. Soderman, & A. Whiren. 1993. *Developmentally appropriate programs in early childhood education.* New York: Macmillan.

Kuhl, P. 1994. Learning and representation in speech and language. *Current Opinion in Neurobiology* 4: 812–22.

Lary, R.T. 1990. Successful students. *Education Issues* 3 (2): 11–17.

Layzer, J.I., B.D. Goodson, & M. Moss. 1993. *Life in preschool: Volume one of an observational study of early childhood programs for disadvantaged four-year-olds.* Cambridge, MA: Abt Association.

Lazar, I., & R. Darlington. 1982. *Lasting effects of early education: A report from the Consortium for Longitudinal Studies*. Monographs of the Society for Research in Child Development, vol. 47, nos. 2-3, serial no. 195. Chicago: University of Chicago Press.

Lee, V.E., J. Brooks-Gunn, & E. Schuur. 1988. Does Head Start work? A 1-year follow-up comparison of disadvantaged children attending Head Start, no preschool, and other preschool programs. *Developmental Psychology* 24 (2): 210–22.

Legters, N., & R.E. Slavin. 1992. Elementary students at risk: A status report. Paper commissioned by the Carnegie Corporation of New York for meeting on elementary-school reform. 1–2 June.

Levy, A.K., L. Schaefer, & P.C. Phelps. 1986. Increasing preschool effectiveness: Enhancing the language abilities of 3- and 4-year-old children through planned sociodramatic play. *Early Childhood Research Quarterly* 1 (2): 133–40.

Levy, A.K., C.H. Wolfgang, & M.A. Koorland. 1992. Sociodramatic play as a method for enhancing the language performance of kindergarten age students. *Early Childhood Research Quarterly* 7 (2): 245–62.

Malaguzzi, L. 1993. History, ideas, and basic philosophy. In *The hundred languages of children: The Reggio Emilia approach to early childhood education*, eds. C. Edwards, L. Gandini, & G. Forman, 41–89. Norwood, NJ: Ablex.

Mallory, B. 1992. Is it always appropriate to be developmental? Convergent models for early intervention practice. *Topics in Early Childhood Special Education* 11 (4): 1–12.

Mallory, B. 1994. Inclusive policy, practice, and theory for young children with developmental differences. In *Diversity and developmentally appropriate practices: Challenges for early childhood education*, eds. B. Mallory & R. New, 44–61. New York: Teachers College Press.

Mallory, B.L., & R.S. New. 1994a. *Diversity and developmentally appropriate practices: Challenges for early childhood education*. New York: Teachers College Press.

Mallory, B.L., & R.S. New. 1994b. Social constructivist theory and principles of inclusion: Challenges for early childhood special education. *Journal of Special Education* 28 (3): 322–37.

Marcon, R.A. 1992. Differential effects of three preschool models on inner-city 4-year-olds. *Early Childhood Research Quarterly* 7 (4): 517–30.

Maslow, A. 1954. *Motivation and personality*. New York: Harper & Row.

Miller, L.B., & R.P. Bizzell. 1984. Long-term effects of four preschool programs: Ninth and tenth-grade results. *Child Development* 55 (4): 1570–87.

Mitchell, A., M. Seligson, & F. Marx. 1989. *Early childhood programs and the public schools*. Dover, MA: Auburn House.

Montessori, M. 1909/1964. *The Montessori method*. New York: Schocken.

Morrow, L.M. 1990. Preparing the classroom environment to promote literacy during play. *Early Childhood Research Quarterly* 5 (4): 537–54.

NAEYC. 1987. *NAEYC position statement on licensing and other forms of regulation of early childhood programs in centers and family day care*. Washington, DC: Author.

NAEYC. 1991. *Accreditation criteria and procedures of the National Academy of Early Childhood Programs*. Rev. ed. Washington, DC: Author.

NAEYC. 1993. *Compensation guidelines for early childhood professionals*. Washington, DC: Author.

NAEYC. 1994. NAEYC position statement: A conceptual framework for early childhood professional development, adopted November 1993. *Young Children* 49 (3): 68–77.

NAEYC. 1996a. NAEYC position statement: Responding to linguistic and cultural diversity—Recommendations for effective early childhood education. *Young Children* 51 (2): 4–12.

NAEYC. 1996b. NAEYC position statement: Technology and young children—Ages three through eight. *Young Children* 51 (6): 11–16.

NAEYC & NAECS/SDE (National Association of Early Childhood Specialists in State Departments of Education). 1992. Guidelines for appropriate curriculum content and assessment in programs serving children ages 3 through 8. In *Reaching potentials: Appropriate curriculum and assessment for young children, volume 1,* eds. S. Bredekamp & T. Rosegrant, 9–27. Washington, DC: NAEYC.

NASBE (National Association of State Boards of Education). 1991. *Caring communities: Supporting young children and families*. Alexandria, VA: Author.

Natriello, G., E. McDill, & A. Pallas. 1990. *Schooling disadvantaged children: Racing against catastrophe*. New York: Teachers College Press.

NCES (National Center for Education Statistics). 1993. *The condition of education, 1993*. Washington, DC: U.S. Department of Education.

NCSL (National Conference of State Legislatures). 1995. *Early childhood care and education: An investment that works*. Denver: Author.

NEGP (National Education Goals Panel). 1991. *National education goals report: Building a nation of learners*. Washington, DC: Author.

New, R. 1993. Cultural variations on developmentally appropriate practice: Challenges to theory and practice. In *The hundred languages of children: The Reggio Emilia approach to early childhood education*, eds C. Edwards, L. Gandini, & G. Forman, 215–32. Norwood, NJ: Ablex.

New, R. 1994. Culture, child development, and developmentally appropriate practices: Teachers as collaborative researchers. In *Diversity and developmentally appropriate practices: Challenges for early childhood education*, eds. B. Mallory & R. New, 65–83. New York: Teachers College Press.

Nye, B.A., J. Boyd-Zaharias, & B.D. Fulton. 1994. *The lasting benefits study: A continuing analysis of the effect of small class size in kindergarten through third grade on student achievement test scores in subsequent grade levels—seventh grade (1992–93), technical report*. Nashville: Center of Excellence for Research in Basic Skills, Tennessee State University.

Nye, B.A., J. Boyd-Zaharias, B.D. Fulton, & M.P. Wallenhorst. 1992. Smaller classes really are better. *The American School Board Journal* 179 (5): 31–33.

POSITION
STATEMENT

Parker, J.G., & S.R. Asher. 1987. Peer relations and later personal adjustment: Are low-accepted children at risk? *Psychology Bulletin* 102 (3): 357–89.

Phillips, C.B. 1994. The movement of African-American children through sociocultural contexts: A case of conflict resolution. In *Diversity and developmentally appropriate practices: Challenges for early childhood education*, eds. B. Mallory & R. New, 137–54. New York: Teachers College Press.

Phillips, D.A., K. McCartney, & S. Scarr. 1987. Child care quality and children's social development. *Developmental Psychology* 23 (4): 537–43.

Piaget, J. 1952. *The origins of intelligence in children*. New York: International Universities Press.

Plomin, R. 1994a. *Genetics and experience: The interplay between nature and nurture*. Thousand Oaks, CA: Sage.

Plomin, R. 1994b. Nature, nurture, and social development. *Social Development* 3: 37–53.

Powell, D. 1994. Parents, pluralism, and the NAEYC statement on developmentally appropriate practice. In *Diversity and developmentally appropriate practices: Challenges for early childhood education*, eds. B. Mallory & R. New, 166–82. New York: Teachers College Press.

Pramling, I. 1991. Learning about "the shop": An approach to learning in preschool. *Early Childhood Research Quarterly* 6 (2): 151–66.

Resnick, L. 1996. Schooling and the workplace: What relationship? In *Preparing youth for the 21st century*, 21–27. Washington, DC: Aspen Institute.

Rogoff, B. 1990. *Apprenticeship in thinking: Cognitive development in social context*. New York: Oxford University Press.

Rogoff, B., J. Mistry, A. Goncu, & C. Mosier. 1993. *Guided participation in cultural activity by toddlers and caregivers*. Monographs of the Society for Research in Child Development, vol. 58, no. 8, serial no. 236. Chicago: University of Chicago Press.

Ross, S.M., L.J. Smith, J. Casey, & R.E. Slavin. 1995. Increasing the academic success of disadvantaged children: An examination of alternative early intervention programs. *American Educational Research Journal* 32 (4): 773–800.

Ruopp, R., J. Travers, F. Glantz, & C. Coelen. 1979. *Children at the center: Final report of the National Day Care Study*. Cambridge, MA: Abt Associates.

Sameroff, A., & S. McDonough. 1994. Educational implications of developmental transitions: Revisiting the 5- to 7-year shift. *Phi Delta Kappan* 76 (3): 188–93.

Scarr, S., & K. McCartney. 1983. How people make their own environments: A theory of genotype—environment effects. *Child Development* 54: 425–35.

Schrader, C.T. 1989. Written language use within the context of young children's symbolic play. *Early Childhood Research Quarterly* 4 (2): 225–44.

Schrader, C.T. 1990. Symbolic play as a curricular tool for early literacy development. *Early Childhood Research Quarterly* 5 (1): 79–103.

Schweinhart, L.J., & D.P. Weikart. 1996. *Lasting differences: The High/Scope preschool curriculum comparison study through age 23*. Monographs of the High/Scope Educational Research Foundation, no 12. Ypsilanti, MI: High/Scope Press.

Schweinhart, L.J., H.V. Barnes, & D.P. Weikart. 1993. *Significant benefits: The High/Scope Perry Preschool Study through age 27*. Monographs of the High/Scope Educational Research Foundation, no. 10, Ypsilanti, MI: High/Scope Press.

Schweinhart, L.J., D.P. Weikart, & M.B. Larner. 1986. Child-initiated activities in early childhood programs may help prevent delinquency. *Early Childhood Research Quarterly* 1 (3): 303–12.

Seefeldt, C., ed. 1992. *The early childhood curriculum: A review of current research*. 2d ed. New York: Teachers College Press.

Seifert, K. 1993. Cognitive development and early childhood education. In *Handbook of research on the education of young children*, ed. B. Spodek, 9–23. New York: Macmillan.

Seppanen, P.S., D. Kaplan deVries, & M. Seligson. 1993. *National study of before and after school programs*. Portsmouth, NH: RMC Research Corp.

Shepard, L. 1994. The challenges of assessing young children appropriately. *Phi Delta Kappan* 76 (3): 206–13.

Shepard, L.A., & M.L. Smith. 1988. Escalating academic demand in kindergarten: Some nonsolutions. *Elementary School Journal* 89 (2): 135–46.

Shepard, L.A., & M.L. Smith. 1989. *Flunking grades: Research and policies on retention*. Bristol, PA: Taylor & Francis.

Slavin, R., N. Karweit, & N. Madden, eds. 1989. *Effective programs for students at-risk*. Boston: Allyn & Bacon.

Smilansky, S., & L. Shefatya. 1990. *Facilitating play: A medium for promoting cognitive, socioemotional, and academic development in young children*. Gaithersburg, MD: Psychosocial & Educational Publications.

Spodek, B., ed. 1993. *Handbook of research on the education of young children*. New York: Macmillan.

Sroufe, L.A., R.G. Cooper, & G.B. DeHart. 1992. *Child development: Its nature and course*. 2d ed. New York: Knopf.

Stern, D. 1985. *The psychological world of the human infant*. New York: Basic.

Stremmel, A.J., & V.R. Fu. 1993. Teaching in the zone of proximal development: Implications for responsive teaching practice. *Child and Youth Care Forum* 22 (5): 337–50.

Taylor, J.M., & W.S. Taylor. 1989. *Communicable diseases and young children in group settings*. Boston: Little, Brown.

Tobin, J., D. Wu, & D. Davidson. 1989. *Preschool in three cultures*. New Haven, CT: Yale University Press.

U.S. Department of Health & Human Services. 1996. *Head Start performance standards*. Washington, DC: Author.

Vandell, D.L., & M.A. Corasanti. 1990. Variations in early child care: Do they predict subsequent social, emotional, and cognitive differences? *Early Childhood Research Quarterly* 5 (4): 555–72.

Vandell, D.L., & C.D. Powers. 1983. Day care quality and children's freeplay activities. *American Journal of Orthopsychiatry* 53 (4): 493–500.

Vandell, D.L., V.K. Henderson, & K.S. Wilson. 1988. A longitudinal study of children with day-care experiences of varying quality. *Child Development* 59 (5): 1286–92.

Vygotsky, L. 1978. *Mind in society: The development of higher psychological processes*. Cambridge, MA: Harvard University Press.

Wardle, F. 1996. Proposal: An anti-bias and ecological model for multicultural education. *Childhood Education* 72 (3): 152–56.

Wertsch, J. 1985. *Culture, communication, and cognition: Vygotskian perspectives.* New York: Cambridge University Press.

White, S.H. 1965. Evidence for a hierarchical arrangement of learning processes. In *Advances in child development and behavior,* eds. L.P. Lipsitt & C.C. Spiker, 187–220. New York: Academic.

Whitebook, M., C. Howes, & D. Phillips. 1989. *The national child care staffing study: Who cares? Child care teachers and the quality of care in America.* Final report. Oakland, CA: Child Care Employee Project.

Wieder, S., & S.I. Greenspan. 1993. The emotional basis of learning. In *Handbook of research on the education of young children,* ed. B. Spodek, 77–104. New York: Macmillan.

Willer, B. 1990. *Reaching the full cost of quality in early childhood programs.* Washington, DC: NAEYC.

Willer, B., S.L. Hofferth, E.E. Kisker, P. Divine-Hawkins, E. Farquhar, & F.B. Glantz. 1991. *The demand and supply of child care in 1990.* Washington, DC: NAEYC.

Witkin, H. 1962. *Psychological differentiation: Studies of development.* New York: Wiley.

Wolery, M., & J. Wilbers, eds. 1994. *Including children with special needs in early childhood programs.* Washington, DC: NAEYC.

Wolery, M., P. Strain, & D. Bailey. 1992. Reaching potentials of children with special needs. In *Reaching potentials: Appropriate curriculum and assessment for young children, volume 1,* eds. S. Bredekamp & T. Rosegrant, 92–111. Washington, DC: NAEYC.

Zero to Three, National Center for Infants, Toddlers, & Families. 1995. *Caring for infants and toddlers in groups: Developmentally appropriate practice.* Arlington, VA: Author.

Developmentally Appropriate Practice: The Early Childhood Teacher As Decisionmaker

Sue Bredekamp

The ideas presented in this section were constructed through a collaborative process by the members of NAEYC's Panel on Revisions to Developmentally Appropriate Practice. Inspired by our encounters with our colleagues in Reggio Emilia, Italy, and challenged in our thinking by each other and by many of our American colleagues, the Panel members argued, confronted differences of opinion, challenged each other's perspectives, and collectively grew and changed as a result of the experience.

As an early childhood professional, ask yourself which of the following practices are developmentally appropriate.

1. A teacher conducts an activity for 30 minutes with young 3-year-olds who mostly observe, listen, and watch the teacher.

2. A teacher reads a picture book to a group of 4-year-olds.

3. A kindergarten teacher provides one hour of free-choice time during which children play with blocks, dress up, and use table toys and other typical early childhood materials.

4. A teacher stands at the blackboard conducting a whole-group math lesson with second-graders.

Many early childhood educators might assume that numbers 2 and 3 are developmentally appropriate, while 1 and 4 are not. However, many other early childhood professionals might say that they cannot decide because they don't have enough information. The examples above leave the reader to infer a great deal about how these teachers are actually supporting children's development and learning and about the individual children in each class and the social and cultural context (Kostelnik 1993). Let's take a closer look.

Assuming that most young 3-year-olds have limited attention spans, are egocentric, and are more likely to learn when actively engaging than when sitting in a group, many early childhood professionals might question the appropriateness of the 30-minute passive activity in the first example. However, this classroom is in a rural program serving a Native American community of which the teacher is a member. In this cultural context, children do much of their learning through observation, imitation, and nonverbal communication, and the culture values interdependence over independence (Little Soldier 1992; Williams 1994). Their teacher is experienced at using the tools and processes of the culture to help children develop valued skills. She is very attuned to their verbal and nonverbal messages and watches for signs of fatigue. The children have opportunities throughout the day to explore, play, and interact with materials. Knowing the context and observing that in the activity described all the children are engaged, interested, participating, and learning, we may recognize that the situation *is* both culturally congruent and developmentally appropriate for these children.

In the second example, the 4-year-olds are enrolled in a public school prekindergarten program. All the children speak Spanish as their home language, and only a few know much English. The teacher is reading an English-language alphabet book to the children that illustrates each letter of the alphabet with a picture of a word that begins with the letter. The children struggle to make sense of the teacher's words. Some of the objects depicted are completely unfamiliar to them. Several children appear bored and become fidgety or talkative with their friends. A few children walk away from the group and the assistant teacher makes them sit in time-out. One child, Carlos, is hearing impaired, and no one is available to sign for him. Observing this situation, a professional equipped with a knowledge of child development and second-language acquisition would seriously question the appropriateness of the choice of book and the format. Young children learn a second language much the same way they learn their first language—through comprehensible, meaningful input (Krashen 1992). Because the teacher's reading of the alphabet book is incomprehensible for most of the children and individually inappropriate for Carlos—he does not hear the words at all—it is *not* developmentally appropriate practice.

In the third example, the kindergarten children love free-choice time, but the materials available to them have not been changed for six months. Many children wander from one activity to another without serious engagement while others continue to do the same things (build a racetrack with blocks or set the table in the housekeeping corner) that they have done every day for months. The teacher generally ignores the children except to correct misbehavior, using the children's free-play time to correct the worksheets they completed yesterday. Children's play and self-selected activity can be a valuable learning experience in many ways. But without planning,

variety, interest, or adult support, the value of play for learning and development is severely diminished. Although providing time for play in kindergarten would typically be considered a good example of developmentally appropriate practice, this teacher's use of play could not be considered developmentally appropriate for these children.

The second-grade classroom in the fourth example seems to embody cornerstone elements of highly traditional educational practice—whole-group, teacher-directed instruction. Yet a closer look tells a different story. The children have been working on these math concepts for several weeks, using a variety of math manipulatives and other methods to develop their understanding of double-digit numbers, addition, estimation, and hypothesis testing. Today, the teacher, Ms. Parker, writes a problem on the board:

$$\begin{array}{r} 22 \\ + 48 \\ \hline \end{array}$$

The children take a few moments to silently add the numbers in their heads. Building on children's intuitive understandings of number, the teacher asks the children to report their estimates, polling them then to see which answers they agree with. Estimates are 54, 60, 70, and 66. The children describe verbally how they got their answers. Carver says, "2 and 2 is 4 and 4 and 8 are 12, so I thought it was 16. But that wasn't a big enough number, so I guessed 66." Elizabeth explains, "48 is almost 40 and 22 is almost 20, so I answered 60." Taneesha says, "20 and 40 are 60, 2 and 8 are 10, and 60 and 10 are 70." Hearing these explanations, some children recognize the errors in their reasoning and decide to change their answers. Ms. Parker asks them to explain why. She continues to involve all the children in the problem solving, observing which children begin to grasp the concepts and which children continue to guess wildly. Later she plans small-group activities to help children at different ability levels to consolidate their understanding of adding large numbers and to move forward. Although the children are in their seats, they are mentally active, engaged in problem solving, working collaboratively, and learning important math concepts, not just memorizing a trick to get the right answer. This second-grade math lesson includes key elements of developmentally appropriate practice (Kamii 1985, 1989).

There is no formula for developmentally appropriate practice. Teachers make decisions day by day, minute by minute, based on knowledge of how children develop and learn, the individual children and families in question, and the social and cultural context.

Overview and NAEYC's definition of developmentally appropriate practice

From these examples and countless others that could be cited, we see that decisions about developmentally appropriate practice are not possible apart from information about the context and the individual children. The purpose of this section is to elaborate on what we mean when we use the term "developmentally appropriate practice" and to demonstrate the complexity of the professional decisions that such practice requires. NAEYC defines developmentally appropriate practice as resulting from

The process of professionals making decisions about the well-being and education of children based on at least three important kinds of information or knowledge:

1. what is known about child development and learning—knowledge of age-related human characteristics that permits general predictions within an age range about what activities, materials, interactions, or experiences will be safe, healthy, interesting, achievable, and also challenging to children;

2. what is known about the strengths, interests, and needs of each individual child in the group to be able to adapt for and be responsive to inevitable individual variation; and

3. knowledge of the social and cultural contexts in which children live to ensure that learning experiences are meaningful, relevant, and respectful for the participating children and their families. (See Part 1, pp. 8–9.)

From this definition, it is clear that the concept of developmentally appropriate practice is not limited in applicability to young children but can be applied throughout the life span. For example, the need for developmentally appropriate education in middle school and adolescence is well documented (Task Force on Education of Young Adolescents 1989; Carnegie Council on Adolescent Development 1996). Others have begun to apply the principles in teacher education, not to teach adults in the same way children are taught but to teach adults in ways that consider the three sources of knowledge.

The NAEYC position statement provides general principles to guide the complex decisions of teachers; it cannot—and should not attempt to—prescribe actual behavior because so many important factors, including the specific context and individual children and families, vary across classrooms. In this

section, first, we elaborate on each of the three pieces of important information that must be considered in decisions about teaching young children and provide some examples of the interrelatedness of this knowledge. Next, we raise the issue of contradictions that inevitably arise, given this paradigm of decisionmaking. For example, teachers see it as inappropriate to use physical punishment, but some parents hold a strong cultural or religious value that sanctions spanking. What does the professional do to resolve this conflict? This section concludes with a discussion of a suggested process for addressing and working through such conflicts in ways that are beneficial for all involved.

Using knowledge about child development and learning to inform practice

To make valid decisions about how to teach young children, teachers must know how children develop and learn. This statement may appear self-evident, and yet it has been the subject of much debate and even controversy in the early childhood profession since NAEYC's publication of its earlier position statement on developmentally appropriate practice (Bredekamp 1987). Critics have raised legitimate questions about the usefulness of the existing child development knowledge base for informing practice, particularly as to whether it is valid across cultures (Spodek 1991; New 1994; Lubeck 1996); this issue is discussed more fully later in this section. Further, scholars in the field have a persistent concern about the too-frequent assumption that child development knowledge is the only important information that early childhood teachers need (Spodek 1991; Goffin 1996; Stott & Bowman 1996). Of course, they are correct in pointing out that child development knowledge, though necessary, is not a sufficient basis for good practice. Yet thinking of child development knowledge as merely information about universals— "ages and stages"—is a major misconception, perhaps exacerbated by the "age-appropriateness" language of the 1987 version.

The revised position statement includes the fundamental principle that there are observable differences in human beings related to their age (for example, 2-year-olds everywhere in the world are more like each other than they are like 7-year-olds).

But because there are serious limitations to the use of age-related data, the revised NAEYC position statement clearly delimits the use of this information to "permit[ting] general predictions within an age range about what activities, materials, interactions, or experiences will be safe, healthy, interesting, achievable, and also challenging to children" (see Part 1, p. 9). This may help to avoid the misuses of age-related data that seem to arise from the failure to recognize two things. First, averages or norms never tell more than a small part of the story; far more informative is the range, that is, how individuals' levels of growth or performance are distributed.

Second, because the mean is a statistical tool, there is no one whom it fits exactly. In other words, while children of about the same age all over the world are alike in some ways, every child is different.

A further limitation on the use of age-based norms is the practice of using majority-culture norms and failing to recognize developmental equivalences across cultural groups (Brice-Heath 1988; Bowman & Stott 1994).

In addition, the revised position statement clearly emphasizes that to make such predictions, teachers need to know not only about child development but also about how children learn and the interaction

Our knowledge of child development and learning allows us to make predictions—but only general predictions—about the kinds of activities or experiences that will interest children within a certain age range and further their development and progress.

that occurs between learning and development. An example from the domain of physical development illustrates this point. Motor development is perhaps the domain of development in which it is easiest to see straightforward, age-related change (Gallahue 1993). So, let's examine a relatively common motor skill—learning to ride a two-wheel bike without training wheels. I once conducted an informal survey of physical education teachers about when they learned to ride a bike (a show of hands during a conference session, certainly not a random sample). A few learned at age 4, a few more at 5, most at 6 or 7, some at 8 or 9. One person learned to ride a bike at 21!

What can we conclude from these data, which are fairly consistent with more scientific research on motor development? By age 6 or 7 most young children have developed the fundamental movement skills (control of large muscles, balance, coordination of both sides of the body, and visual acuity) necessary to master the complex skill of bike riding. (Recently, more children are learning to ride bikes at 4 and even at 3 years of age, not because human physiological development has changed, but because equipment manufacturers have begun to produce two-wheel riding vehicles that are lower to the ground, easier to control, safer, and more developmentally appropriate for young children.) A few children arrive at this developmental level earlier and, with appropriate experience and coaching, can master the skill. Others may take more practice, more time to grow, or more assistance to achieve the skill at a later age. Physical development alone does not account for physical skill. For example, the person who learned to ride a bike as a 21-year-old reported that, as a child, she was somewhat fearful and her parents were overprotective, and they simply never taught her how. Once she had achieved the prerequisite level of development, this particular child also needed instruction from an adult or more capable peer and did not get it.

As the bike-riding example illustrates, knowledge about child development and learning is a vital guide to professionals in planning curriculum and teaching. For, if our goal were to teach a group of 3-year-olds to ride two-wheelers, we would undoubtedly fail miserably despite the amount of instruction and practice we provided. At the same time, we would be entirely wrong in judging as motor delayed a 7-year-old who couldn't ride a two-wheeler but had never had a chance to learn.

Most schools, of course, do not include bike riding among the essential objectives of learning. But learning to read is a goal of every primary-grade school in America. Because it affects all of children's later learning in school and in life, reading is a vital achievement. Here again, knowledge of child development and learning is essential to making informed judgments about appropriate expectations and practices related to acquiring literacy.

As with other skills, reading is an outcome that results from the continual interplay of development and learning. Given exposure to appropriate literacy experiences and good teaching in early childhood, most children learn to read at age 6 or 7, a few learn at 4, some learn at 5, and some need intensive individualized support to learn to read at 8 or 9. Some children who do not explore books and other print during their early years are likely to need more focused support for literacy development when they begin preschool or kindergarten. Other children who enter school speaking little or no English are likely to need instructional strategies in their home language. Nevertheless, given the range within which children typically master reading, even with exposure to print-rich environments and good teaching, we could predict that the goal of beginning reading is achievable for most children by age 7 (or by the end of what is traditionally second grade). To establish this goal for every child in a group of 5-year-olds is to set children up for failure. And what results from such an arbitrary standard is that children who are developing normally but need more time to learn to read are retained in kindergarten, assigned to a transition class, or fail first grade (Shepard & Smith 1986; Smith & Shepard 1987).

There are many reasons why some children struggle in the early years of school, but one cause—developmentally inappropriate expectations—is not justifiable (Bredekamp & Shepard 1989). Adults should have high expectations for all children's learning, but those goals should be realistic and achievable. A developmentally appropriate framework of education uses knowledge about child development and learning to set achievable but challenging goals for all children. It also adapts for the individual variation that exists—the dimension of professional decisionmaking to which we turn now.

Using knowledge of individual children to inform practice

As the preceding discussion reveals, it is not possible to talk about child development without introducing the concept of individual variation. "Individual differences" is certainly among the most widely acknowledged principles of human development, but it is also among the most frequently ignored factors in making educational decisions, as illustrated in our previous discussion of reading. Anyone who has ever known even two children has observed the phenomenon of individual variation. Nevertheless, parents are almost always surprised by how different their two (or more) children are. Likewise, educational institutions continue to be structured in ways that give insufficient recognition to or adaptation for individual differences. There is a fundamental disconnect between knowing that children are different and expecting them all to learn the same way at the same time.

In 1987 we talked about two dimensions of developmental appropriateness—age appropriate and individually appropriate—as though these were somehow separable. The interaction of age appropriateness and individual appropriateness became particularly apparent as early childhood educators and early childhood special educators engaged in serious debate about the applicability of principles of developmentally appropriate practice to children with disabilities or special learning and developmental needs (Safford 1989; Mallory 1992, 1994; Wolery, Strain, & Bailey 1992; Bredekamp 1993). In some of those discussions, the argument was that "age appropriateness" might be the most important consideration for typically developing children, but "in-dividually appropriate" was the guiding principle of early childhood special educators. An unintended consequence of this distinction may be the persistent tendency to equate "difference" with "deficit."

The revised position statement takes a clearer and more inclusive stand on developmentally appropriate practice, partly as a result of NAEYC's collaboration

A developmentally appropriate framework of education uses knowledge about child development and learning to set achievable but challenging goals for all children.

with members of the Division for Early Childhood of the Council for Exceptional Children (DEC/CEC). In the past, some people have equated "developmentally appropriate" with "age appropriate." But the 1996 position clearly argues for a definition of developmentally appropriate that encompasses knowledge of and responsiveness to every child's individuality. Children's individuality is related to genetic and experiential factors, both cultural and contextual. Historically, early childhood educators have given greater attention to genetic or developmental variation, usually based on majority-culture norms, than to cultural or contextual variation (Kagan, Moore, & Bredekamp 1995). Unfortunately, assessments of children that fail to recognize cultural and contextual variation can have negative consequences. For instance, such assessment might be used to con-sign to special education a child who has physical disabilities but no intellectual ones, or a child who does not speak English. A gifted preschooler from a low-income neighborhood might not have his talents recognized (Kagan, Moore, & Bredekamp 1995).

The goal is for teachers to support the learning and development of all children. To achieve this goal, teachers need to know children well and use everything they know about each child—including that individual's learning styles, interests and preferences, personality and temperament, skills and talents, challenges and difficulties. Children are more likely to achieve a positive sense of self if they experience more success than failure in the early school years. The teacher must support a positive sense of self-identity in each child. Children's identities are shaped by many factors, among which are their gen-

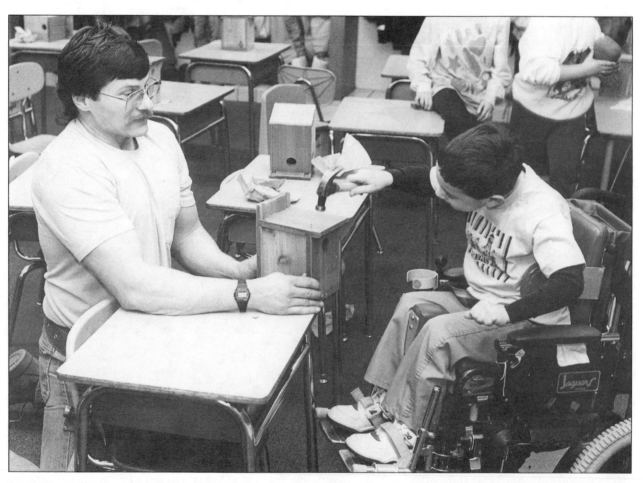

To support children's learning and development, teachers need to know each child well and use what they know—including that child's learning styles, interests and preferences, personality and temperament, skills and talents, challenges and difficulties.

der, race (including biracial or multiracial), language, cultural and family background, religion, abilities, life experiences, and circumstances (Wardle 1996).

The NAEYC revised position statement is explicit in applying developmentally appropriate practice to *all* children. Just as knowledge of individual variation must be used in making decisions about typically developing children, so too must knowledge of typical child development be used in providing services for children with disabilities or developmental delays. In addition, guidelines for practice emphasize that, to be responsive to individual children, teachers need to use various strategies, provide a variety of materials, and plan many different learning opportunities.

Because responsiveness to children as individuals requires knowing them and their families well, the NAEYC position statement encourages early childhood programs to support development of relationships among teachers, children, and families. Continuity of relationships is especially important for infants and toddlers, but its value with preschoolers and primary-school-age children is increasingly recognized. In the infant-toddler centers and preschools of Reggio Emilia, Italy, for example, groups of children stay with the same two teachers for three years (Gandini 1993). The Reggio Emilia approach includes many impressive features (Edwards, Gandini, & Forman 1993; Katz & Cesarone 1994), but certainly among the factors that contribute to the intellectually interesting project work that Reggio children produce is the degree to which the teachers know each child, document observations and experiences, and use this knowledge to effectively support the child's development and learning.

The quality and consistency of care provided for infants and toddlers in Reggio Emilia and other programs that make continuity of the caregiver-child relationship a priority are not possible when child care centers move babies to a new group every six months (NAEYC 1996). Apparently some directors justify this practice on the grounds that parents like it because their babies don't get attached to anyone else but them. Such practice not only ignores what is known about healthy infant development (see Part 3) but also severely inhibits a caregiver's ability to get to know a baby and the baby's family. Without such knowledge, a caregiver could not make informed professional decisions about her practice.

Perhaps one reason that individual differences sometimes become invisible in descriptions of developmentally appropriate practice is that the written word is capable of communicating general concepts but less capable of communicating all the nuances that occur in reality. For this reason we recognize the importance of stressing throughout this publication that developmentally appropriate practice rests on making professional judgments, not on following a list of described practices as if they constituted a recipe. Judgments about developmentally appropriate practice are constructed each day by teachers in relation to a specific group of children and within a specific social and cultural context.

Using knowledge of the social and cultural context to inform practice

Among the differences between NAEYC's revised position statement and the 1987 version is the recognition now given to the role of cultural context in development and learning. The earlier statement was relatively silent on the issue, leading to justifiable criticism from individuals representing widely diverse perspectives. The position statement (see Part 1) now explicitly acknowledges the powerful influence of context on all development and learning. Given the current political climate in the United States in which "culture" has been used as a wedge issue to divide people—stressing differences and ignoring commonalities—advocates of developmentally appropriate practice will need to clearly communicate their position on the significant role of cultural context.

The 1987 position subsumed cultural background as a dimension of individual variation. However, group cultural differences should not be confused with individual differences. "Every person develops a unique personality as a result of their personal history, and at the same time develops within a cultural context with some behavioral characteristics that are shared with other members of the group" (Phillips 1991, n.p.). Carol Brunson Phillips describes culture as a process that encompasses several related concepts, which we can only summarize here.

Culture consists of a set of rules or expectations for the behavior of group members that are passed on from one generation to the next. Cultural experiences

When teachers understand children's cultural context, they are better able to use the full range of children's interests and skills to help them achieve the learning goals of the school.

are not limited to the artifacts or products of culture, such as holiday celebrations, foods, or music. These products are what can be seen easily but they are not the culture itself, which is that set of underlying rules of custom or habit that yield or shape the visible products. Understanding culture requires an understanding of the rules that influence behavior, rules that give meaning to events and experiences in families and communities (Phillips 1994).

Growing up as members of a family and community, children learn the rules of their culture—explicitly through direct teaching and implicitly through the behavior of those around them. Among the rules they learn are how to show respect, how to interact with people they know well as compared to those they just met, how to organize time and personal space, how to dress, what and when to eat, how to respond to major life transitions or celebrations, how to worship, and countless other behaviors that humans perform with little apparent thought every day.

Individual children may be members of more than one cultural group and may be embedded in their cultures to different degrees. In addition, Phillips (1991) reminds us that cultures borrow and share rules and cultures change over time. As with other aspects of the early childhood knowledge base, we as teachers cannot learn a fixed set of facts or behaviors and assume we know about culture. Instead, we must learn a set of principles and remain open to increasing our cultural understanding throughout our careers. Culture is like many complex phenomena—the more you learn about it, the more you realize how little you know.

Because the United States, like a number of the world's countries, is a society composed of people from many diverse cultural groups, teachers' understanding and applications of knowledge of the social and cultural context in practice can be a complex and even daunting task. The first step seems to be for each of us to acknowledge that we all are influenced by our cultural experiences and that, just as children's development and learning is influenced by the context within which they live, teachers also are largely products of their experiences. This recognition is the beginning of increased awareness, sensitivity, and responsiveness to other people's points of view.

We often hear teachers report that culture is not an issue in their community because "we are all alike here." In these situations, culture is actually a considerable issue, but it becomes less visible without contrasting perspectives. This point of view was best expressed by Luis Hernandez (1996), a Cuban American early childhood professional from Miami, during his visit to Minneapolis. When a local group of professionals told him that there was no culture there, his shocked reply was, "What do you mean? With all these Swedish and Norwegian Americans, I feel like Margaret Mead here!"

In fact, ignoring or misunderstanding the role of culture in children's development is a serious proposition and can lead to many different problems in practice. As children grow, they "learn to balance their needs and wishes with the constraints and freedoms of the social world in which they live—to express their developmental predispositions in ways that are consistent with their family's and culture's practices" (Bowman & Stott 1994, 120). When the cultural rules of the home and the early childhood program are congruent, the process of learning is eased. However, when the expectations of the cultures of the home and the school or child care program are different or conflicting, children can be confused or forced to choose which culture to identify with and which to reject. In these situations, young children who identify with family and friends may appear to reject the school culture or vice versa. For example, a Latino father teaches his son to show respect for the teacher by looking down, but the Anglo teacher complains to her friend that she can't reach this child because he won't even look her in the eye.

While one reaction is to ignore the role of culture, a worse error is to treat cultural differences in children as deficits. Such situations hurt children whose abilities within their own cultural context are not recognized because they do not match the cultural expectations of the school (Feagans & Haskins 1986; Hale-Benson 1986; Brice-Heath 1988). Failing to recognize children's strengths or capabilities, teachers may greatly underestimate their competence. Teachers also miss valuable opportunities to use the full range of children's interests and skills to help them achieve the learning goals of school. In other situations, well-intentioned adults attempt to be responsive to cultural diversity but treat children's cultures superficially in terms of artifacts or outward manifestations of culture, such as holiday celebrations or food preferences to be acknowledged occasionally. These practices communicate that a child's culture is exotic or foreign, marginalized compared to the "mainstream" or majority culture.

Early childhood programs exist in contexts. Those contexts are influenced by many factors—among them are parents' preferences, community values, societal expectations, demands of institutions at the next level of education, and broadly defined values of American culture, such as personal freedom and individual responsibility. To further complicate the situation, the demands of each of these forces can be contradictory or conflicting. At times teachers find their own values and beliefs in direct contradiction to those of some families they serve. But whether or not a teacher and the children in the program share the same social and cultural context, each child's own context is no less a powerful influence on his or her development and learning. Therefore, decisions about how to care for and educate young children—decisions about developmentally appropriate practice—cannot be made without knowledge of that context in relation to knowledge about child development and learning and knowledge of individual children. The actual decisionmaking process simultaneously draws on all this information and more, as the following examples illustrate.

Using multiple sources of knowledge in professional decisionmaking

In any given situation, the early childhood professional uses knowledge from multiple sources in deciding what course of action is appropriate. Following are three situations in which adults support children's development—promoting children's independent functioning, providing nutritious food, and responding to a baby's cues—performing tasks that appear to be universal. But in each of these cases, the adults' actions are based on decisions that must incorporate their knowledge not only about child development but also about the individual child and the cultural context.

*   *   *

As children develop, they move toward greater degrees of independent functioning. Such a general principle has important implications for age-appropriate expectations. Infants are perceived to be totally dependent on others for all of their physical needs. Toddlers begin asserting their autonomy but still require constant supervision. Greater self-regulation skill—especially in toileting, dressing, feeding, and other self-help behaviors—is a typical goal for preschool years, while the assumption in the school-age years is that children are able to function on their own (ride the school bus, read, etc.). At first glance, these expectations for developing independence appear to be age-related human characteristics, and yet, to a large extent, they reflect the demands of the American cultural context. Other cultures place different requirements on children for independent functioning at different ages (Edwards & Gandini 1989; Rogoff et al. 1993; Woodhead 1996). In addition, some cultural groups within the United States promote interdependence and cooperation with the group over independence in their children (Soto 1991; Little Soldier 1992; Williams 1994). Likewise, individual characteristics of children also influence development. For example, the temperament, learning style, or specific disability of a particular child may inhibit the development of independent functioning.

* * *

Children all need nutritious food. Knowledge of age-appropriate expectations informs adults about what types of food children generally need, in what textures and quantities. This knowledge helps prevent inappropriate or dangerous responses, such as serving babies foods they can choke on or allowing preschoolers to eat too much junk food. As a general rule, more flexible feeding schedules help to avoid irritability in infants. Likewise, withholding food from preschoolers as punishment for misbehavior is not recommended. This age-appropriate information gives general guidance about feeding, but to determine a response that is truly developmentally appropriate, one must have more information about the cultural context and the individual child's needs. Perhaps children will not eat the food offered at the child care center because it is unfamiliar or even forbidden by their religion. Every individual child has food preferences and aversions. Some individual children have food allergies. An individualized education plan (IEP) may recommend that a favorite food be used to encourage self-help skills

of a child with cerebral palsy. So we see that even in the case of a universal physiological need such as food, adults have decisions to make, and sound decisions take into account the needs of individual children as well as the constraints of the context.

* * *

A seemingly simple situation is one in which a baby begins to fret and fuss. Yet the child's cues trigger a cycle of decisionmaking on the part of the family child care provider that draws on her knowledge of the individual child and the context.

The adult observes the infant and quickly asks herself what this particular sound communicates. Hunger? Discomfort? Or some other condition? The adult decides what she thinks is most likely and proceeds from there. If the child is hungry, wet, or otherwise in need, the adult response will be influenced by the culture (types of food, for instance) and by the individual child (who may be lactose intolerant). The adult then must reflect on the outcome of this interaction, and the process continues. Does the baby want to be held or carried or rocked? Is he overly sensitive to touch? Again, the response will be influenced by the cultural context.

If this child's family culture matches that of the caregiver, her spontaneous responses may be relatively congruent with those of the family, which she has noticed when observing the parent comforting the child. In this situation the caregiver smoothly and simultaneously employs what she knows about infant development and communication, the cultural context, and the individual child and family.

Each of these situations illustrates the constant decisionmaking that confronts early childhood educators. The decisions are based on application of professional knowledge (drawing on multiple perspectives about child development and learning, about individual children, and within a context), reflection, and adaptation.

But what if the perspectives are contradictory? What if a teacher finds herself in a situation in which a family's perspective about a policy or practice conflicts with another important consideration? We turn now to an exploration of this very real situation and suggest an approach for addressing it.

Teachers sometimes find themselves in situations in which a family's perspective differs from their own judgment about how to support the child's learning.

Resolving contradictions

What if the parents want you to spank their child? This is inevitably the first question, it seems, when we introduce the issue of cultural context for consideration by early childhood professionals. The spanking issue is among the easiest to resolve because most states prohibit corporal punishment in child care or school; in those that do not, early childhood educators can turn for guidance to their profession's code of ethical conduct, which clearly considers the practice unethical (Feeney & Kipnis 1992). But more important than finding a simple answer to the dilemma, which might actually cut off communication with the parents, a professional could see the apparent contradiction as the opening for a dialogue.

If parents want their child spanked, they probably have concerns about the child's behavior, perhaps his social skills or emotional control. They may be worried that the child will be a problem in school and will not acquire the important skills needed for the future. Without continuing a dialogue with the family, the teacher may make incorrect assumptions about the family's concerns and priorities or about the child's needs. The first step then in resolving what appears to be a conflict between the family and the teacher is to open communication with families, not close it (Delpit 1988).

The ensuing dialogue will be more productive if the professional has thought through the rationale for her decisions about practice. Equally important, the teacher should be aware of her own perspective and values and how these influence her practice, open to learning new information, and respectful of others whose perspective or values may differ from her own. With such a basis for communication, the potential conflict may be more easily negotiated and resolved (Phillips 1994; Neuman et al. 1995). A successful negotiation is one in which both parties change as a result of the interaction, not a situation in which one party loses and the other wins. For instance, one outcome of the conflict over spanking could be the teacher gaining respect for the family's deep concern for their child's well-being and information about his behavior and experiences at home (i.e., he is the youngest of a large family and frequently must defend himself from older siblings). As a result, the teacher may modify her own tendency to ignore the child's disruptive behavior in favor of more direct coaching of impulse control. For their part, the parents may learn some more effective strategies for disciplining their son.

Many dilemmas faced by early childhood professionals are far less clear-cut than the unacceptability of spanking by teachers. One quandary that preschool teachers often encounter is how to respond to children's play with violent themes—superheroes, archvillains, and the like. Teachers not only confront parents' views, often widely divergent, but they also must consider what children get out of the play, the result of different policies (for instance, banning the play may drive it underground and remove the potential for teachers to help children learn constructive alternatives), and a host of values-related issues.

Individuals preparing to become early childhood professionals must learn that one aim of their work is to deal with these kinds of tensions, which inevitably arise in the real world of practice. Because teachers must mediate between the knowledge base in the discipline and the children and their parents, contradictions are bound to emerge. Rather than striv-

The teacher should be aware of her own perspective and values and how these influence her practice, open to learning new information, and respectful of others whose perspective or values differ from her own.

ing to remember the "right answer," teachers must see themselves as thinkers and problem solvers who construct new understanding from discussing questions with parents and colleagues and stay open to transformations in children, in parents, and in themselves as teachers.

Below are some vignettes that illustrate the process of resolving apparent contradictions when they arise in our practice. The purpose of these vignettes is to convey the transactional character of the teaching and learning process, the reality of which can never be clearly communicated in a set of principles or examples. In practice, contradictions arise between the facts of what we think we know about development, what we know and learn about cultures, and what we learn about individual children. These vignettes illustrate that there is no single right answer for most dilemmas, although there are better and more informed answers. When contradictions arise, the early childhood educator begins a process of information gathering, decisionmaking, reflection, and communication.

Resolving contradictions in practice: A strategy for making decisions and negotiating conflicts

Antonia Lopez (1994), former education director for the Foundation Center Programs in California, uses a wonderful, true story to help people understand how the process described above becomes possible when they remain open to it. She illustrates how two views that initially sound like irreconcilable opposites can, with thought, be resolved.

The Foundation Center operated a child care program in a Mexican American community where the program's goal was to be an extension of values in the community. Staff were hired from among the families, and the school worked hard to build a sense of collaboration between school culture and community culture. However, one behavior rooted in the Mexican American culture—the giving of gifts to teachers as expressions of parents' esteem—seemed to be causing problems. The gift giving was generating feelings of pressure and competition between families that school personnel feared would work against the spirit of community they wanted to build. In short, the cultural practice (giving gifts to teachers) appeared to contradict or undermine other values the school sought to promote (cooperative rather than competitive relationships). Yet teachers feared that to simply ban the gift giving would be perceived by the parents as personal rejection.

Recognizing what was at stake in choosing either extreme of the dilemma, Antonia and the teachers made two rules:

Rule 1: You cannot accept the gifts.

Rule 2: You cannot reject the gifts.

Their challenge was to reconcile these seemingly contradictory rules. They worked out a strategy to accept gifts on behalf of the entire center and to work them into the operation of the program for the general benefit of the entire community. Once they made a commitment to resolve the contradiction without choosing between the values of the families and the school, the question became, "How can we receive the gifts in the spirit in which they are offered?"

When teachers confront situations in which parents' cultural expectations, values, or traditions appear to contradict the values or knowledge base of early childhood educators, the two rules generated from the teachers at the Foundation Center should prove to be useful: you cannot accept *and* you cannot reject. This exercise forces the professionals to reflect on their cherished beliefs and negotiate a compromise acceptable to them and the families they serve.

Antonia Lopez describes a four-step process that her staff uses to approach such apparent contradictions. Four questions are asked:

1. Are the concepts clear?

2. Can you restate the concepts? (When the concepts are restated, they may appear less contradictory.)

3. So what? (Upon analysis, does the issue really matter to children's well-being?)

4. What are the cultural implications or incongruities? (Is the issue really a matter of culture, a difference of opinion, or a difference in information?)

These questions and the process they provoke can provide an excellent framework for resolving other types of conflicts or contradictions as well, as illustrated in the following situation.

Considering children's individual needs in decisions about developmentally appropriate practice

Tommy is a 5-year-old child with Down syndrome. He has attended a public preschool program for the past two years and is now in a morning kindergarten class that includes a number of children with identified special needs. Tommy's social relationships with the other children have been generally positive, especially with several children from the same preschool program. Recently, however, both Tommy's parents and teachers have noticed that other classmates have begun to tease Tommy, and former playmates are less interested in including him in their play unless he takes on the role of the baby. In fact, as one playmate points out, "Tommy still wets his pants, so he has to be the baby."

Tommy's teacher, Mrs. Evans, was trained in early childhood education and has very little experience in or knowledge about special education. She strives to provide learning experiences for children in her class that are interesting enough to keep them engaged. She believes strongly in activating children's intrinsic motivation to learn rather than using external reinforcements like stickers or happy faces. Her previous school practiced a schoolwide discipline strategy that required marking children's names on the board for misbehavior and imposing specific punishments for infractions. She felt uncomfortable using this technique with kindergartners and actually changed schools to find a more compatible job.

She has developed a relationship with Tommy and his parents in the months he has been in her class, and together they discuss strategies to help him become more accepted by his peers. Both the parents and teacher believe that Tommy is physically capable of self-toileting and, in fact, the pediatrician agrees. All adults involved want to allow Tommy to achieve this developmental milestone on his own terms. The dilemma they confront is weighing the risk of waiting longer, while Tommy continues to experience rejection by his peers, against the risk of Tommy possibly becoming dependent on extrinsic reinforcement. Their growing concern about the social costs of peer rejection or infantilization of Tommy leads them to decide on a behavioral intervention. Therefore, the teacher and parents, in consultation with the special education team members, decide to initiate a behavioral intervention that uses operant conditioning. Beginning with concrete reinforcers (in this case, stickers that Tommy selected) for appropriate toileting behavior, the reinforcement eventually shifts to more abstract tokens (which entitle Tommy to extra time on the classroom computer).

As a result of this intervention, Tommy has become more aware of his physical stimuli and gradually has learned to anticipate and respond appropriately to his toileting needs. As a result of this direct teaching strategy, Tommy not only experiences the intrinsic satisfaction of controlling his own toileting practices, but this functional achievement also significantly contributes to an improvement in his social status in the classroom. No longer is he relegated to the role of the baby on every occasion.

In this situation, Mrs. Evans made a decision about practice that drew on all the available information: what she understood about motivation in learning, what she knew about Tommy, her knowledge of the demands of the social context in which Tommy had to function, and other information she obtained that expanded her knowledge. Although Mrs. Evans holds to the idea that in a good early childhood classroom external, tangible reinforcements are rarely needed, she sees the decision in this situation as a valid one.

Considering families' concerns and the wider social context in decisions about developmentally appropriate practice

Ms. Graef is a Head Start teacher in a suburban community outside a major metropolitan area. She is a firm proponent of developmentally appropriate practice and has seen the problems caused by "push-down" curriculum and highly formal academic instruction. She remembers how her own daughter, who loved books and preschool, became frustrated, tense, and fearful in kindergarten until she switched her to another school. However, many middle-income parents in the community voluntarily hold back their children an extra year in preschool to make sure they are ready for the rigorous expectations of kindergarten.

The first parent meeting of the year arrives for Ms. Graef's class, and she is stunned by the challenges to her teaching that the parents raise. "When are you going to start teaching these kids?" "How

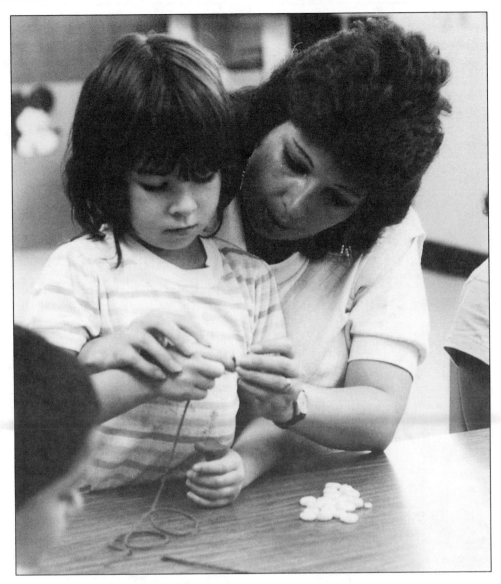

How much assistance to give a child—as well as when to give it and in what way—is one of the many judgment calls that teachers must make.

are they going to be ready for kindergarten?" "They can play at home; we send them here to learn something." Initially, Ms. Graef thinks, These parents don't really understand development. I'll educate them about theory and research and then they'll agree with me.

But before becoming defensive or escalating the conflict, Ms. Graef stops for a minute. She realizes that citing research now would be interpreted as a lack of respect for parents' genuine concerns about their children's future. She decides instead to probe further about their goals for their children. She asks them to restate their concerns and writes them down. One father, Mr. Johnson, explains that his son doesn't

know any letters, and when his daughter started kindergarten last year, her teacher wanted to put her in special education. Mr. Johnson wants to be sure that this doesn't happen to another one of his children. Several other parents express similar concerns.

Ms. Graef concludes the meeting with a promise to carefully evaluate her practice and the children's progress and continue the conversation with the parents at the next meeting. During the next few days, Ms. Graef takes a hard look at the curriculum she provides for children. She also does more systematic observations of several of the children, including James Johnson, and gets a clearer picture of each

Honoring parents' concerns and developing an open dialogue about how their goals for their children can best be achieved are vital in decisions about developmentally appropriate practice.

child's emergent literacy skills. She is disappointed to find that her informal teaching methods are not proving equally successful with all the children.

At first Ms. Graef considers purchasing a workbook series for the class. As she reflects further, she realizes that a better use of the same funds would be to purchase inexpensive children's books on a range of topics that she knows will interest her children, especially books that depict characters and situations congruent with each child's race, language, and culture. She builds many learning experiences around children's favorite books, setting up a classroom lending library so that the children can take the books home along with teacher tips about how parents can help. She continues many of the same valuable early childhood activities she has initiated in the past, but now she takes care to communicate to parents in specific terms how these activities benefit the children and to indicate the link to future skills.

In addition, Ms. Graef works harder at enriching children's play with literacy experiences (writing grocery lists before playing store, for instance) and now and then plays a role in the play to extend children's use of language ("Do you have any fruit for sale that isn't very expensive?"). Then she plans several specific games and experiences for small groups of children to promote phonemic awareness. Finally, she arranges with the fourth-grade teacher for a buddy program. Each day, several fourth-graders spend a half hour in her classroom reading a story to one or two of the preschoolers. James Johnson's buddy is a boy who likes racing cars as much as James does. They read together, and after his buddy leaves, James continues to examine the book, often copying the words or drawing detailed, elaborate pictures of cars. When Ms. Graef meets with James's father a few months later, Mr. Johnson talks with excitement about how his son tries to read the names of cars in the parking lot of their apartment building and now recognizes most of the initial consonants.

Ms. Graef's year of teaching is not as smooth as she had hoped. Confronting the seeming tension between her knowledge of good practice and the demands of the context in which she works is not easy. Yet by seeing the situation as the beginning of a conversation, she is able to use it as a learning experience for herself and the parents. Both she and the parents change their views as a result, and the children are the greatest beneficiaries.

Conclusion

Real life cannot be tied up neatly in five paragraphs. Resolving conflicts is much more complex, and most often the resolution of one problem leads to identification of a new problem. Education and development are, after all, ongoing processes that continue throughout life. As early childhood professionals, we have an especially daunting challenge. Decisions about our practice are based on knowledge that is always changing: our understanding about child development and learning, individual children, and social and cultural contexts. This is why NAEYC's position statements must be periodically revised, and this is also why we cannot risk becoming rigid in our practice. As educators and developmentalists, early childhood teachers have to become comfortable with paradox—stability and change, individual and group, structure and freedom, flexibility and predictability. For early childhood professionals, resolving apparent contradictions is just another part of our day at work.

References

Bowman, B., & F. Stott. 1994. Understanding development in a cultural context: The challenge for teachers. In *Diversity and developmentally appropriate practices: Challenges for early childhood education*, eds. B. Mallory & R. New, 119–34. New York: Teachers College Press.

Bredekamp, S., ed. 1987. *Developmentally appropriate practice in early childhood programs serving children from birth through age 8*. Exp. ed. Washington, DC: NAEYC.

Bredekamp, S. 1993. The relationship between early childhood education and early childhood special education: Healthy marriage or family feud? *Topics in Early Childhood Special Education* 13 (3): 258–73.

Bredekamp, S., & L. Shepard. 1989. How best to protect children from inappropriate school expectations, practices, and policies. *Young Children* 44 (3): 14–24.

Brice-Heath, S. 1988. Language socialization. In *Black children and poverty: A developmental perspective*, ed. D. Slaughter, 29–41. San Francisco: Jossey-Bass.

Carnegie Council on Adolescent Development. 1996. *Great transitions: Preparing adolescents for a new century*. New York: Carnegie Corporation of New York.

Delpit, L. 1988. The silenced dialogue: Power and pedagogy in educating other people's children. *Harvard Educational Review* 58: 280–98.

Edwards, C., & L. Gandini. 1989. Teachers' expectations about the timing of developmental skills: A cross-cultural study. *Young Children* 44 (4): 15–19.

Edwards, C., L. Gandini, & G. Forman, eds. 1993. *The hundred languages of children: The Reggio Emilia approach to early childhood education*. Norwood, NJ: Ablex.

Feagans, L., & R. Haskins. 1986. Neighborhood dialogues of black and white 5-year-olds. *Journal of Applied Developmental Psychology* 7: 181–200.

Feeney, S., & K. Kipnis. 1992. *Code of ethical conduct and statement of commitment*. Washington, DC: NAEYC.

Gallahue, D. 1993. Motor development and movement skill acquisition in early childhood education. In *Handbook of research on the education of young children*, ed. B. Spodek, 24–41. New York: Macmillan.

Gandini, L. 1993. Fundamentals of the Reggio Emilia approach to early childhood education. *Young Children* 49 (1): 4–8.

Goffin, S. 1996. Child development knowledge and early childhood teacher preparation: Assessing the relationship. *Early Childhood Research Quarterly* 11 (2): 117–33.

Hale-Benson, J. 1986. *Black children: Their roots, cultures and learning styles*. Rev. ed. Baltimore: Johns Hopkins University Press.

Hernandez, L. 1996. Nurturing children and respecting families of all cultures: Principles and practices. Presentation at the 5th Annual Conference of the National Institute for Early Childhood Professional Development, 7 June, Minneapolis, Minnesota.

Kagan, L., E. Moore, & S. Bredekamp, eds. 1995. *Reconsidering children's early development and learning: Toward common views and vocabulary*. Washington, DC: National Education Goals Panel, Goal 1 Technical Planning Group.

Kamii, C. 1985. *Young children reinvent arithmetic*. New York: Teachers College Press.

Kamii, C. 1989. *Young children continue to reinvent arithmetic, 2nd grade*. New York: Teachers College Press.

Katz, L., & B. Cesarone, eds. 1994. *Reflections on the Reggio Emilia approach*. Urbana, IL: ERIC Clearinghouse.

Kostelnik, M. 1993. Recognizing the essentials of developmentally appropriate practice: A look at DAP in the real world. *Child Care Information Exchange* (March/April): 73–77.

Krashen, S. 1992. *Fundamentals of language education*. Torrance, CA: Laredo.

Little Soldier, L. 1992. Working with Native American children. *Young Children* 47 (6): 15–21.

Lopez, A. 1994. Personal communication.

Lubeck, S. 1996. Deconstructing "child development knowledge" and "teacher preparation." *Early Childhood Research Quarterly* 11 (2): 147–67.

Mallory, B. 1992. Is it always appropriate to be developmental? Convergent models for early intervention practice. *Topics in Early Childhood Special Education* 11 (4): 1–12.

Mallory, B. 1994. Inclusive policy, practice, and theory for young children with developmental differences. In *Diversity and developmentally appropriate practices: Challenges for early childhood education*, eds. B. Mallory & R. New, 44–61. New York: Teachers College Press.

NAEYC. 1996. Using NAEYC's code of ethics—Reader responses to Dottie Derman's dilemma. *Young Children* 51 (6): 41–45.

Neuman, S., T. Hagedorn, D. Celano, & P. Daly. 1995. Toward a collaborative approach to parent involement in early education: A study of teenage mothers in an African-American community. *American Educational Research Journal* 32 (4): 801–927.

New, R. 1994. Culture, child development, and developmentally appropriate practices: Teachers as collaborative researchers. In *Diversity and developmentally appropriate practices: Challenges for early childhood education*, eds. B. Mallory & R. New, 65–83. New York: Teachers College Press.

Phillips, C.B. 1991. Culture as a process. Unpublished paper.

Phillips, C.B. 1994. The movement of African-American children through sociocultural contexts: A case of conflict resolution. In *Diversity and developmentally appropriate practices: Challenges for early childhood education*, eds. B. Mallory & R. New, 137–54. New York: Teachers College Press.

Rogoff, B., J. Mistry, A. Goncu, & C. Mosier. 1993. *Guided participation in cultural activity by toddlers and caregivers*. Monographs of the Society for Research in Child Development, vol. 58, no. 8, serial no. 236. Chicago: University of Chicago Press.

Safford, P. 1989. *Integrated teaching in early childhood: Starting in the mainstream*. White Plains, NY: Longman.

Shepard, L., & M. Smith. 1986. Synthesis of research on school readiness and kindergarten retention. *Educational Leadership* 44 (3): 78–86.

Smith, M., & L. Shepard. 1987. What doesn't work: Explaining policies of retention in the early grades. *Phi Delta Kappan* 69 (2): 129–34.

Soto, L.D. 1991. Understanding bilingual/bicultural children. *Young Children* 46 (2): 30–36.

Spodek, B. 1991. Early childhood curriculum and cultural definitions of knowledge. In *Issues in early childhood curriculum*, eds. B. Spodek & O. Saracho, 1–20. New York: Teachers College Press.

Stott, F., & B. Bowman. 1996. Child development knowledge: A slippery base for practice. *Early Childhood Research Quarterly* 11 (2): 169–83.

Task Force on Education of Young Adolescents. 1989. *Turning points: Preparing American youth for the 21st century*. Washington, DC: Carnegie Council on Adolescent Development.

Wardle, F. 1996. Proposal: An anti-bias and ecological model for multicultural education. *Childhood Education* 72 (3): 152–56.

Williams, L. 1994. Developmentally appropriate practice and cultural values: A case in point. In *Diversity and developmentally appropriate practices: Challenges for early childhood education*, eds. B. Mallory & R. New, 155–66. New York: Teachers College Press.

Wolery, M., P. Strain, & D. Bailey. 1992. Reaching potentials of children with special needs. In *Reaching potentials: Appropriate curriculum and assessment for young children, volume 1*, eds. S. Bredekamp & T. Rosegrant, 92–111. Washington, DC: NAEYC.

Woodhead, M. 1996. *In search of the rainbow: Pathways to quality in large-scale programmes for young disadvantaged children*. The Hague, Netherlands: Bernard van Leer Foundation.

Developmentally Appropriate Practice for Infants and Toddlers

Growing numbers of infants and toddlers are cared for in settings outside their homes, and many receive excellent care. Yet mediocre and inadequate care is more commonplace for infants and toddlers than for any other age group (Cost, Quality, & Child Outcomes Study Team 1995). Because low-quality, inappropriate care endangers infants' development and future prospects (Carnegie Task Force 1994), it is essential to consider the nature of developmentally appropriate practice in this age range.

This part begins with an overview of children's development in the first three years of life, a period of very rapid growth and development. To help readers consider applying the guidelines for decisions about developmentally appropriate practice (Part 1, pp. 16–22) to this age group, we provide examples of appropriate and inappropriate practices in caring for infants and a comparable set of examples for toddlers. Part 3 concludes with a list of references and resources.

Development in the First Three Years of Life[†]

J. Ronald Lally, Abbey Griffin, Emily Fenichel, Marilyn Segal, Eleanor Szanton, and Bernice Weissbourd

During the past 30 years, careful observation of infants and toddlers around the world has yielded an ever-increasing awareness of the importance of early development. Every day, it seems, we learn more about the capacities of newborns, the differences among very young children, the influence of family and community culture on early development, and the ability of infants and toddlers to cope with developmental challenges. We are also learning that group care of infants and toddlers presents special challenges and opportunities for promoting healthy development and supporting families.

Perhaps most important, we have learned to appreciate the role of relationships in every aspect of early development. Infants and toddlers develop expectations about people's behavior and about them-

selves based on how parents and others treat them. Through daily interactions with responsive, affectionate adults, babies experience their first positive love relationships. Trust and emotional security develop when infants learn that their needs will be met predictably and consistently. Self-confidence develops as babies and toddlers learn to communicate their needs and master challenges in their world.

Infants and toddlers thrive when they encounter challenges they can meet. Infants flourish when they are free to explore and when they feel that caring adults encourage and take pleasure in their emerging interests and skills. Children's sense of belonging and ability to understand their world grow when there is continuity between the home and child care setting.

The overview of infant and toddler development that follows offers a series of snapshots of babies' growing capacities, the experiences of children and parents, and what the family-caregiver relationship might look like at different points in the first three years. Readers are encouraged to consult the references and

[†] Pages 55–69, reprinted by permission, are taken from the first chapter of *Caring for Infants and Toddlers in Groups: Developmentally Appropriate Practice,* published by ZERO TO THREE: National Center for Infants, Toddlers, and Families. The publication and related materials may be ordered directly from ZERO TO THREE, 734 15th Street, NW, Suite 1000, Washington, DC 20005; 800-899-4301.

Ben and Jennifer started at the child care center at 4 months of age and were assigned the same primary caregiver. Ben was quiet and calm, unaffected by sudden occurrences and gracious about waiting to be fed. Jennifer was his opposite. Jen was tight-bodied and highly sensitive to changes in her environment. She cried loudly and persistently when hungry, sleepy, or upset. Their caregiver, Teresa, and respective family members saw that after only a month together, at 5 months of age, Ben and Jen were fascinated by each other. One would light up when the other arrived—Ben smiling and opening his eyes wide with anticipation; Jennifer wiggling every part of her body, making high-pitched sounds. Lying on their tummies looking at each other was a favorite activity. Both would arch their backs and heads until they could hold them up no more, then collapse. When one was face down, the other would use body and voice to summon the partner back.

*   *   *

Ben and Jennifer's primary caregiver and parents are keen observers and ready to follow the interests of their babies. Teresa encourages the interaction by putting them face to face when both are alert and active. Besides the very early show of mutual interest, Teresa had noticed that they had a positive effect on each other. Often Jen could be soothed by Ben's calm presence; in return, Ben was enlivened by Jen's intensity.

resources list of this section, which includes classic studies of early development, recent works, and ongoing sources for new information.

Although there are many ways to define and describe "ages and stages" within the rapid course of development in the child's first three years, we have chosen to look at three periods, characterized by mobility and age range:

- young infants (birth to 9 months);
- mobile infants (8 to 18 months); and
- toddlers (16 to 36 months).

Each age period describes what can generally be expected of the child, the appropriate response of the caregiver, and how families and caregivers work together (the alliance). Thus, each age range has three focus areas: the child, the caregiver, and the alliance.

The overlap in ages reminds us of the importance of individual differences among young children's rates of development. Chronological age alone is not a good indicator of child development but is used here to remind us that the competent caregiver will need to provide different environments, experiences, and interactions for children as they grow.

Regardless of their level of development, infants need a caregiver's help in each stage as they learn about security, exploration, and identity. During the different stages of infancy and early childhood, the type of help children need will change. For example, caregiver practices that help young infants feel secure (keeping a child physically close) can thwart a mobile infant's emerging urge to explore or block a toddler from learning more about how to depend on herself. Developmentally appropriate practice with infants and toddlers requires the ability to adapt a pattern of care quickly to meet children's rapidly changing needs.

Young infants (birth to 9 months)

The baby from birth to 8 or 9 months of age needs security most of all. The young infant thrives on the warmth and caring that come from a close relationship with the caregiver. Feelings about security influence the baby's inclination to explore and become part of the child's identity. Young infants need to know that someone special will come promptly when they feel distressed. Learning that they can count on being cared for helps babies build a sense of security.

The child

Every baby is unique. Newborns differ in their biological rhythms and the way they use their senses (sight, hearing, touch, smell, and taste) to learn about the world around them. They differ in their responses to loud noises or sudden changes in lighting and in the ways they like to be held. What all newborns share is a need for good health and safety; warm, loving relationships with their primary caregivers; and care that is responsive to their individual differences.

Babies enter the world ready for relationships. They use sounds, facial expressions, and movements to communicate their needs and feelings. Very young infants show a particular interest in the people around them. They like to look and listen; they follow the father's voice as well as the mother's. They look intently at the light and dark contours of the human face and can discriminate between an accurate drawing of a human face and one in which the main features are out of place. Babies a few months old show their pleasure and involvement with a caregiver through looking, joyful smiling and laughing, arm and leg movements, and other gestures.

Babies delight in hearing language. They coo when talked to and develop different types of cries to express different needs. Long before they speak in words, infants coo, then babble, then make sounds that imitate the tones and rhythms of adult talk, particularly those of their families and home culture. Before they understand even simple word combinations, they read gestures, facial expressions, and tone of voice. Babies begin quickly to participate in the turn taking of conversation. For example, as a young infant, the child vocalizes as a partner in a

conversation—one partner talks, one listens; if one disengages, the other calls her back into the dialogue. Some particularly social babies can be observed "conversing" with each other.

Babies learn through movement. As they move their arms, legs, and other body parts and through touching and being touched, babies become more aware of how their bodies move and feel. They soon discover they can change what they see, hear, or feel through their own activity—how delightful to kick and then see the mobile move!

Young infants become deeply engrossed in the practice of a newly discovered skill, like putting their hands together to grasp an object. Through the repetition of actions, they develop their motor skills and physical strength. They explore objects, people, and things by kicking, reaching, grasping, pulling, and releasing objects by opening their hands.

Young infants show their pleasure and involvement with a caregiver through looking, joyful smiling and laughing, arm and leg movements, and other gestures.

The family pediatrician for David (7 months) had suggested a strict daily eating and sleeping schedule because the baby was very active and easily distracted. Mattie, the family child care provider, adopted the routine, but as she got to know David, she became increasingly convinced that he needed a more flexible schedule. At first, she simply reported to David's parents that she had a hard time getting David to sleep or that he was very cranky and hungry a half hour before his scheduled feeding time or that he got very angry when she insisted he finish his bottle. But soon, because she felt she was failing David and was slighting the two toddlers she also cared for, she decided to have a serious discussion with his parents about the possibilities of giving up the fixed schedule. Mattie described what she observed and asked whether either parent was seeing similar behavior at home. They said that, while they thought the schedule was worth trying, they too were beginning to recognize early signs of hunger or fatigue and David seemed much happier when they responded right away. Mattie was relieved and began to talk freely about ways to catch David's early signs and reduce possible distractions so that he could learn to follow his own body signals.

*   *   *

Mattie was relieved because such negotiations do not always go so well. There are many reasons parents might want a particular routine—it is what they know from their own upbringing; it may be valued in their culture; they may have read something that suggested this approach was best for their baby; or, as in David's case, a health professional may have suggested the schedule. David's parents came from a community in which medical professionals were highly respected authorities. This caregiver's good communication skills, conviction based on careful observation, knowledge of child development, and respectful approach helped her and David's family trust their own shared, developing understanding of this particular child's emerging needs. "Talking through the child," as Mattie did, is a communication technique that uses observed behaviors to keep parents focused on their child. It is a way to avoid slipping into a confrontation about who knows what is best for the child—a kind of competition the experienced caregiver knows is almost never productive.

Babies use their senses and emerging physical skills to learn about the people and objects around them; they engage their senses by touching different textures and putting things in their mouths. They learn to anticipate how familiar adults will respond to them, a skill that will evolve much later into an ability to "read" people and anticipate how to behave in new situations. Ideally, young infants are learning that their needs are understood and will be met. They are learning that new skills and new experiences most often bring pleasure and that with determined efforts they will succeed—and, most important, that those they love will share in the joys of their discoveries. These early experiences affect a child's approach to learning far into the future.

The caregiver

It is through responsive interactions with parents and a few other special caregivers that infants develop a sense of a safe, interesting, and orderly world where they are understood and their actions bring pleasure to themselves and others. Like dancers, the caregiver and infant synchronize their interactions, each responding to and influencing the other.

Because each baby is unique, the caregiver's task is to learn the baby's individual eating and sleeping rhythms, how she approaches new objects and people, and how she prefers to be held for feeding, sleeping, or comforting. While the adult becomes able to predict what the infant needs and how she will respond to different kinds of stimuli, the baby is learning what to expect. The infant's sense of safety, security, and confidence grows with her sense that the people and the world about her are predictable and offer interesting experiences.

The young infant's day revolves around caregiving routines—diapering, dressing, eating, and sleeping. Caregiving routines are important times, offering unique opportunities for one-to-one interaction and for visual and tactile learning. In the child care setting, each area where these routines take place must be carefully planned so that the caregiver's time in preparation and sanitation procedures, like getting needed supplies and careful handwashing, can be handled efficiently, leaving more time for interaction with the baby. Pictures and objects at the infant's eye level capture his interest, while clean, safe, warm surfaces help him feel comfortable and secure. When routines are pleasurable, infants learn that their needs and their bodies are important.

Young infants need many opportunities to sample a variety of sensory and motor experiences. Before they can creep or crawl, babies depend on adults to carry them to or present them with an interesting object or activity. However, too much stimulation (bright lights, too many children in one group, constant loud noise, too many objects in a clutter) can be overwhelming. A well-organized environment, where objects are placed on low shelves and where there is a variety of visual, tactile, and physically challenging choices to capture the infant's attention, encourages curiosity and exploration and lets each infant engage his world at his own pace.

The caregiver/family alliance

Entering child care is a transition that, among other things, means building new relationships. By the time an infant enters group care, parents have learned a great deal about their baby. The baby has also learned. She has learned to expect a certain pattern of response from her immediate family—a pattern that reflects the values, culture, and child-rearing beliefs of the family and community. The infant will expect this pattern from her primary caregiver in the group care setting. It will take time for her to adjust to differences in touch, tone of voice, and the sights and sounds of a new environment.

To build solid relationships at the beginning of an infant's child care experience, caregivers need to learn from the experiences, knowledge, culture, and child-rearing beliefs of family members. When caregivers value the family as the primary caregivers and the constant in the baby's life, the parent-caregiver relationship becomes one of mutual support and learning about how best to care for the infant. An alliance is created.

Establishing and maintaining the alliance between parent and caregiver require regular communication. The caregiver sets aside time, particularly at the beginning and/or end of the baby's day, to communicate with parents through written notes, telephone calls, casual conversation, and scheduled meetings. Thus, family and caregiver can keep abreast of the baby's health; sleeping, eating, and elimination patterns; interests; and accomplishments. The knowledgeable caregiver can anticipate new developmental challenges and help the parent adjust to the changes in behavior and moods that often accompany a baby's intense effort to master a new skill.

Families and caregivers of young infants may have different perspectives on what a baby needs or on the best way to meet his needs. The skilled caregiver watches for such differences and approaches them as opportunities to learn more about the family and its community. These are opportunities to build the alliance, creating for the baby an environment that reflects his home experience.

The caregiver uses her observational skills to learn more about the individual baby's needs, interests, preferences, and particular ways of responding to people and things. Communication skills help the caregiver learn from the baby's family how his behaviors and reactions reflect his individual style, physical needs, and home experience. Communication skills, which take time and training to develop, also help the caregiver discuss differences openly with the family and arrive at a mutually satisfying agreement. This becomes easier as the family-caregiver relationship grows stronger.

Leaving one's young infant in the care of someone else is difficult. Parents feel differently about this experience and express their feelings in different ways. Some are clearly grieving and need emotional support and reassurance. Others steel themselves by acting aloof; they may even appear uncaring. Still others become overbearing "managers," sometimes competitive with the caregiver, often demanding. To become sensitive to differences in how parents express their feelings requires time and training.

Infants and toddlers evoke strong feelings in adults—both family members and caregivers. Recognizing, accepting, and working to overcome conflicting feelings is one of the major challenges of sharing care. Communicating with all parents regularly and taking every opportunity to reflect their baby's need and love for them will help parents leave their baby in the child care setting comfortably while staying emotionally close, certain that they are still the most important people in their baby's life.

Young infants thrive on responsive caregiving, a stimulating environment, and unhurried time to experience the simple joys of relating. Knowledge of early development and skill in observation help both parents and caregivers be more responsive to babies, whose needs and moods and interests vary

Samantha (3 months) had been a fussy baby, and her parents and caregiver had learned to respond quickly to the first signals of hunger, fatigue, or wet diaper discomfort because her cries became unbearably loud within seconds. One day her mother entered the center, grinning. She reported with pride that she awoke to Samantha's first morning call for breast-feeding and had rushed to the crib, saying, "Mommy's coming, I know you're hungry. Mommy's coming." Rather than the usual red-faced screaming baby, she found Samantha with her thumb in her mouth, intently watching her kicking feet. Samantha had learned to soothe and entertain herself. In their excitement, caregiver and parent marveled at Samantha's new mastery and shared words and responses they might use to build on her trust. They talked about ways Samantha could build her repertoire of self-soothing behaviors.

* * *

This parent and caregiver clearly have a good relationship. One of the many rewards of such a relationship are the opportunities for shared enthusiasm. Another is that through sharing their observations and thoughts, parents and caregivers can learn from each other. When one discovers a caregiving strategy that works, the other can follow suit. This creates continuity and reinforces the baby's ability to anticipate adult responses.

Very young infants are frequently fussy as their central nervous system, digestive system, and other physical capacities develop. Depending on how adults respond, infants learn very different lessons about themselves and their world. Responsive, consistent care helped Samantha trust that those who loved her would relieve her distress. When physically capable and emotionally and cognitively ready, she could soothe her own physical discomfort, trusting that the sound of a familiar voice meant that relief was on its way.

Samantha's first successful attempt at self-soothing reflects multiple domains of learning. Physically, Samantha is using her thumb to satisfy the urge to suck and her kicking to distract her from her hunger. Cognitively, she can now associate the adult's voice with relief. Socially, she has taken an important step toward self-regulation and will receive the rewards of happier and more relaxed caregiving. Emotionally, she has taken a giant step toward trust and attachment, gaining a new sense of both her own competence and the trustworthiness of others. When the caregiver understands such normal developmental challenges and achievements in the first nine months of life, she can offer encouragement, insight, and support to both infants and family members.

from moment to moment. The alliance between parent and caregiver has many benefits for the adults, but most important, it helps them provide better and more responsive care for the baby.

Mobile infants (8 to 18 months)

Exploration takes center stage as the infant becomes more mobile. Often curious and on the move, the mobile infant seems to get into everything in a quest to learn more about the world.

The mobile infant begins to build an identity as an explorer and increasingly ventures out when she feels secure. Caregivers can provide trustworthy support and encouragement to mobile infants by making eye contact with them, talking with them, and gesturing to them. Under a warm and watchful eye, mobile infants will develop feelings of confidence and competence. It is important for caregivers to remember that at this stage infants *practice* independence but very much need trusted adults as a secure base of support.

The child

Mobility opens new worlds for infants. They can now move to what or whom they want by scooting, using their hands and bouncing forward; commando-crawling with stomach on the ground; one-legged-stand crawling; crawling on all fours; walking with assistance; and, finally, toddling. For the mobile infant, the world is full of inviting experiences. Most are exciting, challenging, or pleasurable. Some are painful, frustrating, or frightening. Freedom to move about safely is vital for infants who are beginning to crawl or walk.

Mobile infants are fascinated with the daily activities and belongings of the adults around them. They imitate, holding a comb to a doll's head, patting an adult's cheek to comfort as they have experienced comfort, and mimicking facial expressions of sadness or anger they have seen. Imitation is the first step into the world of dramatic play, in which the child practices what she experiences and sees. During this period of development, infants create mental images of how things work and of sequences of adult behaviors that will soon become part of their rich repertoire of dramatic-play themes.

experiences, almost all infants during this period show anxiety ("stranger fear") around unfamiliar people. A clown face, Santa Claus, a firefighter in uniform, or a mask can be terrifying. Infants at this age can be fearful and upset when a trusted adult leaves their sight.

While distressing to infants and the adults who love them, these powerful emotions reflect new social, emotional, and cognitive understanding. Mobile infants recognize that they are separate people from their caregivers. They express their strong emotional ties to the adults they love, and they are acutely aware of their vulnerability when their loved ones are gone. A cherished object (a "lovey"), like a blanket, a piece of their parent's clothing, or a stuffed toy, can be very helpful as mobile infants navigate this very complicated and important emotional voyage toward independence.

As they play, mobile infants can be totally absorbed. Opening and shutting, filling and dumping, and picking up and dropping are all activities that challenge infants' mobility and dexterity as well as their ideas about objects and what they can do. Physical activity and learning are intricately con-

As they play, mobile infants can be totally absorbed. Opening and shutting, filling and dumping, and picking up and dropping are activities that challenge infants' dexterity and their ideas about objects.

Infants at this stage make use of new physical, cognitive, social, and emotional abilities and the connections among them to discriminate between familiar and unfamiliar people and to seek an object or person that is out of sight. Playing peek-a-boo or hide-and-seek and finding an object hidden in a box are among the many ways infants explore this new understanding of how the world of objects and people works. While they respond with differing degrees of intensity, based on both individual temperament and

nected, as infants discover, test, and confirm that objects can be out of sight (inside a box or in a cabinet) and then found; that objects can be all together, separated into pieces, and put together again; and that adults can be resources for reaching what has been dropped.

During this period, infants develop small-muscle skills as they grasp, drop, pull, push, throw, and mouth objects. They develop their large muscles as they creep, crawl, cruise, walk holding onto furniture,

Joan (10 months) was in motion. She used a large yellow truck to pull herself up to a standing position, dropped to her knees, crawled and scooted about the room, crawled up the two-step platform, sat for a moment to survey the room, and called to Gina, her primary caregiver, with her eyes. They smiled at each other. Joan rolled onto her tummy and slid down the carpeted steps, where she sat and, again, looked over toward Gina. When Gina picked up another child, Joan crawled across the floor and pulled herself up, holding Gina's knee, pouting. Gina stroked her hair, knelt down, and, putting her free arm around Joan, said, "I can't hold you now, but I can come watch while you climb up." Joan returned Gina's smile, burrowed her head into Gina's thigh, then crawled back to the platform. She looked back to be sure Gina had followed and called, "Ji! Ji! Ji!" in an excited voice.

*   *   *

This baby and her caregiver have many ways of communicating. Eye contact is mutual and regular. Adult and child are in tune and check in regularly. A gesture of the arms, a sound, or a pout expresses to the adult what Joan needs. Gina responds gesturally (by putting her arm around Joan to soothe her and reinforce their connection) and also puts Joan's physical communication into words. Joan does not understand the words, but she knows from the tone and all she can read in Gina's face that she can have her attention even when she has to share it with another baby. This brief interaction reinforces Joan's sense of herself as someone who is able to communicate, get what she needs, and control intense feelings, and whose achievements are valued by an adult she loves and trusts.

The younger baby in Gina's arms benefits from the interaction as well. From his perch, he can watch and share in the excitement about skills he has not yet developed. "Ordinary" interactions between an adult and a baby or between older and younger infants offer important opportunities for learning. For example, Joan's desire to use words to communicate grows as she hears Gina talk; the younger baby can share the excitement of physical feats he cannot yet perform.

climb up onto couches and ramps, and descend stairs. Learning to sit unassisted marks infants' readiness to do things for themselves (as they see adults and older children doing), such as feeding themselves and playing with blocks, water, or other materials.

Through their exploration of objects and their own physical skills, mobile infants learn rudimentary rules of cause and effect and the use of objects as tools for specific purposes, sequence, classification, and spatial relationships. They begin to group and compare. They use and manipulate tools—for example, using a cup to scoop water.

The mobile infant is both practicing independence and testing new ways to stay connected to those she loves and trusts to protect her as she moves about on her own. Eye contact, vocalizing, and gesturing take on added importance as tools for maintaining that connection. A strong, loving relationship with a trusted adult gives the mobile infant the secure base from which she can explore her world.

The caregiver

Mobile infants' new abilities and understandings have a profound effect on relationships between them and their primary caregivers. Infants can now move away from, and back to, the security of a loving adult. They can get to an attractive object or place on their own, but as they play, they maintain their sense of security by checking in with their primary caregiver through eye contact, a coo, or a gesture. They rely on loving, vigilant adults to create an environment safe for exploration and to reassure them of their safety.

By the time they become mobile, babies have already learned a great deal about language and communication. Now they begin to understand the meaning of words. With language a new era of relatedness emerges. Children's earliest words reflect their social environment—usually the names of important adults, objects, and activities associated in their daily lives. In response, caregivers slow down their own speech and enunciate words clearly. Expanding, repeating, labeling, and using words from the infant's primary language are among the many ways adults help infants add new words to their repertoire and encourage their sense of themselves as effective communicators.

The mobile infant whose family speaks a different language than that of the caregiver will feel supported in using her home language if caregivers learn some key words and songs from her family and get simple picture books with captions in the family's language.

Listening is a critical skill for effective communication that adults can model even as the infant expresses herself in "babble talk," with a few identifiable words. The caregiver demonstrates her interest in understanding the infant by listening, watching, and giving words to the child. The question, "You want the truck?" reinforces the infant's sense that she can communicate her needs and wishes to others. The joy in her eyes when her words are understood or when she hears the caregiver use words spoken at home tells of her excitement and eagerness to join and become competent in this important aspect of the adult world.

Mobile infants are naturally very curious about other children. Friendships are beginning to emerge. Because infants are not yet experienced in interacting with each other, they often require assistance. A mobile infant will grab at another's hair and pull at his clothes with the same interest she shows in sharing a picture book or crawling up a ramp side by side.

Because mobile infants can be so easily stimulated, sensitive adults will ensure that a good balance is maintained in the levels of intensity of play, from active . . . to quiet . . . to sleep. The developmentally appropriate environment supports the infant's new mobility, interest in routines, imitation of the behaviors of adults and older children, and capacity to engage in a wider range of activities. Structures (e.g., low platforms,

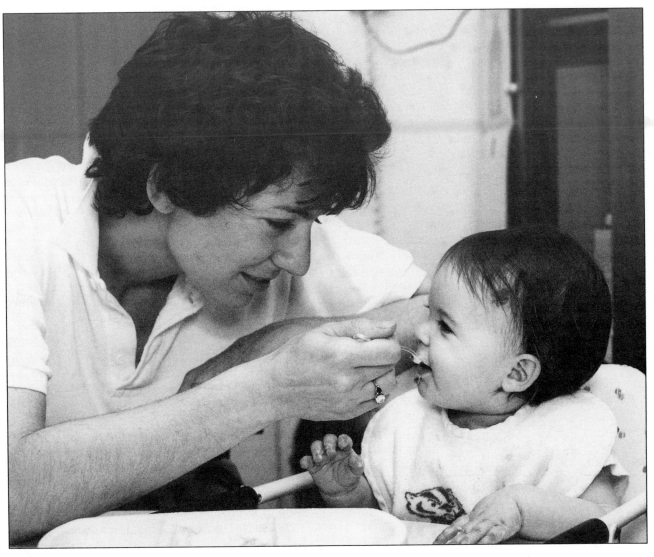

Infants sense whether someone enjoys their company during play and everyday routines.

As a young infant, Maya had moved easily through morning and evening transitions in her family child care, and a warm relationship had developed between Marina, Maya's mother, and Shanita, the family child care provider. At 16 months, however, Maya began clinging to Shanita in the evening, unwilling to let her mother hold her. If Marina arrived while Maya was playing, she was greeted with tears. One evening, when Marina was trying to pick Maya up to go, Shanita, feeling Marina's hurt and concern, stepped in, saying: "You know, Marina, this happens all the time with children. Maya is trying out her new independence and she sees her separation from you very differently than she used to. Now she knows you are gone when you go. She may be telling you she is confused, mad, and, just maybe, that she wants you to spend some time with her playing in her space before you go home." Marina thought about this, looked intently into Maya's eyes, and said in a soft voice: "Maya, do you want Mama to play with you?" Maya, with bright eyes, repeated, "Mama play? Mama play?"

*   *   *

Shanita, knowing how different infants work through the strong emotions associated with their emerging understanding of people and objects, intervenes quickly by telling the mother that what is happening is normal and does not mean that the baby now prefers her caregiver to her mother. By doing so, she avoids the development of jealousy that might undermine her relationship with Marina. By "talking through the child" (described in the vignette on p. 58), Shanita offers Marina several ways to understand Maya's behavior and some strategies the two of them can use to work through the transition together. The alliance is saved. Shanita is using her knowledge and skills to help both mother and baby and negotiate what will be one of many emotionally charged moments.

tunnels) invite the infant to pull herself up, take steps, climb up steps or risers, and crawl into partially enclosed spaces to gain new perspectives on the world. Spaces are organized to invite specific types of activities (a small nook, softly lit and with cushions and books in pockets hung on the wall, says to the baby, "This is a place for quiet activities; books are special, and I am protected while I read").

Ensuring health and safety, always a major concern in group care, demands extra precautionary measures when mobile infants are involved. Caregivers must check the environment regularly for potential dangers. Splinters, unlocked cabinets containing cleaning materials, uncovered electrical outlets, pot handles within the infant's reach, small objects, pieces of balloons, a purse left open, and medications left out are but a few of the long list of potential threats to the infant's health or safety.

The caregiver/family alliance

The mobile infant, his family members, and his caregiver are entering a stage of development that is laced with complicated feelings about separation and attachment, much excitement, and many challenges. At one moment, the baby is consumed with his own movement—crawling, scooting, or toddling off with abandon. In the next, he is fighting to keep the adult close, crying if left for a moment. Each partner in the triangle of relationships may experience different feelings at different times; thus honest communication between parent and caregiver takes on added importance. Working together, they can keep their focus on what is most important for the infant. They can identify and experiment with ways to maintain his sense of security in the child care setting, reinforcing daily his understanding that his parents will be back, that they still love him, and that his caregiver will love and protect him while his family is away.

As with young infants, open and frequent communication is needed to assure continuity between family and caregiver. Parents and caregivers of mobile infants must keep pace with their rapid development by changing the environment and making decisions about how to encourage mobility, independence, and curiosity within safe boundaries. Negotiations with families must be guided by the caregiver's commitment to reaching a mutual understanding. A mutual understanding of the use of "no" is a good example. While mobile infants might be encouraged by the caregiver to use "no" as a tool for self-defense and a statement of independence, many families do not believe that it is appropriate to allow a young child to say "no." In some cultures, such statements of independence, especially when directed toward an adult, are viewed as highly inappropriate. Cultural beliefs and rules about infants' self-feeding, being "loud," and moving without restraint also vary.

The caregiver who anticipates that cultural and child-rearing beliefs will differ among families is ready to open communication. If their beliefs conflict, a caregiver and family can find a mutually acceptable approach by talking over a range of strategies until they reach consensus. This requires strong communication skills on the part of the caregiver as well as a belief that family members are the primary caregivers and a constant, powerful influence on the child's development. The skilled caregiver realizes that being a competent professional requires the ability to listen carefully, explore the parent's perspective fully, and steer the conversation to areas of agreement.

Some parents and caregivers experience deep feelings of loss as the infant becomes more independent. Others feel relief. Whatever feelings are aroused by a young child's development, the alliance between caregiver and parent can be tremendously helpful, as each gives support and insights to the other.

Toddlers (16 to 36 months)

Toddlers are concerned about who they are and who is in charge. Beginning around 18 months of age, identity becomes the dominant developmental issue for children, closely tied to questions of independence and control. Of course, the sense of security that began to develop in the earliest months and the desire to explore (with increasing purposefulness) continue. Caregivers can help toddlers find appropriate ways to assert themselves by supporting their individuality, by giving them choices whenever possible, and by introducing social guidelines. A well-designed environment that offers toddlers chances to be in control and to participate in group play, fantasy play, and independent activity helps the caregiver to foster cooperation and facilitate the toddler's development of a strong sense of self.

The child

Toddlers are learning how to be safe, how to get what they need without taking from others, how to use peers and adults as resources, how to use words to express feelings, and how to act appropriately in different situations. They have a heightened interest in what it is to be a boy or a girl. They are particularly interested in their bodies and those of others.

Donna positioned Haniya, a toddler with cerebral palsy, in her special seat on the countertop so that Haniya could hold her hands under the faucet. Jonathan came in from the adjoining play area to wash his hands before snack. Donna said to Jonathan, "Please turn on the faucet for Haniya." Jonathan did. Haniya glanced at him and gave a faint smile. She stuck her hands under the faucet of running water, seeming to enjoy the cool feeling on her hands. Jonathan stuck his hands under the water also, and they splashed the water together. Haniya's smile filled her face, and they laughed. Jonathan pushed the soap dispenser for Haniya, then for himself. Donna helped both children wash between their fingers, then gave Haniya a paper towel to give Jonathan, who took it gently from her, saying, "Tank you, Hanya."

*　　*　　*

This caregiver knows how to extend this moment of intimacy and cooperation between these two toddlers, letting each use his skills to help the other. She intervenes only to be sure that each child learns proper handwashing. Thus, good habits of personal hygiene, essential for reducing the spread of infection in child care settings, are taught within the context of interaction and cooperation. The bathroom is also set up to offer such opportunities, with a place to sit for the child who needs to be held and a stool for the child who can stand. It allows both children to reach the sink, soap, and paper towels on their own. Teaching proper personal hygiene is critical as toddlers are increasingly capable of doing things by themselves and learning to use the toilet. What could be better than the magic of one toddler helping another and showing off new competence at proper handwashing?

Toddlers' interactions may at times seem very sophisticated (as, for example, when they imitate a gentle, patient, or generous adult). At other times, fatigue, anxiety, or other distress overwhelms them.

The period from 16 to 36 months is filled with exploration, questioning, discovery, and determination to find meaning in events, objects, and words. Through their experimentation with objects, language, and social interactions, toddlers are entering a new phase of mental activity. Toddlers love to divide

During a walk in the park, Richie picked up a branch that had fallen from a tree. As Amy began her customary speech about leaving sticks on the ground because they might poke someone, Richie explained that the stick was his cello. He ran his hand across the branch, singing "de-dah," tapping his toes, and moving his head to the beat. "OK," Amy said, "we'll take the cello back with us." Richie's father, a musician, had recently moved out of the house. Amy thought that the music was a connection with his father. When the group got back to the center, Richie, sitting on a milk crate and using a wooden spoon for a bow, gave the group a concert with his cello. It was the beginning of a ritual. Every afternoon after nap, children would help get the cello out from under the red sofa, and there would be a concert as Richie created a connection with his father.

* * *

In a few critical minutes during an ordinary outing, this caregiver draws on many areas of knowledge, skill, and experience. As Richie picks up a stick, Amy's practiced vigilance about children's safety and health lead her to intervene quickly. But as Richie explains (his experience with Amy must have taught him that she will listen), Amy slows down. Her general knowledge of toddler development helps her to appreciate Richie's emerging capacities to express himself through language and dramatic play. Her awareness of Richie's specific situation helps her to grasp the emotional meaning of the "cello" for Richie and to find a way to support this young child's determined effort to maintain connection with his father. Amy adapts rapidly. She agrees to carry the stick—protecting, simultaneously, the group's safety, the group's respect for safety rules, Richie's dignity, and her individual relationship of trust with Richie. Once back at the center, Amy creates an opportunity for Richie to use his creativity not only to master his own feelings but also to contribute to the shared life of the group. We can imagine that in conversations with Richie's mother and father, Amy will listen for opportunities to let each of them know about the cello concerts and then listen carefully for clues to help her support the whole family during this difficult transition.

objects into categories by shape, size, color, or type. They might line up all the large rubber animals according to their height, put the animals into groups according to their species, and pair a little animal next to a big one, calling them "mommy and baby." They are demonstrating through their play their rudimentary understanding of classification and seriation. What they are learning through play, observation, and exploration is often amazing. For example, while reading a story, a toddler might point to all the cats in a picture, calling them "cats" even though they are different sizes, shapes, and colors.

Toddlers are fascinated by the use of words. Words are new tools for relating to peers and adults. They listen and can follow simple instructions. They ask "why" repeatedly in order to engage adults, as much as to get answers. Words have power. Toddlers can use words to evoke what is not present and to express strong feelings. For example, they often repeat phrases like "Mommy come back" in a ritualistic way to comfort themselves when feeling the sadness of separation and to reassure themselves that the separation is not permanent.

Toddlers who have watched adults and older siblings write, who are read to from books, and who see printed words used to label objects on shelves or names printed on their cubbies become increasingly aware of the importance of written language. Not only do they enjoy being read to, they are more attentive to the words on the page. They label the things they see in illustrations and often join in the telling of the story. As with spoken language, toddlers use their keen powers of observation and desire to imitate the activities of adults and older children around them to learn about various forms of written language before they can read or write.

The social awareness of toddlers is vastly more complex than that of younger infants. Their past experiences in communicating with others enable them to refine their ability to read children's and adults' signals. They demonstrate their growing familiarity with symbols through their dramatic play and their rapidly expanding vocabularies. They are now interested in playing with each other. As they play, toddlers learn from other children's actions and experience the power of "teaching" and guiding others in play. Using their few words, gestural language, and boundless creativity, they can work out simple

The skilled caregiver offers toddlers experiences that support initiative, creativity, autonomy, and self-esteem.

dramatic-play themes, such as pretending that a block is a telephone, dressing up to dance, or carrying a briefcase to "go to work."

Toddlers' exploration of the social world often involves conflict. The most basic is about what is mine and what is yours. Toddlers react impulsively, but their feelings of empathy blossom as they negotiate these conflicts and see that other people have feelings, too. They can easily fall into despair at not getting what they want or feeling the displeasure of a beloved adult; just as easily, they can react with amazing generosity and warmth. Through such negotiations, toddlers build a sense of themselves as social beings competent, cooperative, and emotionally connected.

With Ben, the course of toilet learning was not entirely smooth, though not really difficult. When Ben was 19 months old and his father raised the issue with Carla, Ben's primary caregiver, they agreed to start a toilet routine both at home and at the center. At the center, Carla began suggesting that Ben might like to go to the toilet. When he agreed, they would go to the bathroom together. She would remove his diaper and let him step on the small platform to sit on the toilet. The first day, he wet himself as his diaper was being removed. However, on the second day, he had a bowel movement on the toilet and seemed very pleased with himself. For the next few days, he would occasionally urinate or defecate in the toilet with some pleasure. Then Ben entered a period when he wasn't sure the whole thing was a good idea. At 20½ months, when asked to go to the toilet, he answered vehemently, "No!"

*   *   *

Carla talked to Ben's father, who described the same resistance at home, and they decided not to press him for a while. A few weeks later, Ben's father told Carla that Ben tried to show his baby brother the toilet and suggested this might be a signal. Why not try asking Ben to take a friend to the toilet? Ben seemed eager, and Carla listened as he talked convincingly about toilets and sinks and how they weren't bad. He was still reluctant for short periods of time, and his father and Carla would suggest "helping a friend," which usually worked. By 26 months of age, Ben was using the toilet willingly, standing to urinate; he wore a diaper only at naptime. Soon after that, he either went to the bathroom himself or asked to be taken. He remained a good helper to his friends and was particularly skilled as a handwashing instructor.

The caregiver

The skilled caregiver offers toddlers experiences that support initiative, creativity, autonomy, and self-esteem. Yet she recognizes that while striving to be independent and self-reliant, toddlers count on the understanding and vigilance of the adults who love them. The caregiver must be prepared to prevent injuries and handle conflicts as toddlers learn to defend themselves, share, and cooperate with others. The competent caregiver knows that her toddlers are capable and want to test their social skills. She

gives them opportunities to "take responsibility" for others and takes advantage of unplanned encounters that allow the toddler to show his competence.

Toddlers need opportunities to be responsible, to make significant choices, and to be challenged or disciplined in ways that keep their dignity intact. They are beginning to understand why certain behaviors must be limited—that rules are fair and judgments just. They need to feel that limits are placed on them by adults who can be counted on and who mean what they say. These are adults who can support them in their frustrations and disappointments and enjoy their pleasures and successes. Toddlers need continuity between the expectations of their family and those of their caregiver. Toddlers can cope with the fact that rules about what is acceptable or unacceptable differ between home and the child care setting, but caregivers and parents must work together to make these differences clear to children.

Adults can expect great variability in emotion and social interaction and learn when to let toddlers work a conflict through themselves and when to intervene. Adults who know a toddler well can recognize the signs of stress and help the child learn to control her impulses; they also know when a toddler is acting out deep emotions and give him the space to work them through.

Unfortunately, many infants and toddlers experience the trauma of fighting in the family, divorce, chronic illness, death of a family member, or violence in the community. Their ability to overcome the hurt and fear depends, in large measure, on whether they are secure in relationships with a few caring adults who understand what they have experienced and give them extra attention, tolerance, and appreciation for how they express their feelings. Often, the caregiver grieves with the child. The caregiver's greatest assets in dealing with such situations are her responsiveness to the child and her commitment to being a resource to the family.

The caregiver/family alliance

A healthy toddler's inner world is filled with conflicting feelings—independence and dependence, pride and shame, confidence and doubt, self-awareness and confusion, fear and omnipotence, hostility and intense love, anger and tenderness, initiative and passivity. These feelings challenge parents' and caregivers' resourcefulness and knowledge, as they work together to provide toddlers with emotional security.

A child's sense of identity is rooted in his family and community. Toddlers feel more secure when they can see that their family members are comfortable with their caregivers. Family-caregiver communication, particularly when there are cultural and language differences, builds mutual understanding and creates continuity between home and child care. If the family child care provider or child care center staff do not know the home language of the child, there are strategies available to meet the challenge. For example, bilingual, bicultural members of the family's community can be recruited to interpret during family-caregiver conferences, interpret important program policies, and help the caregiver learn at least a few important words. There are many ways to show respect and help the family feel welcome in the child care setting.

Toddlers whose home language is different from that used in the group care environment need to hear their own language spoken and see it written. These opportunities help them build upon their home language while learning words to communicate with English-speaking peers and caregivers. In valuing the child's home language, caregivers reinforce his pride in family and community as well as his feelings of competence in mastering the challenges of a culturally and linguistically different environment.

Bowel control and learning to use the toilet are important issues during the third year of life. Toilet learning can be effective only if the child wants to learn and feels responsible. It must be accomplished in a spirit of cooperation and enthusiasm as children reach this milestone in their development. Professionals must ensure that techniques that are common, but inappropriate, such as punishment or shaming children, are not used in the child care setting. The family and caregiver should agree upon an approach for helping the older toddler learn this new aspect of self-control.

Caring for toddlers can be challenging for adults. The toddler's constant movement, short attention span, and bouts of frustration mixed with the pure joy of discovery can be both heartwarming and emotionally draining. It is difficult at times to understand that as he pushes away and hurtles himself into action, the toddler is still very much in need of his special adults and the secure base they offer. Parents and caregivers who have built a good relationship can help each other better understand and help the toddler as they share their experiences and insights and offer each other encouragement.

Although in seeking autonomy the toddler may push adults away at times, the child is still very much in need of his special people and the secure base they offer.

Developmental Milestones of Children from Birth to Age 3

	Interest in others	Self-awareness	Motor milestones and eye-hand skills
The early months (birth through 8 months)	• Newborns prefer the human face and human sound. Within the first two weeks, they recognize and prefer the sight, smell, and sound of the principal caregiver. • Social smile and mutual gazing are evidence of early social interaction. The infant can initiate and terminate these interactions. • Anticipates being lifted or fed and moves body to participate. • Sees adults as objects of interest and novelty. Seeks out adults for play. Stretches arms to be taken.	• Sucks fingers or hand fortuitously. • Observes own hands. • Raises hands as if to protect self when object comes close to face. • Looks to the place on body where being touched. • Reaches for and grasps toys. • Clasps hands together and fingers them. • Tries to cause things to happen. • Begins to distinguish friends from strangers. Shows preference for being held by familiar people.	• The young infant uses many complex reflexes: searches for something to suck; holds on when falling; turns head to avoid obstruction of breathing; avoids brightness, strong smells, and pain. • Puts hand or object in mouth. Begins reaching toward interesting objects. • Grasps, releases, regrasps, and releases object again. • Lifts head. Holds head up. Sits up without support. Rolls over. Transfers and manipulates objects with hands. Crawls.
Crawlers and walkers (8 to 18 months)	• Exhibits anxious behavior around unfamiliar adults. • Enjoys exploring objects with another as the basis for establishing relationships. • Gets others to do things for child's pleasure (wind up toys, read books, get dolls). • Shows considerable interest in peers. • Demonstrates intense attention to adult language.	• Knows own name. • Smiles or plays with self in mirror. • Uses large and small muscles to explore confidently when a sense of security is offered by presence of caregiver. Frequently checks for caregiver's presence. • Has heightened awareness of opportunities to make things happen, yet limited awareness of responsibility for own actions. • Indicates strong sense of self through assertiveness. Directs actions of others (e.g., "Sit there!"). • Identifies one or more body parts. • Begins to use *me, you, I*.	• Sits well in chairs. • Pulls self up, stands holding furniture. • Walks when led. Walks alone. • Throws objects. • Climbs stairs. • Uses marker on paper. • Stoops, trots, walks backward a few steps.
Toddlers and 2-year-olds (18 months to 3 years)	• Shows increased awareness of being seen and evaluated by others. • Sees others as a barrier to immediate gratification. • Begins to realize others have rights and privileges. • Gains greater enjoyment from peer play and joint exploration. • Begins to see benefits of cooperation. • Identifies self with children of same age or sex. • Is more aware of the feelings of others. • Exhibits more impulse control and self-regulation in relation to others. • Enjoys small-group activities.	• Shows strong sense of self as an individual, as evidenced by "No" to adult requests. • Experiences self as a powerful, potent, creative doer. Explores everything. • Becomes capable of self-evaluation and has beginning notions of self (good, bad, attractive, ugly). • Makes attempts at self-regulation. • Uses names of self and others. • Identifies 6 or more body parts.	• Scribbles with marker or crayon. • Walks up and down stairs. Can jump off one step. • Kicks a ball. • Stands on one foot. • Threads beads. • Draws a circle. • Stands and walks on tiptoes. • Walks up stairs one foot on each step. • Handles scissors. • Imitates a horizontal crayon stroke.

Pages 70–71, reprinted by permission, are taken from *Caring for Infants and Toddlers in Groups: Developmentally Appropriate Practice,* published 199 by ZERO TO THREE: National Center for Infants, Toddlers, and Families. Wall charts based on "Developmental Milestones of Children from Birth t Age 3" and related materials may be ordered directly from ZERO TO THREE, 734 15th Street, NW, Suite 1000, Washington, DC 20005; 800-899-4301

Language development/communication	Physical, spatial, and temporal awareness	Purposeful action and use of tools	Expression of feelings
• ...ies to signal pain or ...stress. • ...miles or vocalizes to ini...ate social contact. • ...esponds to human ...ices. Gazes at faces. • ...ses vocal and nonvocal ...mmunication to ex...ess interest and exert ...fluence. • ...abbles using all types of ...ounds. Engages in pri...ate conversations when ...one. • ...ombines babbles. Un...erstands names of famil...r people and objects. ...aughs. Listens to con...ersations.	• Comforts self by sucking thumb or finding pacifier. • Follows a slowly moving object with eyes. • Reaches and grasps toys. • Looks for dropped toy. • Identifies objects from various viewpoints. Finds a toy hidden under a blanket when placed there while watching.	• Observes own hands. • Grasps rattle when hand and rattle are both in view. • Hits or kicks an object to make a pleasing sight or sound continue. • Tries to resume a knee ride by bouncing to get adult started again.	• Expresses discomfort and comfort/pleasure unambiguously. • Responds with more animation and pleasure to primary caregiver than to others. • Can usually be comforted by familiar adult when distressed. • Smiles and demonstrates obvious pleasure in response to social stimulation. Very interested in people. Shows displeasure at loss of social contact. • Laughs aloud (belly laugh). • Shows displeasure or disappointment at loss of toy. • Expresses several clearly differentiated emotions: pleasure, anger, anxiety or fear, sadness, joy, excitement, disappointment, exuberance. • Reacts to strangers with soberness or anxiety.
• ...nderstands many more ...ords than can say. • ...ooks toward 20 or more ...bjects when named. • ...reates long, babbled ...entences. • ...hakes head no. Says two ...r three clear words. • ...ooks at picture books ...ith interest, points to ...bjects. • ...ses vocal signals other ...an crying to gain assis...nce. • ...egins to use me, you, I.	• Tries to build with blocks. • If toy is hidden under one of three cloths while child watches, looks under the right cloth for the toy. • Persists in a search for a desired toy even when toy is hidden under distracting objects, such as pillows. • When chasing a ball that has rolled under sofa and out the other side, will make a detour around sofa to get ball. • Pushes foot into shoe, arm into sleeve.	• When a toy winds down, continues the activity manually. • Uses a stick as a tool to obtain a toy. • When a music box winds down, searches for the key to wind it up again. • Brings a stool to use for reaching for something. • Pushes away someone or something not wanted. • Creeps or walks to get something or avoid unpleasantness. • Pushes foot into shoe, arm into sleeve. • Feeds self finger food (bits of fruit, crackers). • Partially feeds self with fingers or spoon. • Handles cup well with minimal spilling. • Handles spoon well for self-feeding.	• Actively shows affection for familiar person: hugs, smiles at, runs toward, leans against, and so forth. • Shows anxiety at separation from primary caregiver. • Shows anger focused on people or objects. • Expresses negative feelings. • Shows pride and pleasure in new accomplishments. • Shows intense feelings for parents. • Continues to show pleasure in mastery. • Asserts self, indicating strong sense of self.
• ...ombines words. • ...istens to stories for a ...hort while. • ...as a speaking vocabulary ...hat may reach 200 words. • ...evelops fantasy in lan...uage. Begins to play pre...end games. • ...efines use of many ...ousehold items. • ...ses compound sentences. • ...ses adjectives and ad...erbs. Recounts events of ...he day.	• Identifies a familiar object by touch when it is placed in a bag with two other objects. • Uses tomorrow, yesterday. • Figures out which child is missing by looking at children who are present. • Asserts independence: "Me do it." • Puts on simple garments, such as cap or slippers.	• When playing with a ring-stacking toy, ignores any forms that have no hole. Stacks only rings or other objects with holes. • Classifies, labels, and sorts objects by group (hard versus soft, large versus small). • Helps dress and undress self.	• Frequently displays aggressive feelings and behaviors. • Exhibits contrasting states and mood shifts (stubborn versus compliant). • Shows increased fearfulness (of dark, monsters, etc.). • Expresses emotions with increasing control. • Aware of own feelings and those of others. • Shows pride in creation and production. • Verbalizes feelings more often. Expresses feelings in symbolic play. • Shows empathic concern for others.

...te: This list is not intended to be exhaustive. Many of the behaviors indicated here will happen earlier or later for individual infants. The chart ...ggests an approximate time when a behavior might appear, but it should not be rigidly interpreted. Often, but not always, the behaviors appear ...the order in which they emerge. Particularly for younger infants, the behaviors listed in one domain overlap considerably with several other ...velopmental domains. Some behaviors are placed under more than one category to emphasize this interrelationship.

Examples of Appropriate and Inappropriate Practices for Infants

The examples presented here pertain to key areas of practice in caring for infants and toddlers: caregivers-child relationships, the environment, daily experiences, health and safety, relationships with families, and policies. These dimensions of practice roughly correspond to those included in the "Guidelines for Decisions about Developmentally Appropriate Practice" (see Part 1, pp. 16–22) and the NAEYC accreditation criteria (1991).

The examples are based primarily on the previous edition of *Developmentally Appropriate Practice in Early Childhood Programs* (Bredekamp 1987) and *Caring for Infants and Toddlers in Groups: Developmentally Appropriate Practice* (ZERO TO THREE 1995). Among the other resources used were *Caring for Our Children—National Health and Safety Performance Standards: Guidelines for Out-of-Home Child Care Programs,* developed by the American Academy of Pediatrics and the American Public Health Association (AAP & APHA 1992), and NAEYC publications, *Healthy Young Children: A Manual for Programs* (Kendrick, Kaufmann, & Messenger 1995) and *The What, Why, and How of High-Quality Early Childhood Education: A Guide for On-Site Supervision* (Koralek, Colker, & Dodge 1995). Our acknowledgment of these groups and individuals does not imply their endorsement of the following material.

The aim is not to issue a prescriptive formula to be rigidly followed but to encourage those who care for infants and toddlers to reflect on all areas of their practice. Nor is the intent to put the blame for inappropriate practices on individual caregivers, most of whom struggle to do their best, often under very difficult circumstances—including limited training, inadequate ratios of adults to children, low compensation and high staff turnover, and meager resources. Our hope is to help them in their efforts through highlighting important elements of good practice.

Appropriate Practices	Inappropriate Practices
Relationships among caregivers and children	
• There is sufficient continuity of care to ensure that every infant (and family) is able to form a relationship with a primary caregiver. As the caregiver comes to know a few infants very well, she is able to respond to the temperament, needs, and cues of each baby and to develop a mutually satisfying pattern of communication with each child and family.	• Development and maintenance of one-to-one relationships are not given top priority. Infants are shifted from group to group or cared for by whatever adult is available at the moment and thus are unable to form a relationship with one or two caregivers over time.
• Adults engage in many one-to-one, face-to-face interactions with infants. Adults talk in a pleasant, calm voice, using simple language and frequent eye contact while being responsive to the child's cues.	• Infants are left for long periods in cribs, play-pens, or seats, without adults' attention. • Adults interact with infants in a harsh or impersonal manner.
• All interactions are characterized by gentle, supportive responses. Adults observe and listen and respond to sounds that infants make, imitate their vocalizations, and appreciate infants' sounds as the beginnings of communication.	• Adults are rough and inattentive, ignoring the child's imitations and responses. Adults do not wait for infants to finish vocalizing before beginning to talk; that is, they "talk over" babies' vocalizing.
• Warm, responsive interactions with infants occur throughout the day. Observing the infant's cues, the adult is able to judge when the baby would like to be held, carried to a new place, or shifted to a new position. Adults often talk to babies, especially older infants, about what is going on ("Let's go for a little walk. Would you like that?").	• Infants are wordlessly and sometimes abruptly moved about at the adults' convenience.

Appropriate Practices	**Inappropriate Practices**
• Adults are especially attentive to infants during caregiving routines, such as diaper changing, feeding, and changing clothes. The caregiver explains what will happen, what is happening, and what will happen next, asking and waiting for the infant's co-operation and participation.	• Routines are swiftly accomplished without involving the infant in play or communication. Little or no warm interaction takes place during routines.
• Adults recognize that crying and body movements are infants' ways to communicate. Responses to infants' cries or calls of distress are calm, tender, and respectful.	• Crying is ignored or responded to irregularly at the convenience of the adult. Crying is treated as a nuisance. Adults' responses neglect the infants' needs or overwhelm the infant with a rush of activity.
• Adults ensure that every infant receives nurturing, responsive care.	• Adults show favoritism and give most of their attention to certain children.
• Playful interactions with babies are done in ways that are sensitive to the child's interests and level of tolerance for physical movement, loud sounds, or other changes.	• Attempting to be playful, adults frighten, tease, or upset children with their unpredictable behaviors.
• Adults show their respect for infants' play by observing the child's activity, commenting on it verbally, and providing a safe environment. The quietly supportive adult encourages the child's active engagement.	• Infants are interrupted; toys are dangled, put into their hands, or whisked away. Adults impose their own ideas or even play with toys themselves without regard to the child's interest.
• Adults frequently talk with, sing to, and read to infants. Language is a vital, lively part of the communication with infants.	• Infants are ignored or left to watch television. Language is used indiscriminately, either too much or too little, and adults use a very limited range of words.
• Infants and their parents are greeted warmly each morning. The caregiver is available to the infant upon arrival and helps the child become a part of the small group as needed. A peaceful transition time for parent and child is a part of the daily routine.	• Adults receive children hurriedly and without individual attention. Babies are placed in a crib or infant seat with no caregiver interaction.
• Caregivers consistently respond to infants' needs for food and comfort, thus enabling the infants to develop trust in the adults who care for them. In this environment they learn that the world is a secure place for them.	• Adults are unpredictable and/or unresponsive. They act as if children are a bother or cute, doll-like objects.
• Adults adjust to infants' individual feeding and sleeping schedules. Infants' food preferences and eating styles are respected.	• Schedules are rigid and based on adults' rather than children's needs. Food is used to pacify or reward (or is withheld as punishment).

73

Appropriate Practices	**Inappropriate Practices**

Relationships among caregivers and children (cont'd)

• Adults respect infants' individual abilities and respond positively as each baby develops new abilities. Experiencing caregivers' pleasure in their achievements, infants feel competent and enjoy mastering new skills.	• Infants are criticized or laughed at for what they cannot do or for their clumsy struggle to master a skill. They are made to feel inadequate and as if they have no effect on others.
• Adults know that infants are curious about each other. At the same time, caregivers help ensure that children treat each other gently.	• Adults do not allow infants to touch each other, even gently. • Adults push infants to play together when they have no interest in doing so. If one child is very rough with another, adults take no action to protect the child who is being hurt.
• Adults cope well with stress and model the type of interactions with others that they want children to develop.	• Adults exhibit a lack of coping behaviors under stress; they often become tearful, aggressive, or overwrought.
• Adults frequently observe the infant at play. Appropriate games, such as peek-a-boo and This Little Piggy, are played with interested infants, the adult being careful not to intrude upon how the infant wants to play.	• Games are imposed on children regardless of their interest. • Adults are rarely playful with babies.
• Diaper changing, feeding, and other routines are viewed as vital learning experiences for both babies and caregivers.	• Routines are dealt with hurriedly and indifferently, with efficiency as the priority.
• Healthy, accepting attitudes about children's bodies and their functions are expressed.	• Infants are made to feel that their bodies are not to be touched or admired and that bodily functions are disgusting.

Environment and experiences

• Walls are painted with lead-free, easy-to-clean paint. Carpeting and flooring are easy to clean, soft, and neutral in color. Infants enjoy bright colors on quilts, thick vinyl mats, and cushions. These add a lively appearance to areas designated for active play.	• Walls are cluttered with posters and other items or are sterile and bland. There is no carpeting, or an area carpet only partially covers the areas in use.
• Pictures of infants and their family members are hung on walls at such heights that infants can see them.	• Decorations are at adult eye level and do not include family photos.
• Adults provide infants with an auditory environment that is not overstimulating or distracting. They choose music and other recordings that infants enjoy.	• Adults play music they themselves enjoy, often so loudly and constantly as to make it difficult for infants to focus on speech sounds and hear their own vocalizations.

	Appropriate Practices	**Inappropriate Practices**
Play	• The play areas are comfortable; they have pillows, foam-rubber mats, and soft carpeting where babies can lie or be held and read to. A hammock, rocking chair (preferably a glider for safety), overstuffed chair, and big cushions are available for caregivers or parents and infants to relax in together.	• The play areas are sterile, designed for easy cleaning, but without the different textures, levels, or colors that infants need to stimulate their senses. There is no area where an adult can sit comfortably with an infant in her arms and read or talk to the baby.
	• Space is arranged so children can enjoy moments of quiet play by themselves, have ample space to roll over and move freely, and can crawl toward interesting objects. Areas for younger infants are separated from those of crawlers to promote the safe interactions of infants in similar stages of development.	• Space is cramped and unsafe for children who are learning how to move their bodies.
	• Visual displays, such as mobiles, are oriented toward the infant's line of sight and designed so that the interesting sights and effects are clearly visible when the baby is lying on her back. Mobiles are removed when children can grasp them.	• Visual displays are not in an infant's line of sight. They are often used as a substitute for appropriate social interaction of infants with adults.
	• Sturdy cardboard books are placed in book pockets or on a sturdy book stand. Books that the adults read to the babies are on a shelf out of reach. Books show children and families of different racial and cultural backgrounds, and people of various ages and abilities.	• Books are not available or are made of paper that tears easily. They do not contain objects familiar or interesting to children.
	• Toys provided are responsive to the child's actions: a variety of grasping toys that require different types of manipulation; a varied selection of skill-development materials, including nesting and stacking materials, activity boxes, and containers to be filled and emptied; a variety of balls, bells, and rattles.	• Toys are battery powered or windup, so the baby just watches. Toys lack a variety of texture, size, and shape.
	• A variety of safe household items that infants can use as play materials are available, including measuring cups, wooden spoons, nonbreakable bowls, and cardboard boxes.	• Household items that help make the infant room more homelike are not available.
	• Toys are scaled to a size that enables infants to grasp, chew, and manipulate them (clutch balls, rattles, teethers, and soft washable dolls and play animals).	• Toys are too large to handle or so small that infants could choke on or swallow them.

75

Appropriate Practices	**Inappropriate Practices**

Environment and experiences (cont'd)

Play (cont'd)

- Mobile infants have an open area where balls, push and pull toys, wagons, and other equipment encourage free movement and testing of large-muscle skills and coordination. Low, climbing structures, ramps, and steps are provided. Structures are well padded and safe for exploration.

- Open shelves within infants' reach contain toys of similar type, spaced so that infants can make choices. Caregivers group materials for related activities on different shelves (e.g., fill-and-empty activities are on a shelf separate from three-piece puzzles or moving/pushing toys).

- There is ample, accessible storage for extra play materials of a type similar to what is already displayed and for materials with increasing challenge. Caregivers can easily rearrange their space as young infants become mobile. When an infant has explored a toy with his mouth and moved to other things, the toy is picked up for washing and disinfecting and replaced with a similar toy. Everything is nearby, so caregivers do not have to leave the space to replace a toy.

- Room temperature can be controlled; vents are clean and provide an even flow of air. Floors are not drafty. Windows provide natural light and fresh air. Caregivers carry infants to the windows to see outside.

- Adults periodically move infants to a different spot (from the floor to an infant seat, from the seat to a stroller, etc.) to give babies differing perspectives and reasonable variety in what they are able to look at and explore.

- An outside play space adjacent to the infant area includes sunny and shaded areas. It is enclosed by protective fencing. The ground around climbing structures and in some of the open space is covered with resilient, stable surfacing for safety, making it easy for mobile infants to push wagons and ride-on toys. There are soft areas where young infants can lie on quilts.

- Balls and other moving toys are for outdoor use only. Equipment designed for crawling up/down or under/through is not available, or structures are safe only for older, more-mobile children.

- Toys are dumped in a box or kept out of children's reach, forcing them to depend on adults' selection.

- Storage closets are far from the infant space and are poorly organized, making it difficult to rotate materials, bring out more complex materials, or add to the variety of activities in the space.

- The infants' environment suffers from one or more of these deficiencies: the room is either too cold and drafty or too hot; it has little natural light; and/or its windows are not accessible enough for caregivers to hold infants so they can look out.

- Babies are confined to cribs, infant seats, playpens, or the floor for long periods.

- Infants rarely go out because there is no adjacent play area, and nearby parks and playgrounds offer no shaded areas or soft surfaces for babies to lie on or crawl about freely.

- Large group size and inadequate staff-child ratios make outdoor play difficult.

	Appropriate Practices	**Inappropriate Practices**
Eating	• Infants are always held with their bodies at an angle when being fed from a bottle.	• Young infants are strapped into infant seats with their bottles propped on a pillow.
	• Highchairs are used only when needed; they can be folded and stored away from the infant area. T-shaped safety straps are securely installed on highchairs. Waist-high tables with infant chairs that have side arms are used for feeding infants who can sit.	• Highchairs are not carefully selected or maintained. There are no safety straps, and highchairs are not routinely checked to ensure that trays will not fall off. There are no small tables and chairs to invite mobile infants to show their small- and large-muscle motor control.
	• Children who can sit up eat in groups of one or two with a caregiver to ensure adult assistance as needed. Finger foods are encouraged and caregivers allow children to feed themselves, even when their efforts are messy. Small servings of healthy foods are offered, and the child selects how much to eat and when to stop. Eating is considered a sociable, happy time.	• Large groups of children are fed in sequence or left to their own devices. Cookies and other sugary foods are used as treats. Adults are not responsive to children's cues as to what foods they prefer and when they've had enough. Conversation is limited.
	• Adults label each infant's food and bottles and store them separate from medicines in the refrigerator. Individual, labeled bibs hang on hooks near the eating area. Dishes and utensils are not shared and are washed after each use. Bottles and nipples are washed and disinfected after each use. Milk that has been warmed and/or used is never reused.	• Adults stack infant foods in the refrigerator and allow infants to share bottles, utensils, and bibs. Bottles are left out on counters, are not labeled, and are reused.
Sleeping	• The infant sleeping area is separate from active play and eating areas. Babies have their own cribs and sheets brought from home. Family members bring special comforting objects to personalize their baby's crib. Infants' names are used to label every personal item.	• Cribs line the walls of the play area. Cribs are all alike, and a baby is put into whatever crib is available. Infants do not have their own supplies, and there is nothing personal to help the baby feel "this is my place."
	• Cribs are made of wood, metal, or approved plastic. Each has a latching device to secure the drop side. The slats are no more than 2⅜ inches apart, and the height from the top of the mattress to the top of the rail is 36 inches. The mattress fits snugly into the crib—if two adult fingers can be placed between the mattress and the side of the crib, the mattress is too small. Cribs are spaced 3 feet apart so that infants do not breathe directly on each other. Infants are placed on their backs or sides for sleeping.	• Adults are uninformed of health and safety requirements of babies' sleeping areas; for example, pillows are used, or cribs and mattresses do not meet safety requirements.
	• The lighting is dim but not so dark that the caregiver cannot see every infant. The sleeping area is quiet with soft music.	• Sleeping babies are easily awakened by bright lights and the sounds of playing babies or loud music.

Appropriate Practices	**Inappropriate Practices**

Environment and experiences (cont'd)

Diapering

- Infants have their own diapering supplies and extra clothes within easy reach of the changing table. Also within easy reach of the caregiver are protective gloves, changing-table paper on a roll secured to the table, disinfectant stored out of the reach of infants but handy to the caregiver, a foot-operated diaper pail, bags that seal for soiled clothes or cloth diapers, and a handwashing sink and disinfectant soap. Adults carefully follow proper handwashing procedures (see p. 91) before and after diapering.

- Storage for disinfectants, gloves, and plastic bags is clearly labeled. Large graphic reminders of the steps in putting on/taking off protective gloves, proper diapering, and handwashing are prominently displayed at adult eye level.

- Every morning, diaper supplies and extra clothes are stored in individual, labeled bins. Specific instructions for each baby are noted on a card attached to the child's bin.

- Because the diaper-changing area is not well designed or organized, diapering takes a long time and can be irritating to caregiver and infant alike. In the rush to get diapers changed, adults may forget and skip essential steps in the diapering process, such as careful handwashing and proper use of gloves, or fail to ensure that the infant cannot possibly fall.

- Supplies, even disinfectants, do not have a designated space out of the reach of infants, so adults tend to leave them on the diapering counter. There are no visual reminders of proper hygiene.

- Families and caregivers leave infant diaper bags and supplies wherever they can in the diaper area. Before diapering an infant, the caregiver must find, sort, and get what is needed.

Health and safety

- Adults follow health and safety procedures, including proper handwashing methods and universal precautions to limit the spread of infectious disease. There are clearly written sanitation procedures specific to each area. Instructions on the proper diapering sequence (including use of protective gloves), cleaning cribs and play areas, and food storage/food preparation (including dishwashing) are displayed on the walls as visual reminders to adults.

- The diapering and food-preparation areas are separate, and caregivers do not move from one to the other without careful handwashing and other necessary procedures.

- Each day adults prepare a solution of ¼ cup of liquid bleach to 1 gallon of water (or 1 tablespoon to 1 quart of water in a spray bottle) and store it in a place out of the reach of children in each area that must be disinfected on a regular basis. All toys that infants put in their mouths are washed in soapy water, disinfected, and air dried before being used by another infant. Diaper tables are cleaned after each infant has been changed.

- Policies and procedures to ensure a sanitary facility have not been clearly thought through and are not written down. Consequently, adults forget handwashing or other essential steps in diapering, cleaning cribs and play areas, handling food, and cleaning of food-preparation areas.

- Diapering and food-preparation areas are not separate. Caregivers are not consistent in maintaining sanitary conditions and procedures.

- Disinfectants are left out, not stored in any special place. They are difficult for adults to find quickly to clean up spills, diaper areas, or bodily fluids.

Appropriate Practices	**Inappropriate Practices**
• Health records on infants' well-baby checkups, immunizations and particular health problems (e.g., allergies) are filed separately and confidentially for every infant. There are clear policies alerting parents to when infants must be excluded from child care for health reasons.	• Health records are incomplete or outdated. There are no policies informing parents as to when infants must be excluded from child care for health reasons.
• Adults are aware of the symptoms of common illnesses, environmental hazards such as lead poisoning, and food or other allergies. They watch for unusual behavior.	• Staff ignore or fail to notice changes in children's normal behavior or do not know children well enough to detect unusual behavior.
• Families bring in a signed permission form to administer nonprescription or prescription medication, including a physician's written instruction for giving the medicine to a particular child.	• Formal records of medications are not required of parents. Caregivers are likely to make mistakes, giving medicines to the wrong infant or incorrectly because there is no visual reminder of the needs of each child.
• Each infant has a labeled daily record book or clipboard available for caregivers and parents to check and use. Caregivers record the time, date, and amount of medication administered. Caregivers and family members can also record vital information (bowel movements, feedings, arrival/departure times, and notes about the infant's activities and moods).	• Caregivers and families have no regular, effective mechanism for sharing information. Caregivers leave notes on the refrigerator or in the infant's diaper bag where parents may miss them. Caregivers may fail to communicate vital information to families.
• Extra clothes for both indoors and outdoors that fit the baby are available. Caregivers dress infants so they are comfortable, given the temperature, and can move freely.	• Caregivers allow infants to remain in soiled clothing or in clothing that either is too tight or not appropriate for the temperature.
• Caregivers directly supervise infants by sight and hearing at all times.	• Infants are left unattended, for example, at naptime.
• Adults do safety checks of all areas inside and out several times a day (e.g., electric outlets are covered; there are no objects on the floor that an infant could choke on; no splinters, cracks, or exposed nails exist on furnishings and equipment; no pools of water go unprotected).	• Adults do not have a system for doing regular safety checks either indoors or outside, so they may leave electric plugs uncovered or disinfectants in reach of children. Paper clips, pins, or pieces of food are left on the floor where babies can pick up and swallow them.
• Emergency evacuation plans are posted on the wall near the infants' daily record charts; a bag of emergency supplies and child-emergency forms are immediately accessible. Evacuation drills are practiced on a regular basis.	• Caregivers must run around to get what they need for an emergency evacuation. They have no practice in carrying infants, records, and supplies at the same time.

Appropriate Practices	**Inappropriate Practices**

Reciprocal relationships with families

• Caregivers work in partnership with parents, communicating daily to build mutual understanding and trust and to ensure the welfare and optimal development of the infant. Caregivers listen carefully to what parents say about their children, seek to understand parents' goals and preferences, and are respectful of cultural and family differences.	• Caregivers communicate with parents only about problems or conflicts, ignore parents' concerns, or avoid difficult issues rather than resolving them with parents.
• Caregivers help parents feel good about their children and their own parenting by sharing with them some of the positive and interesting things that happened with their children during the day. Parents are viewed as the child's primary source of affection and care. Caregivers should always make parents feel welcome in the child care setting; caregivers warmly receive and support nursing mothers who are able to come in for breastfeeding.	• Caregivers communicate a competitive or patronizing attitude to parents or they make parents feel in the way. Parents view caregivers as the only experts and feel isolated from their child's experience.
• Caregivers and parents confer in making decisions about how best to support children's development or to handle problems or differences of opinion as they arise.	• Caregivers ignore parents' concerns or they capitulate to parent demands or preferences, even when these are at odds with good practice.

Policies

Staff qualifications and development

• Staff enjoy working with infants and are warmly responsive to their communications and needs. Staff have had training specifically related to infant development and caregiving. They know what skills and behaviors emerge during the first few months and support children as they become increasingly competent and knowledgeable. Staff are competent in first aid.	• Staff view work with infants as a chore and as custodial in nature. Staff have little or no training specific to infant development. They have unrealistic expectations for this age group, and/or they project their own perceptions onto the needs of the child. They are unaware of what to look for that might signal problems in development.

Staffing patterns

• The group size and ratio of adults to infants is limited to allow for one-to-one interaction, intimate knowledge of individual babies, and consistent caregiving. Babies need to relate to the same, very few people day after day. A ratio of one adult to no more than three infants is best.	• Group size and staff-child ratio are too large to permit individual attention and constant supervision. Staffing patterns require infants to relate to more than two adults during the caregiving day.
• The staffing pattern is designed to ensure continuity over time for each infant's relationship with a primary caregiver. Priority is given to keeping each infant in the same group for many months (and from year to year if possible) to enable the child and a primary caregiver to form and maintain a reciprocal relationship.	• The staffing pattern shifts caregivers around from infant to infant or group to group, not supporting the formation and maintenance of the infant-caregiver relationship.
	• High staff turnover, due to inadequate compensation and/or working conditions, results in low continuity and frequent disruption of infants' budding attachments to caregivers.

Examples of Appropriate and Inappropriate Practices for Toddlers

Appropriate Practices	Inappropriate Practices

Relationships among caregivers and children

• There is sufficient continuity of care to ensure that every toddler (and family) is able to form a relationship with a primary caregiver. As the caregiver comes to know a few toddlers very well, she is able to respond to the temperament, needs, and cues of each child and to develop a mutually satisfying pattern of communication with each child and family.	• The development and maintenance of one-to-one relationships are not given top priority. Toddlers are shifted from group to group or cared for by whatever caregiver is available at the moment and thus are unable to form a relationship with one or two caregivers over time.
• Adults warmly greet toddlers and their parents by name when they arrive. The day begins with a great deal of adult-child interaction. Caregivers help toddlers settle into the group by reading books or quietly playing with them.	• Children are received hurriedly and given no individual attention. Toddlers are expected to begin the day with free play and little adult interaction.
	• There is no predictable routine to the daily transition.
• An adult initiating a conversation with a toddler gives the child ample time to respond. Caregivers also listen attentively for children's verbal initiations and respond to these. Adults label or name objects, describe events, and reflect feelings to help children learn new words. Caregivers simplify their language for toddlers who are just beginning to talk, saying, "Let's wash our hands. Snacktime!" instead of "It's time to wash our hands and have a snack." Then as children acquire their own words, caregivers expand on the toddler's language (Child: "Mary sock." Adult: "Oh, that's Mary's missing sock, and you found it").	• Adults talk *at* toddlers and do not wait for a response. Adult voices dominate or caregivers do not speak to children because they think they are too young to respond. Caregivers either talk "baby talk" or use language that is too complex for toddlers to understand.
• Caregivers ask parents what sounds and words their toddler uses so that the caregiver will understand what the child is saying when she uses beginning speech or a home language that is not understood by the caregivers.	• Caregivers do not talk with the parents about the toddler's speech patterns or home language and they cannot understand what the toddler is trying to say, which causes the child to be frustrated in her efforts to communicate.

Appropriate Practices	**Inappropriate Practices**

Relationships among caregivers and children (cont'd)

• Adults have appropriate expectations for toddlers and are supportive of toddlers as they acquire skills. Caregivers watch to see what the child is trying to do and provide the necessary support to help the child accomplish the task, allowing children to do what they are capable of doing and assisting with tasks that are frustrating.	• Adults expect too much or too little of toddlers. Caregivers are impatient with toddlers who are learning new skills. Because it is faster, adults do tasks for toddlers that they can do themselves.
	• Adults allow children to become frustrated by tasks they cannot do.
• Children are acknowledged for their accomplishments and helped to feel increasingly competent and in control of themselves.	• Adults criticize toddlers for what they cannot do or for their clumsy struggle to master a skill.
	• Adults foster overdependency; children are overprotected and made to feel inadequate.
• Adults respond quickly to toddlers' cries or other signs of distress, recognizing that toddlers have limited language with which to communicate their needs.	• Crying is ignored or responded to irregularly or at the caregiver's convenience.
• Adults comfort toddlers and let them know they are appreciated through warm responsive touches, such as giving pats on the back or hugs and holding toddlers in their laps. Caregivers are sensitive to ensuring that their touches are welcomed by the children.	• Adults follow "no-touch policies" and do not recognize the importance of touch to children's healthy development.
• Adults respect children's developing preferences for familiar objects, foods, and people. Adults permit children to keep their own favorite objects and provide limited options from which children may choose what they prefer to eat or wear. Children's preferences are seen as a healthy indication of a developing self-concept.	• Adults prohibit favored objects like blankets or toys or arbitrarily take them away or expect toddlers to share them with other children. Children are not given choices, and preferences are not encouraged. Children are all expected to do the same thing.
• Adults respect toddlers' desires to carry favored objects around with them, to move the objects from one place to another, and to roam around or sit and parallel play with toys and objects.	• Adults restrict objects to certain locations and do not tolerate children's hoarding, collecting, or carrying objects about.

Appropriate Practices	**Inappropriate Practices**
• Adults give simple, brief, accurate responses to children's staring at or questions about a child with a disability.	• Adults disregard children's curiosity about a child's disability or adaptive equipment.
	• Adults criticize a child for noticing or asking questions about physical differences.
• Adults model the type of interactions with others that they want children to develop. Caregivers help toddlers resolve their differences by using words to express what is happening and what the toddler is feeling ("You want to play with the car? Carol is playing with the car. Let's see if we can find another car on the shelf").	• Adults show aggression, shout, or exhibit a lack of coping behaviors under stress. Adult attempts to punish or control the aggressive toddler escalate the hostility.
	• Adults do not anticipate actions of toddlers to prevent children from getting hurt or hurting others nor do they model for toddlers the words to say.
• Adults patiently redirect toddlers to help guide them toward controlling their own impulses and behavior. When children fight over the same toy, the adult provides another like it or removes the toy. If neither of these strategies is effective, the caregiver may gently redirect the children's attention by initiating play in another area. Caregivers give clear sanctions for overtly dangerous behavior.	• Adults ignore disputes and other problematic behaviors, leading to a chaotic atmosphere.
	• Adults punish infractions harshly, frightening and humiliating children.
• Adults recognize that constantly testing limits and expressing opposition ("No!") to adults is part of a child developing a healthy sense of self as a separate, autonomous individual. Caregivers try to limit their saying "No!" to situations that relate to children's safety or emotional well-being. Adults give positively worded directions ("Bang on the floor"), not just restrictions ("Don't bang on the table").	• Adults are constantly saying "No!" to toddlers or becoming involved in power struggles over issues that do not relate to the child's health or well-being. Caregivers punish children for asserting themselves or saying "No."
	• Adults do not acknowledge children, the behavior escalates, and children begin to feel that they cannot affect their environment.

<u>**Appropriate Practices**</u>   <u>**Inappropriate Practices**</u>

Living and learning with toddlers

- Time schedules are flexible and smooth, dictated more by children's needs than by adults'. There is a relatively predictable sequence to the day to help children feel secure.

- Adults adapt schedules and activities to meet individual children's needs within the group setting. Recognizing toddlers' need to repeat tasks until they master the steps and skills involved, caregivers allow toddlers to go at their own pace. They have time to assist a child with special needs because the group of toddlers knows what is expected and is engaged.

- Adults create an "inclusive" classroom, making sure that spatial organization, materials, and activities enable all children to participate actively; for example, a child with a physical disability eats at the table with other children.

- Adults engage in reciprocal play with toddlers, modeling for children how to play imaginatively, such as playing "tea party." Caregivers also support toddlers' play so that children stay interested in an object or activity for longer periods of time and their play becomes more complex, moving from simple awareness and exploration of objects to more complicated playlike pretending.

- Adults respect toddlers' solitary and parallel play. Caregivers provide several of the same popular toys for children to play with alone or near another child. Caregivers realize that having three or four of the same sought-after toy is better than having one each of many different toys.

- Adults frequently read to toddlers, to one individually on a caregiver's lap or to groups of two or three. Caregivers sing with toddlers, do fingerplays, act out simple stories or folktales with children participating actively, or tell stories using a flannel board or magnetic board and allow children to manipulate and place figures on the boards.

- Activities are dictated by rigid adherence to time schedules, or the lack of a time schedule makes the day unpredictable.

- Adults lose patience with toddlers' desires for repetition. Toddlers must either do things in groups according to the caregivers' plan or follow adult demands that they spend a certain amount of time at an activity. Caregivers have little time for a child with special needs.

- Caregivers do not include children with special needs in all activities; for example, a child who requires adaptive equipment or special procedures eats or plays apart from other children.

- Adults do not play with toddlers because they feel self-conscious or awkward. Caregivers do not understand the importance of supporting children's play, and they control or intrude in the play.

- Adults do not understand the value of solitary and parallel play and try to force children to play together. Adults arbitrarily expect children to share. Popular toys are not provided in duplicate and are fought over constantly, while other toys are seldom used.

- Adults impose "grouptime" on toddlers, forcing a large group to listen or watch an activity without providing opportunity for children to participate.

Appropriate Practices

- Toddlers are given appropriate art materials, such as large crayons, watercolor markers, and large paper. Adults expect toddlers to explore and manipulate art materials and *do not* expect them to produce a finished art product. They use nontoxic materials but avoid using food for art because toddlers are developing self-regulatory skills and must learn to distinguish between food and other objects that are not to be eaten.

- Children have daily opportunities for exploratory activity, such as water and sand play, painting, and clay or playdough manipulation.

- Adults recognize that routine tasks of living, such as eating, toileting, and dressing, are important opportunities to help children learn about their world, acquire skills, and regulate their own behavior. Meals and snacks include finger food or utensils that are easier for toddlers to use, such as bowls, spoons, and graduated versions of drinking containers from bottles to cups. Children's attempts to dress themselves and put on shoes are supported and positively encouraged.

- Adults respect children's schedules with regard to eating and sleeping. Toddlers are provided snacks more frequently and in smaller portions than older children. For example, two morning snacks are offered at earlier hours than the usual snacktime for preschoolers. Liquids are provided frequently. Children's food preferences are respected.

- Adults work cooperatively with families in encouraging children to learn to use the toilet. When toddlers reach an age when they feel confident and unafraid to sit on a toilet seat, caregivers invite them to use the toilet, help them as needed, provide manageable clothing, and positively reinforce them. The toilet, with a step stool, is in a well-lit, inviting, relatively private space. Children are taken to the toilet frequently and regularly in response to their own biological needs.

Inappropriate Practices

- Toddlers are "helped" by teachers to produce a product, follow the adult-made model, or color a coloring book or ditto sheet. Because toddlers are likely to put things in their mouths, adults give them edible, often tasty, fingerpaints or playdough.

- Adults do not offer water and sand play, paints, or playdough because they are messy and require supervision. Children's natural enjoyment of water play is frustrated, so children play at sinks whenever they can.

- Adults foster children's dependence by doing for them routine tasks that they could do for themselves. Children feel incompetent because the eating utensils are too difficult for them to manage or because clothes require adult assistance with tiny buttons or laces.

- Children are expected to do things for themselves but are punished for spills or accidents.

- Schedules are rigid and based on adults' rather than children's needs. Food is used for rewards or is withheld as punishment. Children are allowed to become fussy and cranky, waiting for food that is served on a rigid schedule.

- Adults do not discuss toilet learning with families but impose it on children to meet the caregivers' needs, whether children are ready or not. Children are made to sit on the toilet for undue lengths of time. Children are punished or shamed for toileting accidents.

Appropriate Practices	**Inappropriate Practices**

Living and learning with toddlers (cont'd)

• Healthy, accepting attitudes about children's bodies and their functions are expressed.	• Children are made to feel ashamed of their bodies and to think bodily functions are disgusting.
• Caregivers plan a transition into naptime with a predictable sequence of events. They choose a quiet activity, such as reading a story. Toddlers get their own stuffed toys or blankets and go to their cots; soft music or a story tape may be played for toddlers who are still awake.	• There is no transition, and naptime starts when the adult turns off the light. Caregivers expect children to be quiet immediately. • Naptime is chaotic as toddlers wander about the room. Some toddlers sleep; others are disruptive.

Environment

• Walls are painted with lead-free, easy-to-clean paint. Carpeting and flooring materials are selected to provide a soft background so that toddler's eyes are drawn to the materials and activity choices.	• Walls are cluttered or are sterile and bland.
• Floor coverings are appropriate for the activities that occur there—shock-absorbent tiles for open areas where toddlers push and pull toys around and for art, eating, and water and sand play areas. Low-pile, easy-to-clean carpeting or nonslip area rugs cover areas for quiet play.	• Floors are covered with a thick-pile carpet that requires constant cleaning or is left dirty, or the floor covering is hard and cold.
• Toddlers' artwork and other creative projects are hung at a level just above the toddlers' reach but low enough for them to look at. Caregivers display pictures of children and their families.	• Toddlers' art is not displayed or is hung too high for the toddlers to see. There are no family pictures displayed nor any indication of family involvement.
• The environment and schedule have enough predictability and repetition to allow toddlers to form expectations, repeatedly practice emerging skills, and feel the security of a familiar routine.	• Adults do not follow a consistent routine. They lose patience with doing the same things repeatedly and get bored by toddlers' needs to repeat tasks until they master them and to feel secure in a predictable environment.
• Caregivers organize the space into interest or activity areas, including areas for concentrated small-group play, being alone, art/water/sand and other messy activities, dramatic play, and construction. The activity areas are separated by low partitions, shelves, or sitting benches, making it difficult for running toddlers to disturb toddlers engaged in concentrated play, and creating clear traffic patterns.	• Space is open with no clear traffic pattern from one interest area to another. Toddlers wander aimlessly, unable to make choices. Fighting and tantrums occur as running toddlers bump into those who are engaged in concentrated play.

Appropriate Practices

- The environment contains private spaces with room for no more than two children and that are easily supervised by adults.

- A child-size sink with a good supply of paper towels is located near areas designated for messy activities, so toddlers learn that cleaning up and washing their hands follow any messy activity. Smocks are on low hooks so that toddlers can get them themselves. Cups, paint cans, and other containers are small so that toddlers can easily manage them and cleanup is easy. Toddlers can do most activities without assistance.

- Sturdy picture books are provided. People of different ages, racial and cultural groups, family types, occupations, and abilities/disabilities are depicted.

- Children have many opportunities for active, large-muscle play both indoors and outdoors. The environment includes low, soft climbing platform(s), a tunnel for crawling through, and ramps and steps that are the correct size for children to practice newly acquired skills. Toddlers' outdoor play space is separate from that of older children. Outdoor play equipment for toddlers includes small climbing equipment that they can go around and in and out of and solitary play equipment requiring supervision, such as swings and low slides.

- Walks around the neighborhood or to a park and special trips are planned so that toddlers see many outdoor environments.

- The diapering/toileting, sleeping, and eating areas are separate, both for sanitation and to ensure quiet, restful areas.

- The toddler naptime area can be in the play area as long as cots are well separated from each other. The adult plans where each toddler's cot will go according to the toddler's ease or difficulty in resting, distractibility, need for quiet, or length of normal nap.

Inappropriate Practices

- The environment provides no private spaces, or spaces are out of view of adults.

- Adults restrict messy activities and do not allow toddlers to explore the texture and feel of the paints, water, or sand. Toddlers must start and end at the same time so that caregivers can get them ready and clean them up as a group.

- Books are not available because they get torn or soiled, or books do not contain objects familiar or interesting to children.

- Toddlers' indoor space is cramped and unsafe for children who are just learning how to move their bodies and need to run more than walk. Toddlers share outdoor space and equipment designed for older children, unsafe for younger ones. Caregivers spend time attempting to control toddlers' movements.

- Toddlers rarely go outside because it takes so much time for adults to get organized. Caregivers consider toddlers too young to appreciate "field trips."

- Areas are combined and thus very noisy, distracting, and unhealthy.

- Caregivers place cots too close together. No thought is given to planning for the individual toddler's sleeping needs.

Appropriate Practices	**Inappropriate Practices**

Environment (cont'd)

• Each toddler has a cot and bedding that are personally labeled. Getting her own blanket or special stuffed toy is a part of the child's nap routine.	• Cots and sheets are used by all children, with no personal items for their cots. Special items from home are discouraged because "children might lose them" or "they will fight over them."

Health and safety

• To limit the spread of infectious disease, adults follow health and safety procedures, including proper handwashing methods and universal precautions. There are clearly written sanitation procedures specific to each area. Instructions on the proper diapering and handwashing sequence (including use of protective gloves), cleaning cribs and play areas, and food storage/preparation (including dish-washing) are displayed on the walls as visual reminders to adults.	• Policies and procedures to ensure a sanitary environment have not been clearly thought through and are not written and displayed. Consequently, adults forget handwashing or other essential steps in diapering, cleaning cribs and play areas, handling food, and cleaning of food preparation areas.
• Adults daily prepare a solution of ¼ cup of liquid bleach to 1 gallon of water (or 1 tablespoon to 1 quart of water in a spray bottle) and store it in a place out of the reach of children. Diaper-changing areas are routinely disinfected after each change.	• A disinfectant solution is not prepared daily, and diaper-changing areas are not disinfected after each change. • Disinfectants are left out—not stored in any special place; they are difficult for adults to find quickly when cleanup is needed for spills, diaper areas, or bodily fluids.
• Toys that are mouthed are removed when a child has finished playing with them so that they can be cleaned and disinfected before use by another child.	• Toys are scattered on the floor and cleaned occasionally, not at all, or improperly.
• Health records, including immunizations and particular health problems (e.g., allergies) are filed separately and confidentially for every toddler.	• Health records are incomplete or outdated. Daily records are not kept or are incomplete.
• Adults are aware of the symptoms of common illnesses and alert to changes in children's behavior that may signal illness or allergies. Caregivers conduct daily health checks, recording any signs of illness on each toddler's daily record form.	• Adults ignore or do not notice changes in children's behavior, or they do not know children well enough to detect any change in normal patterns of behavior.

Appropriate Practices	**Inappropriate Practices**
• Families bring in a signed permission form to administer nonprescription or prescription medication, including a physician's written instruction for giving the medicine to that particular child.	• Formal records of medications are not required of parents. Caregivers are likely to make mistakes, giving medicines incorrectly or to the wrong infant because there is no visual reminder of the needs of each child.
• A labeled daily record book or clipboard for each child is available for caregivers and parents to check and use. Caregivers record the time, date, and amount of medication administered. Caregivers and family members can also record vital information (bowel movements, feedings, arrival/departure times, and notes about the child's activities and moods).	• Caregivers and families have no regular, effective mechanism for sharing information. Adults leave notes on the refrigerator or in the infant's diaper bag where parents may miss them. Caregivers may fail to communicate vital information to families.
• Extra clothes for both indoors and outdoors are available. Caregivers dress toddlers so they are comfortable, given the temperature, and can move freely.	• Adults allow toddlers to remain in soiled clothing or dress them in clothing that is either too tight or not appropriate for the temperature.
• Caregivers directly supervise toddlers by sight and sound, even when they are sleeping.	• Children are left unattended. Caregivers leave the area when children are playing quietly or sleeping.
• Adults do safety checks of all areas, both indoors and outside, several times a day to ensure that they are safe (e.g., that electric outlets are covered, no objects are on the floor that a toddler could choke on, no splinters or nails are exposed on furnishings and equipment).	• Adults do not have a system for doing regular safety checks both indoors and outside. Children are frequently told "No!" to hazards that should should have been removed.
• Emergency evacuation plans are posted on the wall near the daily record charts. A bag of emergency supplies and child emergency forms are immediately accessible. Evacuation drills are practiced on a regular basis.	• Adults must run around to get what they need for an emergency evacuation. They have no practice in assisting toddlers and carrying their records and supplies.

Reciprocal relationships with families

• Teachers work in partnership with parents, communicating daily to build mutual understanding and trust and to ensure the welfare and optimal development of the toddler. Caregivers listen carefully to what parents say about their children, seek to understand parents' goals and preferences, and are respectful of cultural and family differences.	• Teachers communicate with parents only about problems or conflicts, or they avoid difficult issues rather than resolving them with parents.

Appropriate Practices	**Inappropriate Practices**

Reciprocal relationships with families (cont'd)

• Teachers help parents feel good about their children and their parenting by sharing with them some of the positive and interesting things that happened with their children during the day. Caregivers communicate that they view parents as the child's primary source of affection and care. Parents always are made to feel welcome in the child care setting.	• Caregivers communicate a competitive or patronizing attitude to parents or they make parents feel in the way. Parents view staff as experts and feel isolated from their child's experience.
• Caregivers and parents confer in making decisions about how best to support children's development or handle problems or differences of opinion as they arise.	• Caregivers ignore parents' concerns or they capitulate to parent demands or preferences, even when these are at odds with good practice.

Policies

Staff qualifications and development	• Staff have training in child development/ early education specific to the toddler age group. Caregivers are competent in first aid. Caregivers enjoy working with toddlers, are warmly responsive to their needs, and demonstrate considerable patience in supporting children as they become increasingly competent and independent.	• Staff have no training in child development/early education, or their training and experience are limited to working with older children. They view work with toddlers as a chore and as custodial in nature. Caregivers push children to achieve and are impatient with their struggles, or they expect too little of toddlers. They are unaware of what to look for that might signal problems in development.
Staffing patterns	• The group size and the ratio of adults to children are limited to allow for the intimate, interpersonal atmosphere and high level of supervision that toddlers require. Maximum group size is 12, with one adult for no more than six toddlers, preferably fewer. Staffing patterns limit the number of adults toddlers relate to each day.	• Both group size and staff-child ratio are too large to permit children's individual attention and constant supervision. Staffing patterns require toddlers to relate to several adults during the caregiving day.
	• The staffing pattern is designed to ensure continuity over time for each toddler's relationship with a primary caregiver. Priority is given to keeping each toddler in the same group for many months (and from year to year if possible) to enable the child and a primary caregiver to form and maintain a reciprocal relationship.	• Shifting caregivers around from toddler to toddler or group to group, as a staffing pattern, does not support the formation and maintenance of the toddler-caregiver relationship.
		• High staff turnover, due to inadequate compensation and/or working conditions, results in low continuity and frequent disruption of toddlers' budding, satisfying attachments to caregivers.

Handwashing procedure

Adults

- Wash hands upon arrival.
- Wash hands before preparing food, eating, or feeding a child.
- Wash hands after
- toileting self or a child and
- handling body secretions (e.g., changing diapers, cleaning up a child who has vomited or spit up, wiping a child's nose, handling soiled clothing or other contaminated items).
- Post signs to remind staff and children to wash their hands in the toilet room, the kitchen, and the area where diapers are changed.
- Be sure that the hot water supplied to fixtures accessible to children does not exceed a maximum temperature of 120° F.

How to wash hands

- Check to be sure a paper towel is available. Turn on water to a comfortable temperature.
- Moisten hands with water and apply heavy lather of *liquid* soap.
- Wash well under running water for at least 10 seconds.

- Pay particular attention to areas between fingers, around nail beds, under fingernails, and to backs of hands.
- Rinse well under running water until free of soap and dirt. Hold hands so that water flows from wrists to fingertips.
- Dry hands with paper towel.
- Use paper towel to turn off faucet; then discard towel.
- Use hand lotion, if desired.

Infants/toddlers

Use soap and water at a sink if you can. If a baby is too heavy to hold for handwashing at the sink, use disposable wipes or follow this procedure:

- Wipe the child's hands with a damp paper towel moistened with a drop of liquid soap.
- Wipe the child's hands with a paper towel wet with clear water.
- Dry the child's hands with a paper towel.

*　　*　　*

When children are able to wash hands on their own, teach them to use these procedures and supervise them until they are consistent in doing so.

Adapted from *Healthy Young Children: A Manual for Programs,* 1995 ed., NAEYC.

References and resources

Infant and toddler development

Bornstein, M.H., & H.G. Bornstein. 1995. Caregivers' responsiveness and cognitive development in infants and toddlers: Theory and research. In *Infant/toddler caregiving: A guide to cognitive development and learning*, ed. P.L. Mangione, 12–21. Sacramento: California State Department of Education.

Brazelton, T.B. 1976. *Toddlers and parents: A declaration of independence.* New York: Dell.

Brazelton, T.B. 1983. *Infants and mothers: Differences in development.* New York: Delacorte.

Brazelton, T.B. 1983. *Working and caring.* Reading, MA: Addison-Wesley.

Brazelton, T.B. 1992. *Touchpoints: Your child's emotional and behavioral development.* Reading, MA: Addison-Wesley.

Bruner, J. 1985. *Child's talk: Learning to use language.* New York: Norton.

Erikson, E. 1950. *Childhood and society.* New York: Norton.

Featherstone, H. 1980. *A difference in the family: Life with a disabled child.* New York: Basic.

Fraiberg, S. 1959. *The magic years.* New York: Scribner's.

Galinsky, E. 1987. *The six stages of parenthood.* Reading, MA: Addison-Wesley/Lawrence.

Genishi, C. 1986. Acquiring oral language and communicative competence. In *Early childhood curriculum: A review of current research*, ed. C. Seefeldt, 75–106. New York: Teachers College Press.

Greenspan, S., & N.T. Greenspan. 1985. *First feelings: Milestones in the emotional development of your baby and child.* New York: Viking.

Greenspan, S.I. 1990. Emotional development in infants and toddlers. In *Infant/toddler caregiving: A guide to social-emotional growth and socialization*, ed. J.R. Lally, 15–18. Sacramento: California State Department of Education.

Howes, C., D.A. Phillips, & M. Whitebook. 1992. Threshold of quality: Implications for the social development of children in center-based child care. *Child Development* 63: 449–60.

Howes, C., C. Rodning, D. Galluzzo, & L. Myers. 1988. Attachment and child care. *Early Childhood Research Quarterly* 3: 401–16.

Kopp, C. 1994. *Baby steps: The "whys" of your child's behavior in the first two years.* New York: W.H. Freeman.

Lally, J.R. 1994. *Infant/toddler caregiving: A guide to culturally sensitive care.* Sacramento: California State Department of Education.

Larner, M. 1994. *In the neighborhood: Programs that strengthen family day care for low-income families.* New York: National Center for Children in Poverty.

Leach, P. 1976. *Babyhood.* New York: Knopf.

Lieberman, A. 1994. *The emotional life of the toddler.* New York: Free Press.

Mahler, M., F. Pine, & A. Bergman. 1975. *The psychological birth of the human infant.* New York: Basic.

Musick, J. 1986. *Infant development: From theory to practice.* Belmont, CA: Wadsworth.

Rosenblith, J.F. 1992. *In the beginning: Development from conception to age two.* 2d ed. Newbury Park, CA: Sage.

Schaffer, H.R. 1984. *The child's entry into a social world.* Orlando, FL: Academic.

Segal, M. 1974. *From birth to one year.* Fort Lauderdale, FL: Nova University.

Segal, M., & D. Adcock. 1976. *From one to two years.* Fort Lauderdale, FL: Nova University.

Shatz, M. 1994. *A toddler's life: From personal narrative to professional insight.* New York: Oxford University Press.

Weissbourd, B., & J. Musick, eds. 1981. *Infants: Their social environments.* Washington, DC: NAEYC.

White, B. 1975. *The first three years of life.* Englewood Cliffs, NJ: Prentice-Hall.

Winnicott, D.W. 1987. *Babies and their mothers.* Reading, MA: Addison-Wesley.

Winnicott, D.W. 1987. *The child, the family and the outside world.* Reading, MA: Addison-Wesley/Lawrence.

Zigler, E., & M. Finn-Stevenson. 1987. *Children: Development and social issues.* Lexington, MA: DC Heath & Co.

Components of quality infant/toddler child care

Anderson, P.O., & E.S. Fenichel. 1989. *Serving culturally diverse families of infants and toddlers with disabilities.* Arlington, VA: Zero to Three.

Aronson, S. 1985–96. Ask Dr. Sue (regular column). *Child Care Information Exchange.*

Aronson, S. 1989. Child care and the pediatrician. *Pediatrics in Review* 10 (9): 277–86.

Bailey, D.B., & M. Wolery. 1992. *Teaching infants and preschoolers with disabilities,* 2d ed. Columbus, OH: Merrill.

Barclay, K., C. Benelli, & A. Curtis. 1995. Literacy begins at birth: What caregivers can learn from parents of children who read early. *Young Children* 50 (4): 24–28.

Boutte, G., D. Keepler, V. Tyler, & B. Terry. 1992. Effective techniques for involving "difficult" parents. *Young Children* 47 (3): 18–22.

Bredekamp, S., ed. 1987. *Developmentally appropriate practice in early childhood programs serving children from birth through age 8.* Exp. ed. Washington, DC: NAEYC.

Children's Foundation. 1988. *Better baby care: A training course for family day care providers.* (Designed to accompany *Better baby care: A book for family day care providers.*) Washington, DC: Author.

Children's Foundation. 1990. *Helping children love themselves and others: A professional handbook for family day care.* Washington, DC: Author.

Cryer, D., & T. Harms. 1987. *Active learning for ones.* Reading, MA: Addison-Wesley.

Cryer, D., & T. Harms. 1988. *Active learning for twos.* Reading, MA: Addison-Wesley.

Cummins, D.B. 1967. *Lullabies of the world.* New York: Random House.

De la Brisse, B. 1987. *Children with special needs in family day care homes: A handbook for family day care home providers: Activity and resource book.* (Spanish and English). Washington, DC: El Centro de Rosemount.

Derman-Sparks, L. 1995. Creating an inclusive, nonstereotypical environment for infants and toddlers. In *Infant/toddler caregiving: A guide to culturally sensitive care,* ed. P.L. Mangione, 64–68. Sacramento: California State Department of Education.

Derman-Sparks, L. 1995. Developing culturally responsive caregiving practices: Acknowledge, ask, and adapt. In *Infant/toddler caregiving: A guide to culturally sensitive care,* ed. P.L. Mangione, 40–62. Sacramento: California State Department of Education.

Dittmann, L.L., ed. 1984. *The infants we care for.* Washington, DC: NAEYC.

Fein, G., & M. Rivkin, eds. 1986. *The young child at play: Reviews of research,* vol 4. Washington, DC: NAEYC.

Fredericks, B., R. Hardman, G. Morgan, & F. Rodgers. 1985. *A little under the weather: A look at care for mildly ill children.* Boston: Work/Family Directions.

Garcia, E.E. 1992. Caring for infants in a bilingual child care setting. In *Infant/toddler caregiving: A guide to culturally sensitive care,* eds. P.L. Mangione and C.L. Young-Holt. Sacramento: California State Department of Education.

Gerber, M. 1982. What is appropriate curriculum for infants and toddlers? In *Infants: Their social environments,* eds. B. Weissbourd & J. Musick, 77–85. Washington, DC: NAEYC.

Godwin, A., & L. Schrag, eds. 1996. *Setting up for infant/toddler care: Guidelines for centers and family child care homes.* Rev. ed. Washington, DC: NAEYC.

Gonzalez-Mena, J. 1992. Taking a culturally sensitive approach in infant-toddler programs. *Young Children* 47 (2): 4–9.

Gonzales-Mena, J. 1995. Cultural sensitivity in routine caregiving tasks. In *Infant/toddler caregiving: A guide to culturally sensitive care,* ed. P.L. Mangione, 12–19. Sacramento: California State Department of Education.

Gonzalez-Mena, J., & D.W. Eyer. 1989. *Infants, toddlers, and caregivers.* Mountain View, CA: Mayfield.

Greenberg, P. 1991. *Character development: Encouraging self-esteem & self-discipline in infants, toddlers, and two-year-olds.* Washington, DC: NAEYC.

Greenman, J. 1988. Changing spaces, making places. *Child Care Information Exchange* 62: 3–7.

Greenman, J. 1992. Places for childhoods: How institutional are you? *Child Care Information Exchange* 87: 49–52.

Griffin, A. 1993. Caring for mildly ill infants and toddlers in the context of child care: Emotional, medical, and practical perspectives. *Zero to Three* 13 (4): 15–18, 23.

Griffin, A. 1993. *Preventing preventable harm to babies: Promoting health and safety in child care.* Arlington, VA: Zero to Three.

Guilmartin, K. 1992. *Music and your child: A guide for parents and caregivers.* Audiocassette with songbook and guide. Princeton, NJ: Music and Movement Center.

Harmes, T. 1994. Humanizing infant environments. *Children's Environments* 11 (2): 155–65.

Heideman, S. 1989. *Caring for at-risk infants and toddlers in a family child care setting.* Minneapolis: University of Minnesota Press.

Honig, A.S. 1985. High quality infant/toddler care: Issues and dilemmas. *Young Children* 41(1): 40–46.

Honig, A.S., & D.S. Wittmer. 1990. Socialization guidance and discipline with infants and toddlers. In *Infant/toddler caregiving: A guide to social-emotional growth and socialization*, ed. J.R. Lally, 64–78. Sacramento: California State Department of Education.

Jenkins, E. 1966. *The Ella Jenkins song book for children.* Chicago: Adventures in Rhythm.

Johnston, K., E.M. Bemporad, & E. Tuters. 1990. Attending to the emotional well-being of children, families and caregivers: Contributions of infant mental health specialists to children. *Zero to Three* 10 (3): 7–10.

Kendrick, A.S., R. Kaufmann, & K.P. Messenger, eds. 1995. *Healthy young children: A manual for programs.* Washington, DC: NAEYC.

Koralek, D.G., L.J. Colker, & D.T. Dodge. 1995. *The what, why, and how of high-quality early childhood education: A guide for on-site supervision.* Rev. ed. Washington, DC: NAEYC.

Knitzer, J. 1995. Meeting the mental health needs of young children and families: Service needs, challenges and opportunities. In *Systems of care for children and adolescents with serious emotional disturbances: From theory to reality*, ed. B. Stroud. Baltimore: Paul H. Brookes.

Lally, J.R. 1995. The impact of child care practices and policies on infant/toddler identity formation. *Young Children* 51 (1): 58–67.

Lally, J.R., S. Volkert, C. Young-Holt, & E. Szanton. 1988. *Visions for infant-toddler care: Guidelines for professional caregiving.* Sacramento: California State Department of Education.

Lane, M.B., & S. Signer. 1990. *Infant/toddler caregiving: A guide to creating partnerships with parents.* Sacramento: California State Department of Education.

Lansky, V. 1974. *Feed me! I'm yours.* Deephaven, MN: Meadowbrook.

Leavitt, R.L., & B.K. Eheart. 1985. *Toddler daycare: A guide to responsive caregiving.* Lexington, MA: DC Heath & Co.

Mallory, B.L., & R.S. New. 1994. *Diversity and developmentally appropriate practices: Challenges for early childhood education.* New York: Teachers College Press.

McDonald, D.T. 1979. *Music in our lives: The early years.* Washington, DC: NAEYC.

McLane, J.B., & G.D. McNamee. 1991. The beginnings of literacy. *Zero to Three* 12 (1): 1–8.

Miller, C.S. 1984. Building self-control: Discipline for young children. *Young Children* 40 (1): 15–19.

Miller, K. 1988. *More things to do with toddlers and twos.* Mt. Ranier, MD: Gryphon House.

Money, R. 1995. Enhancing relationships with babies in a group setting. *Educaring* 16 (1 & 2).

Moore, S. 1982. Prosocial behavior in the early years: Parent and peer influences. In *Handbook of research in early childhood education*, ed. B. Spodek. New York: Free Press.

Mussen, P., & N. Eisenberg-Bert. 1977. *Roots of caring, sharing, and helping: The development of prosocial behavior in children.* San Francisco: Freeman.

Olds, A. 1987. Designing settings for infants and toddlers. In *Designing settings for infants and toddlers*, eds. C. Weinstein & T. David. New York: Plenum.

Palmer, H. 1984. *Babysong.* Freeport, NY: Educational Activities.

Palmer, H. 1984. *Tickly toddler.* Freeport, NY: Educational Activities.

Pawl, J. 1990. Infants in day care: Reflections on experiences, expectations and relationships. *Zero to Three* 10 (3): 1–6.

Phillips, C.B. 1995. Culture: A process that empowers. In *Infant/toddler caregiving: A guide to culturally sensitive care*, ed. J.R. Lally, 2–9. Sacramento: California State Department of Education.

Pizzo, P. 1992. Financing family-centered infant child care. Arlington, VA: Zero to Three.

Provence, S., J. Pawl, & E. Fenichel, eds. 1992. *The child care anthology 1984–1992.* Arlington, VA: Zero to Three.

Rogers, D.L., & D.D. Ross. 1986. Encouraging positive social interaction among young children. *Young Children* 41 (3): 12–17.

Ross, H.W. 1992. Integrating infants with disabilities? Can "ordinary" caregivers do it? *Young Children* 47 (3): 65–71.

Rothenberg, B.A., S.L. Harrison, M.L. Harrison, & M. Graham. 1990. *Parentmaking: A practical handbook for teaching parent classes about babies and toddlers.* Menlo Park, CA: Banster.

Segal, M. 1974. *From birth to one year: The Nova University play and learn program.* Fort Lauderdale, FL: Nova University.

Segal, M. 1988. *In time and with love: Caring for the special needs baby.* New York: Newmarket.

Stonehouse, A., ed. 1988. *Trusting toddlers: Programming for one-to-three year olds in child care centers.* Fyshwick ACT, Australia: Canberra.

Surbeck, E., & M. Kelley, eds. 1990. *Personalizing care with infants, toddlers, and families.* Wheaton, MD: Association for Childhood Education International.

Torelli, L., & C. Durrett. 1996. Landscape for learning: The impact of classroom design on infants and toddlers. *Early Childhood News* 8 (2): 12–17.

Wittmer, D. 1995. The importance of relationships in infant/toddler child care: A unique training program and partnership. Denver: University of Colorado. Typescript.

Wittmer, D.S., & A. Honig. 1994. Encouraging positive social development in young children. *Young Children* 49 (5): 4–12.

Zero to Three, National Center for Infants, Toddlers, and Families. 1995. *Caring for infants and toddlers in groups: Developmentally appropriate practice.* Arlington, VA: Author.

Major reports and research on infant/ toddler child care

AAP & APHA (American Academy of Pediatrics and American Public Health Association). 1992. *Caring for our children—National health and safety performance standards: Guidelines for out-of-home-child care programs.* Washington, DC: APHA. Available from AAP, P.O. Box 927, Elk Grove, IL 60009-0927.

Adams, G. 1990. *Who knows how safe? The status of state efforts to ensure quality child care.* Washington, DC: Children's Defense Fund.

Carnegie Task Force on Meeting the Needs of Young Children. 1994. *Starting points: Meeting the needs of our youngest children.* New York: Carnegie Corporation of New York.

Center for Career Development in Early Care and Education. 1994. *Making a career of it: State of the states report.* Boston: Author.

Chang, H.N-L., & L. Sakai. 1993. *Affirming children's roots: Cultural and linguistic diversity in early care and education.* San Francisco: California Tomorrow.

Cost, Quality, & Child Outcomes Study Team. 1995. *Cost, quality, and child outcomes in child care centers, executive summary.* Denver: Economics Department, University of Colorado at Denver.

Family Child Care Quality Criteria Project, Frank Porter Graham Child Development Center. 1995. *Quality criteria for family child care.* Washington, DC: National Association for Family Child Care.

Galinsky, E., C. Howes, S. Kontos, & M. Shinn. 1994. *The study of children in family child care and relative care: Highlights and findings.* New York: Families and Work Institute.

Harms, T., & D. Cryer. 1994. *Infant child care environment rating scale.* New York: Teachers College Press.

Howes, C. 1991. Research in review: Infant child care. *Young Children* 44 (6): 24–28.

Kamerman, S., & A. Kahn. 1994. *A welcome for every child: Child care, education and family support for infants and toddlers in Europe.* Arlington, VA: Zero to Three.

Lally, J.R., P.L. Mangione, A.S. Honig, & D.S. Wittmer. 1988. More pride, less delinquency: Findings from ten-year follow-up study of the Syracuse University Family Development Research Program. *Zero to Three* 13 (4): 13–18.

Lally, J.R., P.L. Mangione, A.S. Honig, & D.S. Wittmer. 1988. The Syracuse University Family Development Research Program: Long-range impact of an early intervention with low-income children and their families. In *Parent education in early childhood intervention: Emerging directions in theory, research and practice,* ed. D. Powell. Norwood, NJ: Ablex.

Larner, M. 1995. *Linking family support and early childhood programs: Issues, experiences, opportunities.* Chicago: Family Resource Coalition.

Lazar, M., R. Darlington, H. Murray, J. Royce, & A. Snipper. 1982. *Lasting effects of early education: A report from the Consortium for Longitudinal Studies.* Monographs of the Society for Research in Child Development, vol. 47, nos. 2–3, serial no. 195. Chicago: University of Chicago Press.

Leach, P. 1994. *Children first.* New York: Knopf.

Modigliani, K. 1990. *Assessing the quality of family child care—A comparison of five instruments.* Boston: Family Child Care Project.

Modigliani, K. 1993. *Child care as an occupation in a culture of indifference.* Boston: Family Child Care Project.

Modigliani, K., ed. 1993. *Readings in professional development in family child care—project-to-project.* Boston: Family Child Care Project.

NAEYC. 1991. *Accreditation criteria and procedures of the National Academy of Early Childhood Programs.* Rev. ed. Washington, DC: Author.

NAEYC. 1996. NAEYC position statement: Responding to linguistic and cultural diversity—Recommendations for effective early childhood education. *Young Children* 51 (2): 4–12.

NAFCC (National Association for Family Child Care). 1985. *Accreditation criteria and self study guide for family day care providers.* (Rev. ed. in press.) Washington, DC: Author.

Osofsky, J., & E. Fenichel, eds. 1994. *Caring for infants and toddlers in violent environments: Hurt, healing, and hope.* Arlington, VA: Zero to Three.

Whitebook, M., D. Phillips, & C. Howes. 1993. *National child care staffing study revisited: Four years in the life of center-based child care.* Oakland, CA: Child Care Employee Project.

Willer, B., ed. 1990. *Reaching the full cost of quality in early childhood programs.* Washington, DC: NAEYC.

Willer, B., S.L. Hofferth, E.E. Kisker, P. Divine-Hawkins, E. Farquhar, & F.B. Glantz. 1991. *The demand and supply of child care in 1990: Joint findings from the National Child Care Survey 1990 and a profile of child care settings.* Washington, DC: NAEYC.

Zero to Three, National Center for Infants, Toddlers, & Families. 1988. *Infants, families and child care: Toward a research agenda.* Arlington, VA: Author.

Zero to Three, National Center for Infants, Toddlers, & Families. 1992. *Head Start: The emotional foundations of school readiness.* Arlington, VA: Author.

Developmentally Appropriate Practice for 3- through 5-Year-Olds

In ever-increasing numbers, children between 2½ and 6 years of age are involved in out-of-home programs, including child care centers, family child care homes, or public and private full- and half-day prekindergartens and kindergartens. This age group is sometimes referred to as preschoolers, a name that has lost its former meaning as "the years before school attendance." The preschool years are now recognized as a vitally important period of human development in its own right, not as a time to grow before "real learning" begins in school. Preschool and kindergarten are no longer considered precursors to formal schooling. Instead, it is now well established that important development and learning occur during these years in all areas of human functioning—physical, social, emotional, and cognitive (including language, perception, reasoning, memory, and other aspects of intellectual development).

It is also well established that optimal development during these years is more likely to occur if children have opportunities to establish positive and caring relationships with adults and other children, benefit from adult guidance and assistance, and explore interesting environments with many things to do and learn. These conditions can and still do occur for many young children at home with their parents. But for those children who attend out-of-home early childhood programs, many hours of their day are spent away from their families. Early child-hood teachers, in collaboration with parents, are responsible for ensuring that the program "promotes the development and enhances the learning of each individual child served" (see Part 1, p. 8); in other words, professionals must ensure that the program is developmentally appropriate.

Part 4 of this book is designed to assist teachers of 3-, 4-, and 5-year-olds in that fundamental task of serving each child, and it includes the following:

- an overview of the integrated nature of learning and development;

- sketches of children's development in various domains during this period as well as the ways children vary as individuals and members of cultural groups;

- descriptions of individual children to convey the reality of how each preschool or kindergarten child is unique;

- discussion of ways to help children and families negotiate transitions; and

- examples of practices we see as appropriate—that is, consistent with the guidelines articulated in the position statement (see Part 1) and the principles of development and learning from which the guidelines are derived—and those we see as inappropriate or inconsistent with these guidelines and principles.

Development and learning in children age 3 through 5

Considerable growth and change occur in children during these three years in all areas of development—physical, cognitive (language, perceptual, and intellectual), and social-emotional. Yet compared to what occurs in the first three years of life, change is steadier and slower. Three-year-olds are no longer toddlers, but they behave like toddlers at times; at other times their language ability, motor skills, and other behaviors make them seem older than they are. The challenge for the teacher of 3-year-olds is to maintain appropriate expectations, expecting neither too little nor too much of the children. To care for and educate any group of 3- through 5-year-olds, teachers need to fully understand the developmental continuum from toddlerhood through the primary grades.

We include 5-year-olds in this age span because most children at that age have not yet made the major shift in cognition that has been found to occur between 5 and 7 years of age (Piaget 1952; White 1965, 1970; Sameroff & McDonough 1994). Before this well-documented shift occurs, children are developmentally more like preschoolers than like school-age children. The transformation that occurs around age 6 or 7 for most children has been marked throughout time and across cultures as "achieving the age of reason" or "acquiring sense"—that is, an increased ability to assume personal responsibility, self-direction, and logical thinking (Whiting & Edwards 1988). The implications of this cognitive shift are described more fully in Part 5.

Because most 5-year-olds have more in common developmentally with preschoolers than with primary-grade children (Berk 1996), it follows that kindergartens that are much like programs for 3- and 4-year-olds are most appropriate for children at age 5. In the world of educational institutions, kindergarten is sometimes grouped with prekindergarten and first grade and more often is part of primary or elementary schools. School structures, however, are changing rapidly, with more public schools now serving 4-year-olds and even some 3-year-olds (Mitchell, Seligson, & Marx 1989; Adams & Sandfort 1994). Regardless of how preschool and kindergarten are structurally organized, a primary consideration in designing the educational program should be knowledge of the developmental and learning needs of this age group.

Integrated development and learning in early childhood

Among the biggest challenges when describing children's development in various domains (such as physical, social, or cognitive) is to accurately convey the degree to which development and learning are interconnected across and within domains. Countless examples of this integration exist. Among the more obvious is that, as children develop physically during the preschool years, the range of environments and opportunities for social interaction that they are capable of exploring expands greatly, thus influencing their cognitive and social development. Similarly, children's vastly increased language ability enhances the complexity of their social interactions with adults and other children, which, in turn, influences their language and cognitive abilities. Likewise, children's growing cognitive capacity to understand different points of view affects their ability to regulate their own emotions and express empathy for others. Their increasing language capacity enhances their ability to mentally represent their experiences (and, thus, think, reason, and problem solve), just as their improved fine-motor skill increases their ability to represent their thoughts graphically and visually.

The integrated nature of children's development and learning underlies early childhood educators' insistence on not losing sight of the "whole child." This understanding precludes the notion that one can provide a program that focuses on one area of learning or development while neglecting or ignoring others, such as occurs in many programs that stress formal academics with very young children. In a large-scale observational study of preschool and kindergarten programs, Stipek and her colleagues (1992) found that the social context experienced by children was invariably negative and punitive in highly teacher-directed programs emphasizing evaluation of children's academic performance. Because the evidence was so consistent, the researchers concluded that for preschool and kindergarten, "A strong emphasis on academic achievement and teacher-directed instruction appeared to preclude a positive social context" (Stipek et al. 1992, 14). Given other evidence of the powerful influence of positive, social relationships on children's development (e.g., Howes 1988; Hartup & Moore 1990), early childhood teachers are compelled to use well-researched teaching practices that support children's intellectual development while also enhancing their social, emotional, and physical development (such as project work, play, small-group learning experiences, engagement in real-life tasks such as cooking or woodworking, and other appropriate practices, examples of which are described on pp. 123–35 of this section).

Narrow focusing on academic skills is problematic during the years from 3 to 6, not only because it is potentially damaging to children's social and emotional development but also because it is intellectually limiting. With the astonishing changes that occur during these years in children's ability to think, reason, communicate, and take initiative, children benefit from being intellectually and perceptually challenged (Katz & Chard 1989; Edwards, Gandini, & Forman 1993). They need opportunities to explore deeply and attend in great detail to subjects of interest to them (whether the subject is bugs, shadows, trains, or floating and sinking). Children also need challenging and changing learning environments that provide opportunities for them to function independently, as well as with assistance from adults and peers, in what Vygotsky (1978) called their "zone of proximal development." If the context is boring or unchanging and thus children are not physically and intellectually challenged, the children may become disruptive. Offering uninteresting, unstimulating situations to young children is like asking them to "run in place." But if the context includes a reasonable amount of complexity and challenge, along with sufficient amounts of adult direction and guidance, children are more likely to take initiative, respond to the challenge, express themselves, and acquire important skills and concepts.

In considering good practice for a certain age range, we must give thought to what children of that age are like. For each major area of development, we include a brief sketch of characteristics and widely held expectations for children 3 through 5.

A sketch of physical development in 3-, 4-, and 5-year-olds

"Teddy bear, teddy bear, turn around," a group of kindergarten children chant as they jump rope on a playground. All of the children act out the motions to this chant with little difficulty. Two children turn the rope as several wait their turns to jump in. A short distance away three younger children alternate between giggles and looks of frustration as they try to turn their own ropes and jump. They are 3- and 4-year-olds who have yet to master how to keep the rope going over their heads and how to jump over it. An adult offers some assistance, but all the children continue to experience difficulty. Realizing that children of 3 or 4 have some time to mature before they are likely to master jump rope, she suggests several other play alternatives, such as throwing, catching, and kicking a large ball, that will challenge but not frustrate them.

Physical development is an important aspect of development during early childhood. It involves an interplay between new physical capacities resulting from the child's actual growth and maturation and skills that develop from experience and training provided by adults (Gallahue 1993).

Physical growth

The amount and rate of growth in children between the ages of 3 and 5 vary. Some children grow as much as six inches over the three-year period, and others grow only a few inches, but all children develop a less-toddler-like trunk and become less top-heavy. Growth in this period takes place mostly in the trunk and legs. The physical growth rate during these ages is steadier but slower than during the first three years. On the average, children gain five to six pounds and two to three inches per year during the period of 3 to 6 years of age. However, the amount of growth varies greatly between individuals and also between children of different races.

Children's image of their body often lags behind their increasing size. Learning how to monitor their bodies in space is a challenge to this age group, and frequent mishaps arise from children's lack of awareness of their actual changes in size (as when a child does not believe that a favorite shirt no longer fits) and from their lack of motor-skill planning (as when a child picks the more difficult than simple way to get somewhere).

Maturation

Changes that are less visible also occur as the child ages from 3 to 6. The brain grows from 75% to 90% of its adult size during these years. Coordination improves with each year, as lateralization (each hemisphere of the brain developing separate functions and interconnections) and myelinization (the process of insulating the nervous system with fat) are nearly completed by 6 years. Handedness is fairly well established around 4 years of age, although the wrist contains some cartilage that will not harden into bone until about age 6, placing some constraint on fine-motor capacity (Berk 1996). As a result, most children of this age cannot make fully circular wrist motions like those used in cursive writing; neither do they have the wrist strength to propel themselves on overhead horizontal bars. All 20 deciduous, or baby, teeth have erupted by around 3 years of age. Simply put, the preschooler is physically not an infant anymore. These processes of growth and maturation promote many new abilities in all areas of development.

Sensation and perception

For the most part, the senses of sight, touch, smell, taste, and hearing are well developed in the preschool period. However, children are farsighted and are still developing their coordination of binocular

Between the ages of 3 and 6, gross-motor development progresses rapidly as children begin to develop new skills and refine others.

vision, which is one of the reasons that larger print is used with this age group. While the perceptual abilities of children are generally well developed by this period, the child's use of the incoming information is less complete, because the child has yet to develop some of the cognitive strategies and language refinements to interpret and communicate the sensory data. Processing of information steadily improves throughout the years from 3 through 5 (described in this section under "A sketch of cognitive development," p. 110).

Children at 2 and 3 years of age improve in their ability to perceive patterns and discriminate various forms. Gradually children begin to recognize and then repeat and design visual patterns. Throughout this period, children show increasing interest in producing designs and patterns in art, puzzles, constructions, and letters and words. Even in kindergarten, however, children continue to make letter reversals (confusing q and p or d and b). This confusion is a natural one because in the physical world an object has the same function and name regardless of its directional orientation.

Young children's sense of hearing is well developed by preschool age. Nevertheless, the ability to perceive subtle phonological distinctions in sounds, such as consonant blends (necessary for mastering all the phonetic combinations of language), is not well developed until about age 6 in most children (Dale 1976). For example, most adults have observed that no matter how often they enunciate the sp sound, their preschoolers still insist on eating "basghetti." Chronic middle-ear infection during infancy or toddlerhood can also impair hearing during these years and affect later reading.

Preschool children's sense of touch, smell, and taste are fully developed. In fact, preschool children's sense of taste is actually more acute than that of adults because they have additional taste buds in the cheeks and throat, which partially accounts for their reputation as "picky eaters" (Harris 1986).

Perceptual development is influenced by experience but is largely dependent on brain and central-nervous-system development, the exact timing of which varies widely, even among typically developing children. When a child's perceptual development or coordination appears to lag significantly behind that of peers, early childhood professionals may decide to recommend screening or diagnostic evaluation, which may result in suggested interventions that teachers help to implement. All young children need to experience in their daily environment an array of objects and events that they can explore and learn about with the senses. Throughout the preschool years, children benefit from materials, experiences, and teaching strategies that help them learn the distinctive features of objects, graphic symbols, and other stimuli.

Gross-motor development

Physical growth during this age lowers the child's center of gravity, making more steady and surefooted movements possible. Gross-motor development includes increased functional use of limbs for such activities as jumping, running, and climbing. Yet, because the nervous system is still immature, the preschooler's reaction time is generally much slower than that of a 6- or 7-year-old. Variation in motor development is due to a combination of genetic and environmental factors, including maturation, motivation, experience, and adult support. Differences between racial groups in motor development have been documented; for instance, norms of motor development among African American children exceed those of Caucasian children in walking, running, and jumping (Lee 1980). While some 3- and 4-year-olds are already demonstrating the gross-motor abilities of 5-year-olds, the sequences in which children acquire motor skills and the age-related generalizations about physical development hold true for children in this age range.

Developmental characterizations of an age group provide rough guidelines that enable teachers to make general program plans. Expectations for children in a particular classroom should come from teacher observation of children in a variety of actual physical activities and settings. For instance, watching a group of children running is not very helpful in identifying the more able or less able children in this age range. Most children, unless they have experienced some developmental difficulty or delay, are able to perform basic gross-motor skills like running. One gets a fuller picture of children's individual levels of gross-motor skill by watching each child go through an obstacle course that includes a balance beam and something to jump into, out of, and over (such as hoops and tunnels). Most 3- and 4-year-olds are

Gross-Motor Development—Widely Held Expectations

For 3-year-olds —

- walks without watching feet; walks backward; runs at an even pace; turns and stops well
- climbs stairs with alternating feet, using hand rail for balance
- jumps off low steps or objects; does not judge well in jumping over objects
- shows improved coordination; begins to move legs and arms to pump a swing or ride a trike, sometimes forgetting to watch the direction of these actions and crashing into objects
- perceives height and speed of objects (like a thrown ball) but may be overly bold or fearful, lacking a realistic sense of own ability
- stands on one foot unsteadily; balances with difficulty on the low balance beam (four-inch width) and watches feet
- plays actively (trying to keep up with older children) and then needs rest; fatigues suddenly and becomes cranky if overly tired

For 4-year-olds —

- walks heel-to-toe; skips unevenly; runs well
- stands on one foot for five seconds or more; masters the low balance beam (four-inch width) but has difficulty on the two-inch-wide beam without watching feet
- walks down steps, alternating feet; judges well in placing feet on climbing structures
- develops sufficient timing to jump rope or play games requiring quick reactions
- begins to coordinate movements to climb on a jungle gym or jump on a small trampoline
- shows greater perceptual judgment and awareness of own limitations and/or the consequences of unsafe behaviors; still needs supervision crossing a street or protecting self in certain activities
- exhibits increased endurance, with long periods of high energy (needing increased intakes of liquids and calories); sometimes becomes overexcited and less self-regulated in group activities

For 5-year-olds —

- walks backward quickly; skips and runs with agility and speed; can incorporate motor skills into a game
- walks a two-inch balance beam well; jumps over objects
- hops well; maintains an even gate in stepping
- jumps down several steps; jumps rope
- climbs well; coordinates movements for swimming or bike riding
- shows uneven perceptual judgment; acts overly confident at times but accepts limit setting and follows rules
- displays high energy levels; rarely shows fatigue; finds inactivity difficult and seeks active games and environments

just beginning to work on skills such as balancing, jumping, and hopping and are challenged by such an obstacle course. At these children's ages, specific motor difficulties will become more apparent to parents and teachers, who may need to involve specialists (early childhood special educators, physical therapists, or occupational therapists) in assessing and planning appropriate intervention and support for children's physical development. If observers conducted a careful observation of groups of 3s, 4s, and 5s, their general observations of children's gross-motor skills might resemble those in the boxes on page 102 (see also Harris 1986; Nebraska/Iowa 1993).

Considerations for early childhood educators in supporting gross-motor development

The physical development of 3- through 5-year-olds should be considered throughout the learning environment and across the curriculum. Plans should provide for physical activity throughout the young child's day. In any part of the curriculum, requiring too much sitting is at odds with young children's characteristic mode of learning through activity—through moving, exploring, and acting on objects. It is also important to provide preschool children who have developmental disabilities with ways of being active and mobile. Adaptations of equipment or the environment may be necessary, such as making playgrounds and equipment wheelchair accessible or using signs and symbols to help a child with hearing loss participate in music or movement.

Between the ages of 3 and 6, gross-motor development progresses rapidly as children begin to develop new skills and refine others. Daily activities should include many opportunities for young children to develop competence and confidence. For example, as part of the daily routine, children carry objects, take nature walks, exercise and move to music, and engage in role-playing actions and short dramas. Play equipment for indoors can promote gross-motor skills, with adaptation to provide access for children with disabilities. A diversity of equipment could include cup stilts, a small trampoline, steps, a balance beam, hoops for jumping, jump ropes, bean bag toss, scooter boards, a puppet show, ring toss, a parachute, floor puzzles, hollow blocks, large Legos, and strollers for dramatic play. Large floor areas (carpeted and not) are needed inside

for movement and other activities, such as throwing and jumping.

The outdoors is an ideal environment for promoting gross-motor development, but its use must be planned and supervised. Equipment is needed, such as a small net and beach balls for playing volley ball, foam bats and balls, trikes, or scooter boards. Teachers can plan outdoor activities that include parachute games, hoop activities, ball games, an obstacle course, group games (e.g., Fruit Basket), and an exercise station with a balance beam, ladder, climbing pole, and tires.

Children in this age range enjoy and engage in many gross-motor activities for the first time; therefore, a significant amount of direct adult supervision is necessary because preschoolers' perceptual judgments are still immature. The physical environment should have pieces of equipment that vary in skill level according to the degree of balance and coordination required. Under climbing structures, six to twelve inches of appropriate cushioning material is necessary to protect children from falls, a major cause of childhood injury (see AAP & APHA 1992; Kendrick, Kaufmann, & Messenger 1995). Planned outdoor activities should challenge children to use a range of motor skills, as obstacle courses do, but allow for and be adapted to a wide range of difference among children due to maturational rates; motivation level; experience, practice, and adult coaching; nutrition; and identified or potential disabilities and exceptional abilities.

Fine-motor development

Young children do not attain sophisticated manual dexterity during the years from 3 through 5. They may experience failure and frustration if they often are expected to perform tasks involving precise control of the hand muscles, careful perceptual judgment involving eye-hand coordination, and refined movements requiring steadiness and patience.

From 3 through 5, and even beyond, children benefit from activities that develop their hand muscles and fine-motor skills, such as drawing and painting, working with playdough, or constructing with Duplos or Legos. Such open-ended activities—along with plenty of time and encouragement—engage children and prepare them for the demands of handwriting and other skills developed later. Children can learn to use their hands and fingers by watching others, and when a task has several steps, such as in making a clay figure or building a house with Legos, they may need to have it broken down into perceivable elements.

Children experience different degrees of difficulty at doing fine-motor tasks. Some children are far more facile than others at fine-motor tasks, and gender differences are observable as well. Girls tend to be more advanced than boys in fine-motor skills and gross-motor skills requiring precision, such as hopping and skipping, and boys on the whole hold an edge in physical skills that require force and power, such as running and jumping (Berk 1996). When children have certain kinds of identified disabilities, the usual fine-motor activities may require adaptation. For example, through assistive technologies that include modified keyboards, switches, pointing devices, and graphics programs (Behrmann & Lahm 1994), children unable to use their hands are able to draw and construct.

Observers seeking a picture of 3- through 5-year-olds' fine-motor skills might observe children using open-ended materials, drawing, and engaging in personal care. A summary of what observers would be likely to see is presented in the boxes on page 105.

Considerations for early childhood educators in supporting fine-motor development

Fine-motor development progresses slowly during the preschool years but can be fostered by providing ample opportunities, appropriate tools, and adult support, as can be seen in settings where children's experiences and the cultural expectations are highly conducive to fine-motor skill development (Reggio Emilia Department of Education 1987; Tobin, Davidson, & Wu 1989). Nevertheless, more narrow-gauged efforts to merely accelerate fine-motor development by pushing children too early into fine-motor tasks are likely to be unsuccessful or frustrating for children. Too much focus on performance in this area may create feelings of inadequacy and stress. Acknowledging what children can do and supporting their efforts to try new activities result in fewer discouraged young learners. By kindergarten, children are able to engage in fine-motor activities more readily and for longer periods of time; they are less likely to experience frustration. When children seem interested and persistent in writing their name and

forming letters, adults should offer assistance, both formal and informal.

Three- through 5-year-olds should have access to many kinds of materials and objects to help them develop and practice fine-motor skills, such as small objects to sort and count; pegboards and beads to string; clothing and things that zip, button, and tie for dress-up play; dolls and accessories; drawing and writing materials; scissors, paint, and clay; and opportunities to practice functional skills, such as pouring milk, setting the table, eating, and dressing. Using assistive technology and modified tools, children with disabilities can also practice these fine-motor skills (e.g., Velcro shoes or weighted bowls and utensils allow children to feed themselves in the group).

A sketch of language and communication development in 3-, 4- and 5-year-olds

Although language and communication are inextricable from cognition, they are such major developments in these years that we discuss them as an area in their own right. The speed with which young children become speakers of their home languages without directly being taught is one of nature's marvels and provides strong evidence of a biological basis for language acquisition (Chomsky 1968). At the same time, the development of communicative competence—the ability to use the full array of human-language skills for expression and interpretation—is strongly influenced by children's experiences and environment (Hart & Risley 1995). During the preschool and kindergarten years, interactions with adults and other more-mature speakers of the language play an important role in supporting children's growing ability to communicate.

The early childhood years are also an optimal time to acquire fluency in a second language. For instance, when children learn other languages before about age 12, they are more likely to speak those languages as native speakers do (Ladefoged 1969; Flege 1981). The optimum conditions for learning a second language are similar to those for learning a first—within the context of a trusting, ongoing relationship with a fluent speaker of that language. Programs serving one or more children whose first language is not English should provide support for maintaining the home language while the child acquires English (Wong Fillmore 1992; NAEYC 1996). In addition, second-language learning

Fine-Motor Development—Widely Held Expectations

For 3-year-olds —

- places large pegs into pegboards; strings large beads; pours liquids with some spills
- builds block towers; easily does puzzles with whole objects represented as a piece
- fatigues easily if much hand coordination is required
- draws shapes, such as the circle; begins to design objects, such as a house or figure; draws objects in some relation to each other
- holds crayons or markers with fingers instead of the fist
- undresses without assistance but needs help getting dressed; unbuttons skillfully but buttons slowly

For 4-year-olds —

- uses small pegs and board; strings small beads (and may do so in a pattern); pours sand or liquid into small containers
- builds complex block structures that extend vertically; shows limited spatial judgment and tends to knock things over
- enjoys manipulating play objects that have fine parts; likes to use scissors; practices an activity many times to gain mastery
- draws combinations of simple shapes; draws persons with at least four parts and objects that are recognizable to adults
- dresses and undresses without assistance; brushes teeth and combs hair; spills rarely with cup or spoon; laces shoes or clothing but cannot yet tie

For 5-year-olds —

- hits nails with hammer head; uses scissors and screwdrivers unassisted
- uses computer keyboard
- builds three-dimensional block structures; does 10–15-piece puzzles with ease
- likes to disassemble and reassemble objects and dress and undress dolls
- has basic grasp of right and left but mixes them up at times
- copies shapes; combines more than two geometric forms in drawing and construction
- draws persons; prints letters crudely but most are recognizable by an adult; includes a context or scene in drawings; prints first name
- zips coat; buttons well; ties shoes with adult coaching; dresses quickly

Interactive, collaborative activities, such as block building and dramatic play, provide rich opportunities for language development.

should occur (as primary-language acquisition does) through meaningful, comprehensible experiences.

At around 2 years of age, children have a vocabulary of about 50 words on the average. To keep a conversation going, adults make surmises and fill in actual words to match the child's presumed intent. From 3 to 5 years of age, language development seems to explode, with children learning an average of 50 new words per month. As this dramatic acceleration continues, the child's working vocabulary reaches 8,000 to 14,000 words by age 6. Sentence length also increases each year, as does the use of abstract words. The chatter of the 2-year-old turns into increasingly complex conversations. Young children are talkers. They are also attracted to and endlessly enjoy listening to stories read aloud in small groups or on adults' laps. They like to share favorite books, "read" books, and retell stories.

During these years from 3 to 5, children also become familiar with and use various "scripts" for communicating in different contexts, such as talking on the phone, ordering in a fast-food restaurant, or going to a birthday party (Sroufe, Cooper, & DeHart 1993, 343). Familiarity with these scripts—that is, the sets of actions and language that are conventionally used in a range of situations—frees children from attending solely to the cognitive demands of the situation and enables them to spend more cognitive energy on speech production. Knowing the appropriate script for a given context greatly facilitates the child's communication. Similarly, if a child is unaware of conventional scripts or has learned scripts in a cultural or social context that differs from that of the school or center, communication is more difficult (Bowman 1994).

Oral language development not only plays a significant role in children's social development, but also provides tools for mental representation or what Vygotsky (1978) calls "verbal mediation"—the ability to attach labels to objects and processes, which is necessary for concept development, generalization, and thought. The increasing capacity of preschool-age children to use language in thought is a key development of this period and enables children to solve new problems without relying solely on trial and error (e.g., a child builds her tower away from the doorway because she knows the door will open).

Another indication of this emerging ability in children is their use of private speech—the tendency for preschoolers to think out loud or control their own behavior by literally talking to themselves ("Don't let the paint run down. Quick, stop it!"). Vygotsky (1978) demonstrated the usefulness of this form of speech for children in problem solving and coping with stressful or frustrating situations. He also observed the developmental changes that occur in how private speech is used. Younger children use it to announce the completion of an activity ("There, I did it"). With age, children begin to make use of private speech as they work on a task. Still more mature is children's use of private speech to plan in advance what they will do or how they will proceed. A similar progression takes place in children's naming of their drawings (Smart & Smart 1973).

Children with disabilities that affect speech production, of course, learn to think and solve problems, but they need to be provided with alternative ways of communicating, such as American Sign Language for hearing-impaired children, computer-assisted communication, or a communication board or device that is revised as the child develops new concepts, skills, and emotions. For example, a kindergartner with Down syndrome has made rapid progress in communication abilities since she has been included in a regular classroom, but her communication board still contains only the six basic symbols (such as for *potty* or *hungry*) that she used in preschool, which severely limits what she is able to convey.

Observing and talking with 3-, 4-, and 5-year-old children, an adult would first be aware of the enormous variation and complexity of children's language development. "Children vary in the language forms and structures they have acquired at any point in time and in the rate of mastery over time . . . . [There are] considerable individual differences among children from very similar cultural and social backgrounds" (Kagan, Moore, & Bredekamp 1995, 32). Of course, a primary function of language is to meet personal and cultural objectives of communication, so it is not surprising that a growing body of research demonstrates that cultural and social differences exist in children's acquisition and use of language (Miller 1982; Shuy & Staton 1982; Hale-Benson 1986; Brice-Heath 1988).

Watching and listening to groups of children, an observer would note age-related differences in children's

Language and Communication Development—
Widely Held Expectations

For 3-year-olds —

- shows a steady increase in vocabulary, ranging from 2,000 to 4,000 words; tends to overgeneralize meaning and make up words to fit needs
- uses simple sentences of at least three or four words to express needs
- may have difficulty taking turns in conversation; changes topics quickly
- pronounces words with difficulty; often mistakes one word for another
- likes simple finger plays and rhymes and learns words to songs that have much repetition
- adapts speech and style of nonverbal communication to listeners in culturally accepted ways but still needs to be reminded of context
- asks many *who*, *what*, *where*, and *why* questions but shows confusion in responding to some questions (especially *why*, *how*, and *when*)
- uses language to organize thought, linking two ideas by sentence combining; overuses such words as *but*, *because*, and *when*; rarely makes appropriate use of such temporal words as *before*, *until*, or *after*
- can tell a simple story but must redo the sequence to put an idea into the order of events; often forgets the point of a story and is more likely to focus on favorite parts

For 4-year-olds —

- expands vocabulary from 4,000 to 6,000 words; shows more attention to abstract uses
- usually speaks in five- to six-word sentences
- likes to sing simple songs; knows many rhymes and finger plays
- will talk in front of the group with some reticence; likes to tell others about family and experiences
- uses verbal commands to claim many things; begins teasing others
- expresses emotions through facial gestures and reads others for body cues; copies behaviors (such as hand gestures) of older children or adults
- can control volume of voice for periods of time if reminded; begins to read context for social cues
- uses more advanced sentence structures, such as relative clauses and tag questions ("She's nice, isn't she?") and experiments with new constructions, creating some comprehension difficulties for the listener
- tries to communicate more than his or her vocabulary allows; borrows and extends words to create meaning
- learns new vocabulary quickly if related to own experience ("We walk our dog on a belt. Oh yeah, it's a leash—we walk our dog on a leash")
- can retell a four- or five-step directive or the sequence in a story

---

For 5-year-olds —

- employs a vocabulary of 5,000 to 8,000 words, with frequent plays on words; pronounces words with little difficulty, except for particular sounds, such as *l* and *th*
- uses fuller, more complex sentences ("His turn is over, and it's my turn now")
- takes turns in conversation, interrupts others less frequently; listens to another speaker if information is new and of interest; shows vestiges of egocentrism in speech, for instance, in assuming listener will understand what is meant (saying "He told me to do it" without any referents for the pronouns)
- shares experiences verbally; knows the words to many songs
- likes to act out others' roles, shows off in front of new people or becomes unpredictably very shy
- remembers lines of simple poems and repeats full sentences and expressions from others, including television shows and commercials
- shows skill at using conventional modes of communication complete with pitch and inflection
- uses nonverbal gestures, such as certain facial expressions in teasing peers
- can tell and retell stories with practice; enjoys repeating stories, poems, and songs; enjoys acting out plays or stories
- shows growing speech fluency in expressing ideas

---

vocabulary, sentence length, conversation, oral presentation, nonverbal behaviors, syntactical complexity, and ways of organizing thought, such as those noted in the boxes on the opposite page and above.

Considerations for early childhood educators in supporting language and communication development

Children from 3 through 5 years of age experience phenomenal growth in language ability. Adults serve as language models, of course, but it is children's desire to construct meaning and to communicate, along with their neurological readiness, that propels this rapid development. Providing opportunities for children to talk, carefully listening to children, and offering well-placed expansions of their sentences to enhance the meaning are the most important ways teachers can assist these young language learners. Many errors, as perceived by the adult, may, in fact, be a part of the child's current working model that at this age often includes overgeneralizing of a rule or pattern (e.g., "mouses" or "I goed"). Many of these will be self-corrected at a later stage as the child's model is revised through better auditory perception, memory capacity, and experience. Teachers of young children need to un-

derstand which aspects of children's speech do not need correcting because they are developmental (such as private speech and overgeneralizations) and which aspects may need enriching through learning experiences (for instance, vocabulary and use of directional words like *over, under,* or *around*).

The ability to represent thoughts and feelings verbally allows children to develop new social strategies and to participate with others in many ways. Ideas and experiences can be shared, feelings can be explained, or words can be used to encourage or hurt others. Teachers should recognize the value of expanding children's vocabulary in the course of studying topics of interest. For example, when children are learning about farms, they encounter animal names and words like *harvest* and *plant*. Projects and activities should also encourage children to generate ideas verbally, evaluate solutions, plan, problem solve, and predict outcomes.

Children at this age will vary greatly in their language abilities, yet the progression is toward producing speech in greater quantity and with increased complexity and abstraction; therefore, children with developmental delays or other difficulties are more likely to be noticed when they lag in the amount or kind of change that occurs. Projects and activities should take these differences into account so that all children can participate. For example, teachers should create a supportive context for children who are reticent about speaking in front of a small group, including some of those learning English as their second language. Creating psychological and cultural safety is an important part of any language program. Large-group experiences should involve some opportunities for active participation, such as joining in music or movement activities.

Interactive, collaboration activities such as dramatic play and block building provide rich language-promoting opportunities. Children get involved in negotiating differing perspectives and imitating what adults do and say. They use language to establish roles, symbolic use of objects, and other shared meaning ("Let's pretend this block is the car phone. You be the delivery man"). Recognizing the great value of dramatic play for children's language, cognitive, and social development, teachers actively foster and extend it through a variety of strategies. They provide a range of play props, both realistic replicas and open-ended materials like blocks, that children can use to be different things as their play scenarios require (Copple, Sigel, & Saunders 1984). Teachers' own modeling of make-believe interactions and the scripts of adult roles help children develop more elaborated levels of language and play (Smilansky & Shefatya 1990). The potential of such play for language, literacy, and other learning is well established (Pellegrini & Galda 1982, 1991; Schrader 1989, 1990; Smilansky & Shefatya 1990; Pramling 1991; Pellegrini & Boyd 1993).

Play also provides a safe and highly motivating context within which children can learn a second language (Heath 1983). In recent years, with more developmentally appropriate software available, computers have also proven to be conducive to language and social interaction when children are able to use them collaboratively (Clements & Nastasi 1993; Wright & Shade 1994).

Promoting language development is a major curriculum goal for preschool and kindergarten children. Teachers need to provide many opportunities for social interaction and conversation among children as well as activities that contain varying representational demands (for instance, ask a child to describe something to another child who cannot see the object, explain how a task was done or how something works, or negotiate a social problem with another child through words). Teachers also should make readily available those materials and settings that promote language development, such as a class library and a book-sharing nook (with two copies of some books); construction sets for designing and building a pretend-play town; a book-making or art area with paints, writing tools, paper, wallpaper, pictures, catalogs, rubber stamps, and so on; sets of magnetic letters and wooden letters; chalkboards; puzzles, board games, and card games; and much more.

A sketch of cognitive development in 3-, 4-, and 5-year-olds

As has been seen in the descriptions of both physical and language development (and as will be seen in social and emotional development), dramatic cognitive changes occur during the preschool and kindergarten years. Cognition in children between ages 3 and 6 is qualitatively different from that of infants and toddlers because children have acquired the ability to use language and mental representation. For example, they can think about events that happened weeks ago or those that have not yet happened. Although children's thinking, reasoning, and memory processes will continue to change and be transformed again around age 7, during the years from 3 through 5, children's increasing cognitive capacity enables them to engage in more sophisticated learning activities and social relationships.

Early childhood educators' current understanding of cognitive development in children is grounded in three broad theoretical perspectives—Piaget's theory describing these years as preoperational (1952), Vygotsky's sociocultural theory (1978), and the information-processing theories of short- and long-term memory ability and use of cognitive strategies in young children (Siegler 1983; Seifert 1993). Research related to each of these theories (and others) informs early childhood practice today.

Among the major contributions of Piaget's work has been the now widely accepted recognition that young children actively construct their own understanding of concepts and "operations" (such as cause and effect, number, classification, seriation, and logical reasoning). This constructivist perspective in cognition emphasizes the child's need to act on objects, interact with people, and think and reflect on their experiences. Much of Piaget's research identified ways in which preschool children's thinking and ability to perform such operations are less mature than those of older children, because younger children tend to view the world from their own point of view (egocentrism) and confuse appearances and reality (for instance, a whole cookie broken into pieces appears to be bigger than an unbroken one).

Recent research supports Piaget's view that there are limits on preschool children's cognitive processing, although researchers find that operational processes develop rather gradually over this period as opposed to appearing abruptly at the end of the period, as Piaget assumed. The studies conclude that when young children are given sorting, classifying, and ordering tasks that are simplified and highly relevant to their experience, they perform more successfully than do children in the Piagetian scenarios, which are less familiar and less meaningful to them (see Seifert 1993; Sroufe, Cooper, & DeHart 1993; Berk 1996). For example, Gelman and Meck (1983) have shown that under certain conditions (in their study, watching a puppet counting) children as young as 3 may recognize that each item in a set must be matched with a different number name, numbers must be named in consistent order, and the last number gives the special name to the entire set. Yet, on their own, these same children cannot demonstrate one-to-one correspondence and appear to

Asking a well-timed question that provokes the child's further reflection or investigation is one of the many active strategies a good teacher uses.

lack these understandings basic to the concept of number. Young children's cognitive capacities are increasing enormously during these years, but the cognitive limitations of 3- through 5-year-old children make them significantly different thinkers than school-age children.

The work of Vygotsky (1978; Berk & Winsler 1995) illuminates the role of language development and social interaction in cognitive development. Vygotsky's perspective on private speech was described earlier (see "A sketch of language and communication development," pp. 104-08). According to Vygotsky, young children often use private speech when they are trying to perform a task in their "zone of proximal development"—that is, just beyond their current level of functioning but achievable with another person's assistance or supportive scaffolding. Cues, questions, and other forms of assistance are given by adults and other children. For example, as a child struggles with a puzzle piece, instead of directly showing the child how to place the piece, an adult may say, "What color is it? Where do you see that color on the puzzle?" or "Try turning it around another way." Vygotsky demonstrated that much of children's understanding first occurs in communication with other people, then appears in private speech, and eventually is internalized as thought.

Information-processing theorists look at developmental differences in cognitive performance in terms of children's changing abilities, such as attending to stimuli, holding information in short-term memory, storing it in and retrieving it from long-term memory, and other aspects of processing information. There are age-related differences in these capacities. Although these developmental constraints limit children's capacity to process information, appropriate adult guidance and support can strengthen children's processing skills.

In comparison to physical and language development, children's cognitive development is less easily observed. A visitor to a preschool or kindergarten would not be able merely to observe and expect to make the kind of detailed notes that are possible about a child's motor skills or vocabulary production or sentence length. Understanding how children think, reason, remember, or solve problems necessitates engaging children in tasks requiring these abilities and then devising strategies for assessing what children know and how they think. Accurately assessing children's cognitive development has proven to be

more difficult than it would seem. As most early childhood educators know, children may appear to know or understand more—or less—than they actually do. For instance, many preschool children can count in order up to 20 or higher; a child may even be able to count a group of eight objects but, when asked to "show me 8," points just to the last object in the set (Kamii 1982).

Characteristics of thought in 3- through 5-year-olds

From 3 through 5 years of age, children continue to develop in key areas of cognition. Following is a summary of young children's characteristics of thought, information-processing capacities, and development of social cognition during the preschool and kindergarten years.

Symbolic thought. The most obvious change from toddlerhood is the extraordinary increase in the child's ability to mentally or symbolically represent concrete objects, action, and events. This ability is most apparent in the vast increase in language that allows preschoolers to uncouple thought from action. For example, toddlers continually repeat the same "mistake" and figure things out through an acting on objects and people, but preschoolers can think ahead and anticipate the consequences of their physical actions. This increasing ability to use mental representation allows children to make plans before taking action, and their activities take on a more purposeful, goal-directed character (Friedman, Scholnick, & Cocking 1987). Preschoolers' increased capacity for symbolic thought is also apparent in the significant increase in their use of make-believe play, which becomes more elaborated and more cooperative. Engaging in sociodramatic play, in turn, strengthens children's memory, language, logical reasoning, imagination, and creativity.

Egocentrism, centration, and concreteness. Preschool and kindergarten children's thinking continues to be influenced by their egocentrism—the tendency to take into account only their own point of view—and centration, which is the focusing of attention on one element of a situation and ignoring of all others. These characteristics influence much of young children's thinking and reasoning. For instance, young children have difficulty understanding how the world looks to other people, assuming that other people see and experience things the same way they do. This egocentrism accounts for many of the delightful and amusing things that young children do and say (such as a child giving his blanket to his mother when she is sad or sick, in the belief that she will be comforted by the same object that comforts him). Egocentrism also limits the child's ability to reason logically or perform other operations that older children and adults find simple.

Concreteness is the tendency of young children to focus on the tangible, observable aspects of objects, as is apparent in their use of language. For example, a child may use the word *fuzzy* in relation to a peach skin or a blanket but have difficulty applying it to something abstract, as in "fuzzy thinking."

Reasoning. Preschoolers typically reason from the particular to the particular ("My dog is friendly, so this dog is friendly"). They also tend to presume a causal relationship if two events are closely associated in time or in some other way, and they focus on attributes that are actually superficial to the events they are linking. For example, a 4-year-old on an airplane may ask another passenger, "Are you going to Grandma's house, too?" Another 4-year-old may say, "My dad's car is bigger than yours, so we can go faster." Over time, children's reasoning abilities become more logical.

Young children's reasoning is also influenced by their tendency toward magical thinking and animism—that is, giving lifelike qualities to inanimate objects. These perspectives account for many typical fears among this age group (e.g., the thunderstorm being God angry with them or the vacuum cleaner being a monster).

Concept acquisition. Young children are organizing information into concepts (e.g., car or chair), based on attributes that define an object or an idea (four wheels and you ride in it or four legs and you sit on it, respectively). They can also describe objects by their appearance and actions (the big, mean dog). At about age 5, children are capable of one-to-one correspondence, but their number concept is not fully developed. They may be confused, for example, when comparing the same number of objects arranged in shorter or longer rows (as in the Piagetian conservation task). While preschoolers have developed a wealth of concepts, they still find abstract concepts like time, space, and age very difficult to use in organizing their experiences.

Classification. From 3 through 5, children show increasing interest in number and quantity (counting, measuring, comparing) and more complex matching and classifying activities. Three-year-olds have difficulty sticking with one feature in sorting objects into a class. Other attributes tend to distract them from using one dimension consistently throughout the task. Preschoolers still have difficulty with seriation tasks, such as putting a group of six or eight sticks in order by size. Because children are just beginning to understand part/whole and hierarchical relationships, they may have difficulty grasping that an object can be in more than one class ("It's not a fruit—it's an apple!") or recognizing that with six girls and four boys there are more children than girls. By 4 or 5, children sort and classify using more than one attribute of an object (e.g., color and size).

Information processing in 3- through 5-year-olds

During early childhood, children's attention and memory are not fully developed, which accounts for some of the limitations in their capacity to reason and solve problems. Compared to primary-school children, preschoolers have difficulty focusing on details and are more distractible (Day 1975; Anderson & Levin 1976; Miller 1985), especially when required to listen passively or work on a prescribed task. Attention becomes more sustained and planful during these years (Cocking & Copple 1987), at least when children's interest is engaged. Although global adult demands to "Pay attention!" or "Listen!" are not helpful, more specific challenges ("Which two are alike?") provide just enough structuring of the task to bring it within the child's reach.

Young children have relatively poor recall of listlike information that is not embedded in meaningful contexts (Istomina 1975; Murphy & Brown 1975). Unlike older children, they do not make effective use of memory strategies, such as rehearsing a list or grouping items into meaningful categories (Perlmutter & Myers 1979; Waters & Andreassen 1983). Even when adults try to teach these strategies for improving memory, younger children do not automatically or accurately apply the strategies in situations requiring memory. Concreteness and egocentrism continue to make children more likely to understand and remember relationships, concepts, and strategies that they acquire through firsthand, meaningful experience. For

Young children are more likely to understand and remember relationships, concepts, and strategies that they acquire through firsthand, meaningful experience.

as to the freeing up of their memory capacity through reliance on routine patterns of behavior—scripts and the like—in familiar situations (Schank & Abelson 1977; Nelson 1978; Frese & Stewart 1984).

Social cognition

Social interaction plays a significant role in children's cognitive development. Children do not construct their own understanding of a concept in isolation but in the course of interaction with others. In developing the notion of "school," for instance, the child uses what she hears people say about school, glimpses of buildings identified by others as schools, and stories about school that she has had read to her. Her initial ideas may be challenged, confirmed, elaborated on, or altered by subsequent interactions with peers, older children, or adults. This process is known as the social construction of knowledge (Vygotsky 1978; see also Shantz 1975, 1982). As children's memory and other aspects of cognition improve and change, their relationships with other people are affected. From their experiences and interactions, children discover that other people have different points of view, which challenges and begins to break down their egocentrism. As children overcome their egocentric perspectives, they become more successful in interacting with other people, although not

instance, preschoolers who cannot recall multiple steps in a direction given repeatedly can relate specific, even sequential, events from highly salient experiences (a trip on an airplane, a visit to a theme park) from as long as a year before. Some of this improvement in long-term memory is related to preschoolers' increased use of organizing strategies as well always consistent in applying this knowledge (Flavell et al. 1968; Shantz 1975). Once again, the highly integrated nature of development and learning is evident. Children's cognition affects their social interaction and their social interaction affects their cognition. These new developments have important implications for children's social, emotional, and moral development.

Considerations for early childhood educators in supporting cognitive development

During the years from 3 through 5, children are gradually developing in problem solving and reasoning, classification and seriation, abstract concept formation, and other cognitive capacities. These processes will take several years to be well developed, in part because the child's concrete, egocentric, and unidimensional focus makes it difficult for the child to adequately represent what he or she experiences. Research on cognitive development in preschool-age children (Seifert 1993; Case & Okamoto 1996) leads to an important conclusion: young children have age-related limits in their cognitive capacities; they also have enormous capacities to learn and often underestimated capacities to think, reason, remember, and problem solve.

Skilled teachers do a great many things to foster children's learning and intellectual development; in some of these the teacher plays a facilitating role. For instance, knowledgeable early childhood teachers ensure ample time for sustained play, realizing its powerful benefits for cognitive development. They skillfully foster children's interaction and collaboration with peers, thus promoting language development, problem solving, perspective taking, and a host of other facets of intellectual growth.

Teachers also take active roles in promoting children's thinking and their acquisition of concepts and skills. These roles range from asking a well-timed question that provokes further reflection or investigation to showing children how to use a new tool or procedure. Early childhood educators have evolved approaches that are very successful in promoting children's engagement in challenging, meaningful problems and enterprises, for instance, by encouraging them to plan and review their work and to represent what they know verbally, pictorially, and through other modes and media (Copple, Sigel, & Saunders 1984; Edwards, Gandini, & Forman 1993; Forman 1994; Hohmann & Weikart 1995). A fuller description of teaching strategies that promote children's cognitive development is given in the section on guidelines for decisions about developmentally appropriate practice (see Part 1, pp. 16–22) and in this section in the examples of appropriate practice (pp. 123–35).

A sketch of social and emotional development in 3- through 5-year-olds

Closely related to children's advances in language and cognitive development during the preschool period are dramatic changes in the social, emotional, and moral domains. True relationships between peers first occur during the preschool years. Peers become important agents of socialization and provide important learning opportunities as well as the rough-and-tumble, playful, and inventive forms of interaction that young children enjoy at these ages. Many 3- through 5-year-olds become capable of playing together for extended periods, though they need periodic adult guidance to learn more socialized patterns of play, positive ways of dealing with others, and more effective verbal communication with peers.

Among the important aspects of social-emotional development during this period is the child's self-concept. Children's diminished egocentrism and improved reasoning ability help them to develop a more constant and stable perception of themselves despite the variation in their behaviors and in the responses they receive from other people. Along with this stable self-concept come feelings and judgments that children make about themselves. Children's self-evaluations and perceptions about their own worth—whether these are positive or negative—constitute their self-esteem.

Supporting children's developing self-concept and sense of positive self-esteem is an important task for parents and teachers of young children. Preschoolers tend to have an undifferentiated sense of their own competence, and they also tend to overestimate their own capabilities. Their overconfidence is partly due to their egocentrism and partly based in the rapid changes in their capabilities from one day to the next. Young children know that they cannot yet do many things, but they have also noticed that what they cannot do today, they can often do tomorrow (whether it is hopping on one foot, whistling, or tying their shoes). Despite their frequent overratings of their own competence, young children can also become quickly discouraged if they experience repeated disapproval, failure, or frustration. During early childhood, helping children develop a sense of themselves as initiators of action and competent actors is an important task of teachers and other adults.

The new cognitive abilities of preschool children allow for another aspect of their emotional development: fears. No other period of the life span is so characterized by fears. Children's increased capacity to think and fantasize lead them to imagine many terrible things happening. This fearfulness is typical development and will be overcome with adult caring and support as children themselves become more rational thinkers. At the same time, today's world *is* for too many young children a scary and unsafe place. Exposure to violence through the media, in the community, and even in their own homes is a real threat to young children's emotional and physical health. Teachers of young children today must help equip them to cope with these real fears and at the same time help them learn to separate reality from fantasy—a daunting task that requires deep understanding and application of principles of child development and learning (Garbarino et al. 1992; Slaby et al. 1995). Garbarino and his colleagues, who study the impact of violence, trauma, and war on young children's development, find that building resilience and healing trauma in children depend on establishing positive adult-child relationships. Trusting the adults in the early childhood setting and experiencing a sense of psychological safety, especially in their play and through their involvement in art, children are able to "reinstate their sense of inner control, reestablish self-worth and self-esteem, and develop relationships of trust" (Garbarino et al. 1992, 204).

Helping children to express strong emotions constructively and control aggression is a related task for early childhood teachers. Toddlers' aggression is most often instrumental, that is, connected to obtaining a toy or getting into a space occupied by another child. During the preschool years, however, children's aggression becomes less instrumental and more hostile, directed at other children who anger them in some way. This typical development of increased aggressive behavior in the preschool years is exacerbated today by the fact that many young children are regularly exposed to aggressive models through the media, requiring more adult attention to help children develop effective conflict-resolution skills (Slaby et al. 1995).

In children and adults alike, morality has emotional, cognitive, and behavioral components—both our feelings and reasoning come into play, and the consequences we experience have powerful effects on our actions (Berk 1997). During the preschool years, children's moral development reflects the significant development taking place in each of these areas, along with the impact of family, peers, schooling, and the wider society. An example of how young children's moral judgments reveal cognitive developmental age is the preschooler's tendency to focus on evident damage and other results of an action rather than the actor's intentions: a child accidentally breaking 20 cups is "badder" than a child intentionally breaking one (Kohlberg 1976).

Young children's social and emotional development is apparent during the preschool years in their play, peer interaction, prosocial behavior, aggression, self-regulation, and expression of feelings—a summary of which appears in the boxes on page 117.

Considerations for early childhood educators in supporting social and emotional development

Preschoolers are capable of engaging in truly cooperative play with their peers and forming real friendships. However, development of these important social skills is not automatic for children. They need coaching and adult supervision to learn and maintain appropriate behaviors with others. With a little assistance they can conduct themselves in positive ways and learn to play well with others. The ability of 3- to 5-year-olds to regulate their own emotions and behavior improves greatly over that of toddlers, but verbal and physical aggression increases. Young children do not learn to control aggression by being harshly punished or shamed; rather, they need teachers to help them learn alternatives to aggression for resolving conflicts, communicate their needs and feelings verbally, and maintain productive relationships with other children (Slaby et al. 1995).

Among the key tasks of early childhood educators is supporting children's developing sense of self. In some classrooms, however, the translation of supporting self-esteem and self-concept is reduced to having a unit called "I am special" (Katz 1995). It is in an environment of encouragement and genuine respect that children are able to develop confidence and competence, not by being told how wonderful or special they are but by being given chances to take initiative, experience success in performing difficult tasks, and figure things out for themselves.

Social and Emotional Development—Widely Held Expectations

For 3-year-olds —

- depending in part on previous experience with peers, may look on from the sidelines or engage in parallel play until becoming more familiar with the other children, or may engage in associative play patterns (playing next to a peer, chatting, and using toys but having separate individual intentions for behaviors)
- shows difficulty taking turns and sharing objects, activity changing form often during a play period; lacks ability to solve problems well among peers; usually needs help to resolve a social situation if conflict occurs
- plays well with others and responds positively if there are favorable conditions in terms of materials, space, and supervision (less likely to engage in prosocial behavior when any of these elements are lacking)
- acts more cooperatively than does toddler and wants to please adults (may revert to toddler behavior of thumb sucking, pushing, hitting, crying if unhappy with the outcome of a social situation)
- can follow simple requests; likes to be treated as an older child at times but may still put objects in mouth that can be dangerous or wander off if not carefully supervised
- expresses intense feelings, such as fear and affection; shows delightful, silly sense of humor

For 4-year-olds —

- still engages in associative play but begins true give-and-take, cooperative play
- shows difficulty sharing (some children more than others) but begins to understand turn taking and plays simple games in small groups
- becomes angry easily if things don't go her or his way at times; now prefers to play with others most often; seeks to resolve negative interactions although lacking verbal skills to resolve all conflicts
- begins to spontaneously offer things to others; wants to please friends; compliments others on new clothing or shoes; shows pleasure in having and being with friends
- exhibits occasional outbursts of anger but is learning that negative acts bring negative sanctions; quickly begins to justify an aggressive act ("He hit me first")
- knows increasingly what self-regulation behaviors are expected but shows difficulty following through on a task or becomes easily sidetracked, forgetting what was asked unless reminded; likes to dress him- or herself; gets own juice or snack; cleans up without constant supervision; unable to wait very long regardless of the promised outcome
- shows greater ability to control intense feelings like fear or anger (no more temper tantrums); still needs adults to help him or her express or control feelings at times

For 5-year-olds —

- enjoys dramatic play with other children
- cooperates well; forms small groups that may choose to exclude a peer
- understands the power of rejecting others; verbally threatens to end friendships or select others ("You can't come to my birthday party!"); tends to be bossy with others, resulting in too many leaders and not enough followers at times
- enjoys others and can behave in a warm and empathetic manner; jokes and teases to gain attention
- shows less physical aggression; more often uses verbal insult or threatens to hit someone
- can follow requests; may lie rather than admit to not following procedures or rules; may be easily discouraged or encouraged
- dresses and eats with minor supervision; reverts easily to younger behaviors when group norms are less than appropriate

Because self-regulation, emotional expression, and positive social relationships are such essential skills for later schooling and life, these are main goals of programs that serve children from 3 through 5. Teachers need to be aware of the fragility of each child's self-concept and self-esteem at this point in development. They need to clearly encourage children toward acceptable behavior and provide real opportunities for initiative taking and competence building. For these reasons, knowledgeable early childhood teachers do not view discipline as something to do so that they can get on with the curriculum. Instead, helping young children acquire self-discipline, self-confidence, and social skill is a large part of the early childhood curriculum. For children the preschool classroom is a laboratory for learning about human relationships; they have opportunities to play and work with other children, make choices and encounter the consequences of those choices, figure out how to enter play situations with others, negotiate social conflicts with language, and develop countless other skills that characterize socially competent human beings.

Self-regulation, emotional expression, and positive social relationships—essential skills for later schooling and life—are key goals of programs that serve children from 3 through 5.

Responding to individual and cultural variation

Putting in print a description of typical child development and learning, as we have done here, is risky. NAEYC's position statement on developmentally appropriate practice strongly stresses that individual and cultural variations are the norm, not the exception. The growing body of cross cultural studies of child development and early childhood practice demonstrates that many previously held tenets of child development do not hold up (Tobin, Davidson, & Wu 1989; Mallory & New 1994; Woodhead 1996).

Because of the limited research across cultures and the significant variation among children, we are not entirely comfortable describing age-related characteristics and expectations, even with many caveats. Such descriptions are often misused to label or categorize individual children.

Although NAEYC recognizes the enormous effects of individual and cultural factors on development, compelling evidence exists of the similarities among children of approximately the same age across cultures (e.g., Weikart 1995). Early childhood itself is still markedly different from middle childhood, adolescence, and adulthood. Unfortunately, failure to recognize young children's learning and developmental characteristics still results in practices, programs, and policies that, at best, miss important opportunities to support healthy development and, at worst, harm children. As Lilian Katz (1995) often reminds educators, the most important decisions are choices of error and one must often choose the "least worst error." Thus, we choose in this publication the error of providing a generalized profile of children at different ages and seek to correct that error by reminding readers of real children who inhabit homes and classrooms—each of whom is like no one else.

Joey, Katelyn, Andres, Nicole, Adam, and Lourdes are children we know. The following brief descriptions provide only a snapshot of the children at one point in time. But even such brief descriptions illustrate two fundamental principles of development and learning: tremendous individual variation exists between children of the same age, and different patterns of development occur within any one child. When one adds the other variables of cultural and contextual variation, understanding child development becomes even more complex. This endless variation is what makes early childhood interesting and

Joey and Katelyn—3-Year-Olds

Joey and Katelyn are cousins who were born on the same day. Joey is an only child and lives with his parents in a suburban community. For the first three years of his life, he has a warm, loving relationship with his family child care provider.

As a baby, Joey suffered chronic ear infections, and tubes were put in his ears at age 1. At 3½ he speaks mostly in one- or two-word utterances. He has resisted learning to use the toilet. It's clear that Joey's receptive language is good because he readily understands messages from many different speakers. He also communicates his wants clearly with words like "juice" and "blankey." Joey has a delightful smile, loves his blanket, runs wherever he goes until he almost drops from exhaustion, but he still fights going to sleep at night.

Concerned about his language development, Joey's parents have a specialist evaluate him and find that his hearing is fine. However, his language development is about six to nine months behind that of most children his age. The specialist gives Joey's parents ideas about reading and talking to him to encourage his language development.

When Joey enters the preschool environment with children older and more verbal than he is, his vocabulary increases rapidly and he is soon speaking in three- and four-word sentences ("Where's those guys?"). With more focused attention, he works on toileting and proudly gives a thumbs-up sign when displaying his "big boy" pants.

Katelyn has a loving, protective brother who is three years older. Her family lives in a rural community not far from where grandparents and aunts and uncles live. For as long as anyone can remember, Katelyn has seemed sure of herself; she won't smile when her picture is taken, and she's very clear about what she likes and doesn't like. She was potty trained at 2 and started talking early.

When she is 3½, she proudly displays her swimming goggles to her family at the beach. Her aunt says, "Oh, Katelyn, you look so official in your goggles." She stares back disdainfully and declares, "I'm not a fish, I'm a kid!" Katelyn's older brother loves working on his mom's computer, and Katelyn herself spends long periods of time with certain software programs she especially loves.

When she starts preschool at 3½, Katelyn is quite shy and rarely speaks; it takes several months for her teacher to begin to discover all her abilities.

Nicole and Andres—4-Year-Olds

Nicole is large for her age and slow in gaining motor control. At 4, she still doesn't alternate her feet when she walks up or down steps. She has a sister who is five years older, and Nicole tries to compete with her on word games and math problems. Nicole's vocabulary and communicative competence are comparable to those of most 7- or 8-year-olds. When given a doll as a gift at age 3, she responded, "Thanks. I really needed this." She also has intuitive understandings of number. When her new kindergarten teacher asks her to count, Nicole honestly inquires, "By 1s, 2s, 5s, or 10s?" Yet she isn't always confident in social situations and sometimes relies on her sister or an adult to help her get into a play situation with other children.

An only child who was born prematurely, at 4 Andres is small for his age. He has excellent coordination, loves sports, and can hit a plastic ball almost every time someone pitches it to him. Andres tends to learn new skills by watching others, and he won't try something unless he first is very sure that he can do it. He has shown little interest in drawing or writing despite his teacher's many attempts to encourage him. Not having scribbled or done much prior practicing, Andres sits down one day and writes his whole name. Andres is empathetic and gets along very well with other children in his child care center, almost intuitively knowing how to negotiate conflicts without fighting.

Adam and Lourdes—5-Year-Olds

Adam is the oldest child in his family and is often described by his grandmother as a "little old man." He is very serious at times and becomes especially anxious during thunderstorms or other events when he is afraid harm will come to his family. He has a December birthday, so, when he starts kindergarten, he is the youngest child in his class. Even though many family friends think the early start unwise, Adam's parents never consider holding him out for a year.

Adam does very well in school and is reading by the end of kindergarten. He attends a church-related school and takes an eager interest in the Bible study. One day when he and his cousins are playing that they are taking a trip, his uncle asks, "Where are you going?" Adam replies seriously, "Jerusalem." His uncle is surprised and asks, "Who told you about Jerusalem?" And Adam answers matter-of-factly, "Moses told me."

Lourdes lives with her mother and sister in a suburban community. When she starts kindergarten, she is almost monolingual in Spanish. She has excellent motor skills, both large and fine, and excels at almost any physical activity she tries.

Lourdes shows artistic ability, producing detailed drawings and paintings at an early age. She loves to dress and undress dolls. She has an affinity for music and learned to play the piano with ease.

In her first year at school, Lourdes struggles to learn English and make friends. She can sometimes be clumsy in approaching other children, so her mother coaches her on what to do and say to help other people get to like her. Together they rejoice when she receives her first birthday-party invitation.

When Lourdes's teacher wants to refer her to special education, her mother refuses and insists on her being moved to another classroom. In the new class Lourdes functions well, her English improves, and her teacher reports that, even though she still has trouble paying attention, she is doing much better.

why good teachers love teaching—because every child, every group of children, is different.

In the same way, each setting in which a child spends time has its own, different demands. Today, young children experience many transitions during early childhood. These transitions can create discontinuity or contribute to development, depending on what adults do to help children. Transitions are discussed here because, for many children, two of the most dramatic transitions occur during this period—the child's first participation in a group program and, at the end of this period, entry into the school setting.

Negotiating transitions: Changes and challenges

Transitions occur throughout early childhood, as

- a toddler enters child care for the first time;

- a 3-year-old moves from the toddler group to the preschool group in a child care center;

- a 4½-year-old moves from Head Start to kindergarten; and

- a first-grader goes from the classroom at 3:00 P.M. each day to the after-school child care group.

All change is stressful. But for young children who have limited experience and few well-developed coping strategies, change can be very stressful. When children move from one program to another or from one group to another within a program, adjustments are always necessary. However, the amount of stress and the time required to make successful adjustments can be lessened significantly if teachers and administrators plan and work together and with parents to implement smooth transitions. The limited research that is available on the topic finds that major tran-

sitions for children, such as entering kindergarten, can be very difficult due to the lack of continuity in teaching practices and absence of systems to ease transitions for children and families (Love et al. 1992). The following are four key elements to consider in helping ensure successful transitions for young children and their families (Glicksman & Hills 1981; ACYF 1987).

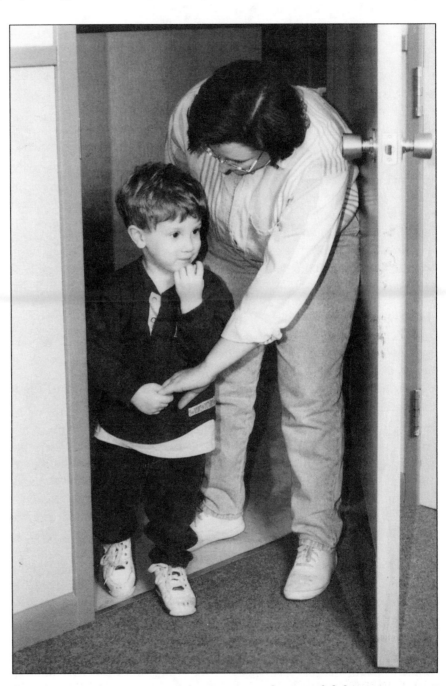

Because entering a new setting or group is stressful for many young children, teachers are ready to give extra support and to help a child join in.

1. Ensure program continuity by providing developmentally appropriate curriculum for all age levels in all educational settings

The more variance between different settings or groups that exists in developmental expectations and teaching practices, the more stressful the transition will be for young children. When the kindergarten program is more like a second grade, with desks and workbooks, than like a preschool, with blocks and dramatic-play props, the change is so abrupt that many children have difficulty adapting. When such a sharp contrast exists, the preschool teacher may introduce inappropriate academic instruction to help her group of children "get ready" for kindergarten. In such a situation, modifying an appropriate preschool program is a misguided attempt to ease the child's transition. The cause of the problem is not the preschool but the kindergarten—its curriculum and teaching practices need attention. Likewise, a similar problem often arises when happy kindergartners move on to a first grade where the expectations are so different that the transition is sometimes called "hitting the wall."

Differences in program content, teaching strategies, and expectations of children are not only usual but desirable. Programs *should* vary depending on the age of children and the needs and interests of individual children and families. Nevertheless, when the program at each age level is developmentally appropriate, children's transitions between different programs or groups will be smoother and more successful.

2. Maintain ongoing communication and cooperation between teachers and administrators at different programs

Children's transitions can be facilitated if teachers in one setting, such as a preschool or child care center, work together with teachers in settings where children will go next, such as a public-school kindergarten. Visits to programs can be arranged for children and parents. Teachers can visit each others' programs to note similarities and differences for which to prepare children. Such cooperation is advantageous for the teacher whose classroom or program the child will attend because the child is better prepared and less fearful. The teacher preparing the transition also benefits by broadening professional

contacts and knowing that she has fulfilled her professional responsibility to meet the developmental needs of the children in her care.

3. Prepare children for the transitions

"Next year you'll be in kindergarten, and then you won't be allowed to do that!"

"You'd better study this now because you have to know it when you start third grade."

"At the center, you'll have to use the potty like a big boy."

Messages like the above may be the only preparation children get for what in childhood are major life changes. Vague warnings about unfamiliar situations only serve to heighten children's anxieties about change. A more appropriate approach is to give children first-hand experiences, preferably by visiting the program setting and meeting the teacher—or getting acquainted in a home visit by the teacher. If such direct contact is impossible, a welcome letter to be read aloud by the parent or a phone call from the new teacher or caregiver are other options. Children need time to talk about their feelings and sensitive adults to listen and help prepare them for the exciting and positive changes that are a natural part of growing up.

4. Involve parents in the transitions

Parents usually feel as anxious as their children do about child care and school transitions, and children sense their stress. If parents' tensions are soothed, children will also face the change more calmly and confidently. Communication is the key to effective involvement of families. Transitions are more successful when teachers work with parents to help children negotiate the changes. Communication with parents is more effective if it is two-way; teachers inform parents about expectations but also listen to parents' concerns and goals for their children.

Attention to these four critical elements will lessen the negative impact of transition. Too often today, children's lives are unnecessarily fragmented. Formerly, transitions occurred once a year; now they occur several times daily. Parents and teachers need to work together to minimize the number of transitions required of children and to ease the transitions that are a necessary and healthy by-product of development.

Examples of Appropriate and Inappropriate Practices
for 3- through 5-Year-Olds

The following examples, which are by no means exhaustive, contrast appropriate, excellent practices in settings for children 3 through 5 years of age with inappropriate, less effective practices. The aim is not to issue a prescriptive set of practices but to encourage educators to reflect on their practice. In Part 1, pages 9–15, we have stated 12 principles of learning and development from which are derived the guidelines for decisions about developmentally appropriate practice (see Part 1, pp. 16–22) and the examples in this chart.

We remain convinced that people construct an understanding of a concept from considering both positive and negative examples. For this reason the chart includes not only practices that we see as developmentally appropriate but also practices we see as inappropriate or highly questionable for children of this age. Of the practices identified as inappropriate, some are harmful to children; others merely waste children's time.

There are many reasons for the persistence of inappropriate practices of the kinds described here. Some teachers are poorly prepared or out of date with the professional knowledge base. Compensation is insufficient to recruit and retain qualified staff. Class sizes are too big and adult-child ratios inadequate—making it difficult for teachers to know children and their families well. Children's emotional and physical needs are not being met, and the program and community lack the resources or services to assist them. The learning environment is unsafe or has insufficient supplies of learning materials. Administrative policies require outdated methods and structures. Any of these factors, or all of them together, could be the root cause for observed practices such as those described as inappropriate in this chart.

Appropriate Practices	Inappropriate Practices

Creating a caring community of learners

Promoting a positive climate for learning

Appropriate Practices	Inappropriate Practices
• Teachers ensure that classrooms or groups of young children function as caring communities. They help children learn how to establish positive, constructive relationships with adults and other children. Teachers support children's beginning friendships and provide opportunities for children to learn from each other as well as adults.	• No efforts are made to build a sense of the group as a community. To maintain classroom order, teachers continually separate children from friends and discourage conversation. Some children who lack social skills are isolated or rejected by peers and receive no help or support from teachers in developing positive relationships with others.
	• For administrative reasons, such as to maintain required staff-child ratios, the composition of the group changes many times in the course of a day or week, making it difficult for teachers to get to know children and for children to establish relationships with adults or each other.

Appropriate Practices	**Inappropriate Practices**

Creating a caring community of learners (cont'd)

Promoting a positive climate for learning (cont'd)

- To develop children's self-confidence and positive feelings toward learning, teachers provide opportunities for them to accomplish meaningful tasks and to participate in learning experiences in which they can succeed most of the time and yet be challenged to work on the edge of their developing capabilities.

- Planned activities often present no real challenge for children, such as when children engage in pasting precut forms.

- Teachers' expectations and requirements of children repeatedly exceed their developmental capabilities. For instance, 3-year-olds are expected to write their names legibly.

Fostering a cohesive group and meeting individual needs

- Teachers know each child well and design activities based on their knowledge of individual children's differing abilities, developmental levels, and approaches to learning. Responsiveness to individual differences in children's abilities and interests is evident in the curriculum, adults' interactions, and the environment (where photos of children and their families and children's work are displayed and spaces are provided for personal belongings).

- Teachers use many strategies to help build a sense of the group as a cohesive community. The children sometimes work on group activities that all can identify with, such as creating a mural for the classroom or planning a surprise event for parents. Teachers engage children in experiences that demonstrate the explicit valuing of each child, such as sending a "We miss you!" card to a sick classmate.

- Teachers bring each child's home culture and language into the shared culture of the school so that children feel accepted and gain a sense of belonging. The contributions of each child's family and cultural group are recognized and valued by others. Children learn to respect and appreciate similarities and differences among people.

- Teachers attempt to move all children through the same subskills in the same timeframe, although some children have already mastered them and others are not ready yet for them.

- The curriculum and environment are essentially the same for each group of children that comes through the program, without adaptation for the identities, interests, or work of that group of individuals.

- The sense of community is undermined by teachers' behaviors and techniques—for example, encouraging or allowing chronic tattling, scapegoating, teasing, or other practices that turn children against each other; or setting up games or situations in which the same children are always chosen and less-popular children are left out.

- Cultural and other individual differences are ignored. Some children do not see their race, language, or culture reflected in the classroom, so they do not feel part of the group.

- Differences among children are stressed to such an extent that some children are made to feel that they do not fit in.

Appropriate Practices	**Inappropriate Practices**
• Recognizing the value of working and playing collaboratively, teachers provide many opportunities for children to work in small, flexible groups that children informally create or the teacher organizes. Whole-group time is used as an opportunity to build a sense of community and shared purpose, such as through book reading, storytelling (about children's experiences), problem-solving as a group, or taking attendance by asking the group of children, "Who is absent today?" As each child encounters what others in the group think, say, and create, the child's own knowledge and understanding grow and change.	• Most of the time, teachers talk to the whole group or expect children all to do and presumably learn the same things at the same time without attention to their individual needs or differences or without opportunities to learn from each other.
	• Teachers frequently group children or set up competing teams by age, gender, or other ways that may diminish children's sense of their being part of a whole group. Teachers do not help children develop feelings of caring and empathy for each other.
• Children with disabilities or special learning needs are included in the classroom socially and intellectually as well as physically, and necessary supports are provided to ensure that their individual needs are met in that context. As much as possible, children with disabilities receive therapeutic or other services within their regular classroom to maintain their sense of continuity and support their feeling of belonging to and acceptance by the group.	• Children with disabilities or special learning needs are nominally assigned to a class, but most of their instruction occurs with special teachers elsewhere in the building. These children have only a vague sense of what is happening in their classroom, and the classroom teacher is unfamiliar with their educational program because she assumes they are getting intensive treatment from the special education teacher. Even while in the classroom, children with special needs may be isolated in a designated area.

Teaching to enhance development and learning

Environment and schedule	• Teachers plan and prepare a learning environment that fosters children's initiative, active exploration of materials, and sustained engagement with other children, adults, and activities. In choosing materials and equipment, teachers consider children's developmental levels and the social/cultural context, for instance, the geographic location of the program and the backgrounds of the children.	• The environment is disorderly, with little structure or predictability; children wander aimlessly without purpose or direction. The environment and materials provide too little variety, interest, or choice for children (for instance, puzzles are too easy or are missing pieces). The noise level is stressful for children and adults, impeding conversation and learning.
		• The organization of the environment severely limits children's interaction with other children and their opportunities to pursue engaging learning experiences. For example, children have to stay in their seats throughout most of the day or have to always ask teachers for materials.

Appropriate Practices

Inappropriate Practices

Teaching to enhance development and learning (cont'd)

Environment and schedule (cont'd)

- Teachers maintain a safe, healthy environment and careful supervision. They anticipate and avoid accidents or problems before these occur. Teachers guard children's safety, while also encouraging children to do what they are capable of doing for themselves. Teachers support children's age-appropriate risk taking within safe boundaries, for instance, supervising children wearing safety goggles as they use real tools for woodworking or children exploring a climb-on apparatus that is securely anchored, with adequate cushioning material in place.

- Teachers organize the daily schedule to allow for alternating periods of active and quiet time, adequate nutrition, and naptime (for younger children). Teachers allocate extended periods of time (at least one hour) for children to engage in play and projects. Children have ample time to explore and learn about the environment, investigate what sparks their curiosity, and experiment with cause-and-effect relationships.

- Teachers are frequently inattentive or careless about supervising children and monitoring the safety of the indoor and outdoor environments.

- Teachers do things for children that they could do themselves, because it is faster or less messy. Children do not have access to playground equipment, woodworking tools, or cooking equipment.

- Teachers overschedule activities, so children become overtired from too much activity without respite.

- Teachers schedule frequent transitions of activity, so children have insufficient time to become involved in a sustained investigation, dramatic-play interaction, or construction activity; children's behavior is restless and frenetic rather than interested and engaged. Playtime is provided only for a brief time early in the morning or late in the afternoon (and some children miss it altogether).

Learning experiences

- Teachers plan a variety of concrete learning experiences with materials and people relevant to children's own life experiences and that promote their interest, engagement in learning, and conceptual development. Materials include, but are not limited to, blocks and other construction materials, books and other language-arts materials, dramatic-play themes and props, art and modeling materials, sand and water with tools for measuring, and tools for simple science activities.

- Learning materials are primarily workbooks, ditto sheets, flash cards, and other materials that focus on drill and practice rather than engaging children's problem-solving and other higher-order thinking skills.

- The primary criterion for planning activities is that they be fun and entertaining to children, with no attempt to build higher-level abilities or connect the activity to intellectual or social goals.

Appropriate Practices	**Inappropriate Practices**
• Teachers provide opportunities for children to plan and select many of their own activities from among a variety of learning areas and projects they make available, based on program goals and information gathered about children's varying interests and abilities. Following their own interests, children choose from among various activities that typically include, but are not limited to, dramatic-play, construction, science and/or math experiences, games and puzzles, books and recordings, computers, art, and music. Teachers also use these various materials and experiences in teacher-planned activities to address learning goals; for example, a dramatic-play restaurant theme includes literacy (menus, order forms) and mathematical materials (play money, cash register).	• The program provides few or no opportunities for children's choices. The teacher does much of the activity for the children, such as cutting shapes or performing steps in an experiment. Children's alternative ways of doing things are rejected; copying the adult's model is considered more important. • The same materials are available day after day. Children have few new experiences from which to choose, either in terms of materials or the degree of challenge.

Language and communication

Appropriate Practices	**Inappropriate Practices**
• Teachers encourage children's developing language and communication skills by talking with them throughout the day, speaking clearly and listening to their responses, and providing opportunities for them to talk to each other. Teachers engage individual children and groups in conversations about real experiences, projects, and current events; they encourage children to describe their products or ideas, and they respond attentively to children's verbal initiatives.	• Adult agendas dominate classroom conversations. Children's responses or reactions are often viewed as interruptions of the adult's talk or work. • Teachers make it a priority to maintain a quiet environment; they ignore, reprimand, or punish children for talking or for not waiting to be called on. Teacher's speech is mostly one-way—for instance, much more often telling children what to do than facilitating back-and-forth exchanges—and usually to the group as a whole. For the most part, teachers address individual children only to admonish or discipline them. • Teachers "talk down" to children, asking questions children are not really meant to answer or using "baby talk" with preschoolers and kindergartners.
• In accordance with children's developing capacities, teachers incorporate experiences to enhance children's ability to actively listen and observe—for instance, children listening to a peer describe an event and then having the opportunity to ask questions for clarification or respond with their own ideas.	• During much of the day, children are expected to sit down, watch, be quiet, or do rote tasks for long periods of time. Teachers expect attentiveness during these times, but children often become restless or tune out. • Children spend a major portion of time passively sitting and waiting—for example, during transition times that are not planned in advance.

127

Appropriate Practices	**Inappropriate Practices**

Teaching to enhance development and learning (cont'd)

Teaching strategies

- Teachers observe and interact with individuals and small groups in all contexts (including teacher-planned and child-chosen learning experiences) to maximize their knowledge of what children can do and what each child is capable of doing with and without coaching, scaffolding, or other supportive assistance. To help children acquire new skills or understandings, teachers select from a range of strategies, such as asking questions, offering cues or suggestions, demonstrating a skill, adding more complex materials or ideas to a situation, or providing an opportunity for collaborating with peers.

- Teachers stimulate and support children's engagement in play and child-chosen activities. Teachers extend the child's thinking and learning within these child-initiated activities by posing problems, asking questions, making suggestions, adding complexity to tasks, and providing information, materials, and assistance as needed to enable a child to consolidate learning and to move to the next level of functioning.

- Teachers provide many opportunities for children to plan, think about, reflect on, and revisit their own experiences. Teachers engage children in discussion and representation activities (such as dictating, writing, drawing, or modeling in clay), which help children refine their own concepts and understanding and help the teacher understand what children know and think; for example, teachers use children's own hypotheses about how the world works to engage them in problem solving and experimentation.

- Teachers are uninvolved in children's play, exploration, and activities, viewing their role as mere supervision. Teachers fail to take an active role in promoting children's learning, assuming that children will develop skills and knowledge on their own without adult assistance.

- Children do much paper-and-pencil seatwork of the type in which there are only right or wrong answers. Thus teachers have little idea about the process of children's problem-solving or their specific areas of difficulty and competence. As a result, teachers do not know how to help children who do not understand and are frustrated or how to further challenge children who get the problem "right."

- Teachers do not help children make good use of choice time. They rarely intervene when children do the same things over and over or become disruptive. Rather than assisting children in developing decision-making skills, teachers overuse time-out or use punishment to control disruptive children.

- During children's play and choice activities, teachers assume a passive role, contributing little or nothing to children's play and learning.

- Teachers expect children to respond with one right answer most of the time. Teachers treat children's naive hypotheses as simply wrong answers rather than clues to how they think. Not realizing how much learning young children are capable of, teachers do not engage them in dialogues in which they take children's ideas seriously, nor do they encourage children to express ideas through other (nonverbal) modes of representation.

- Feeling pressured to cover the curriculum and believing that returning to the same topic or experience is a waste of time, teachers present a topic only once and fail to provide the revisiting opportunities that make fuller, more refined understanding possible.

Appropriate Practices	**Inappropriate Practices**
	• Underestimating children's intellectual ability, teachers do not provide time and support for children to develop concepts and skills.
• Teachers provide many opportunities for children to learn to work collaboratively with others and to socially construct knowledge as well as develop social skills, such as cooperating, helping, negotiating, and talking with other people to solve problems. Teachers foster the development of social skills and group problem solving at all times through modeling, coaching, grouping, and other strategies.	• Children are expected to work individually at desks or tables most of the time. Teacher directions are typically given to the total group, with few opportunities for meaningful social interaction with other children.
	• Teachers rarely use children's social relationships as a vehicle to address learning goals. Teaching strategies are not designed to support children's social competence.

Motivation and guidance

• Teachers draw on children's curiosity and desire to make sense of their world to motivate them to become involved in interesting learning activities. Teachers use verbal encouragement in ways that are genuine and related to an actual task or behavior, acknowledging children's work with specific comments like, "I see you drew your older sister bigger than your brother."	• A preponderance of experiences are either uninteresting and unchallenging, or so difficult and frustrating as to diminish children's intrinsic motivation to learn. To obtain children's participation, teachers typically rely on extrinsic rewards (stickers, privileges, etc.) or threats of punishment. Children with special needs or behavioral problems are isolated or punished for failure to meet group expectations rather than being provided with learning experiences at a reasonable level of difficulty.
In cases of children with special needs, such as those identified on an Individualized Education Plan, those resulting from environmental stress such as violence, or when a child's aggressive behavior continually threatens others, teachers may develop an individualized behavioral plan based on observations of possible environmental "triggers" and/or other factors associated with the behavior. This plan includes motivation and intervention strategies that assist and support the child to develop self-control and appropriate social behaviors.	• Teachers constantly and indiscriminately use praise ("What a pretty picture. That's nice.") so that it becomes meaningless and useless in motivating children.
• Teachers facilitate the development of social skills, self-control, and self-regulation in children by using positive guidance techniques, such as modeling and encouraging expected behavior, redirecting children to more acceptable activities, setting clear limits, and intervening to enforce consequences for unacceptable, harmful behavior. Teachers' expectations respect children's developing capabilities. Teachers are patient, realizing that not every minor infraction warrants a response.	• Teachers spend a great deal of time punishing unacceptable behavior, demeaning children who misbehave, repeatedly putting the same children who misbehave in time-out or some other punishment unrelated to the action, or refereeing disagreements.
	• Teachers do not set clear limits and do not hold children accountable to standards of acceptable behavior. The environment is chaotic, and teachers do not help children set and learn important rules of group behavior and responsibility.

129

Appropriate Practices	**Inappropriate Practices**

Constructing appropriate curriculum

Integrated curriculum

• Curriculum goals address learning in all developmental areas—physical, social, emotional, language, aesthetic, and intellectual.	• Curriculum goals are narrowly focused on a few dimensions of the child's development or on one dimension at a time, without recognition that all areas of a child's development are interrelated.
	• Goals of the program are unclear or unknown.
• Curriculum content from various disciplines, such as math, science, or social studies, is integrated through themes, projects, play, and other learning experiences, so children develop an understanding of concepts and make connections across disciplines. For example, in exploring patterns in math, children use art, music, objects in nature, pegboards, blocks, and other materials.	• Children's learning and cognitive development are seen as occurring in separate content areas, and times are set aside to teach each subject without integration.
	• Teachers create an excessively theme-driven curriculum rather than a curriculum shaped by children's developmental characteristics and the content and skills (including thinking skills) they need to acquire.

The continuum of development and learning

• The curriculum plan is designed to help children explore and acquire the key concepts and tools of inquiry of the various disciplines in ways that are comprehensible and accessible for their age. For example, science experiences include opportunities in which children explore and directly observe changes and phenomena. Teachers are knowledgeable about the continuum of development and learning for preschool children in each content area. For example, teachers understand the continuum of emerging literacy and support individual children as they learn to recognize letter names and initial sounds and to hear and generate rhyming words.	• Curriculum content lacks intellectual integrity and is trivial, unimportant, and unworthy of children's attention. Curriculum expectations are too low, underestimating children's cognitive capacity (such as by limiting math exploration to numbers 1 through 5). Children are given little exposure to print, number concepts, or science.
	• Curriculum expectations are not well matched to children's intellectual capacities and developmental characteristics, so children do not understand what is being taught. Teachers fail to recognize the continuum of learning in the discipline areas and how these apply to children in this age range. For example, teachers expect children to perform the task of addition before they understand one-to-one correspondence and other fundamentals of number.

Appropriate Practices	**Inappropriate Practices**
Coherent, effective curriculum	

Appropriate Practices

Coherent, effective curriculum

• Teachers plan and implement a coherent curriculum to help children achieve important developmental and learning goals. They draw on their knowledge of the content, what is likely to interest children of that age, and the context of the children's experiences. They also recognize that learning experiences are more effective when the curriculum is responsive to the children's interests and ideas as they emerge.

• Teachers plan curriculum that is responsive to the specific context of children's experiences. Culturally diverse and nonsexist activities and materials are provided to help individual children develop positive self-identity, to construct understanding of new concepts by building on prior knowledge and creating shared meaning, and to enrich the lives of all children with respectful acceptance and appreciation of differences and similarities. Books and pictures include people of different races, ages, and abilties, and of both genders in various roles.

Curriculum content and approaches

• Teachers use a variety of approaches and provide daily opportunities to develop children's **language and literacy** skills through meaningful experiences, such as listening to and reading stories and poems; taking field trips; dictating stories; seeing classroom charts and other print in use; participating in dramatic play and other experiences requiring communication; talking informally with other children and adults; and experimenting with writing by drawing, copying, and using their own "invented" spelling. Adults read to children every day in various contexts, such as lap book reading to individuals, guided reading to small groups, as well as occasional large-group storytime. Children have opportunities to develop print awareness, sense of story, appreciation for literature, and understanding of the various uses of the written word, while learning particular letter names and letter-sound combinations and recognizing words that are meaningful to them (such as their names, names of friends, phrases like "I love you," and commonly seen functional words like *exit*).

Inappropriate Practices

• Teachers rigidly follow a prescribed curriculum plan (sometimes commercially prepared or adopted by a district or school) without attention to individual children's interests and needs or the specific and changing context. For example, regardless of where the program is located or the local weather conditions, children study snow in January. Teachers stick with their previously planned topic regardless of current circumstances (the class rabbit just gave birth) or environmental conditions (it's snowing).

• Teachers do not adequately plan curriculum; experiences are random; and there is no accountability for children's learning.

• Children's cultural and linguistic backgrounds and other individual differences are ignored or treated as deficits to be overcome.

• Multicultural curriculum reflects a "tourist approach" in which the artifacts, food, or other particulars of different cultures are presented without meaningful connections to the children's own experiences. Some children's cultural traditions are noted in ways that convey that they are exotic or deviations from the "normal" majority culture.

• In reading and writing instruction, teachers follow a rigid sequence of prerequisites; for example, children do not have experiences with books or other meaningful text until they have mastered the whole set of predetermined phonics skills. A single approach is used for all children regardless of what some can already do. For instance, letters are introduced one at a time and with insufficient context in words; some children are bored because they already know all the letters, and other children are confused because they cannot make sense of isolated bits of information.

• Teachers miss opportunities to encourage children's language and emergent literacy abilities, discouraging children's conversation or failing to support children's interest in and knowledge of books and print. Teachers only read stories occasionally and always to the whole group.

Appropriate Practices	**Inappropriate Practices**

Constructing appropriate curriculum (cont'd)

Curriculum content and approaches (cont'd)

- Teachers use a variety of strategies to help children develop concepts and skills in **mathematics, science, social studies, health**, and other content areas through a variety of meaningful activities. For example, teachers design activities for children to seek solutions to concrete problems; construct with blocks; measure sand, water, or ingredients for cooking; observe and record changes in the environment; work with wood and tools; classify objects for a purpose; explore animals, plants, water, wheels, and gears; use art media, music, movement, and other modes to represent what they see, understand, and feel; learn and practice routines of healthy living.

- Children have daily opportunities for **aesthetic expression** and appreciation through art and music. Children experiment and enjoy various forms of dramatic play, music, and dance. A variety of art media, such as markers, crayons, paints, and clay, are available for creative expression and representation of ideas and feelings.

- Children have opportunities throughout the day to move freely and use large muscles in planned movement activities. Planned indoor and outdoor activities, involving balancing, running, jumping, and other vigorous movements, are provided to increase the child's understanding of movement and to support **gross-motor development**.

- Children have opportunities throughout the day to develop **fine-motor skills** through play activities such as pegboards, beads to string, construction sets, and puzzles; drawing, painting, clay sculpting, cutting, and other similar activities; and such routines as pouring juice or dressing themselves.

- Instruction focuses only on isolated skill development through memorization and rote, such as circling an item on a worksheet, memorizing facts, reciting in unison, or drilling with flash cards.

- Teachers are inattentive or uninvolved in children's play and do not look for opportunities to support intellectual development during play activities and daily routines.

- Art and music are seen only as diversions or once-a-week activities, disconnected from the goals and activities of the rest of the program. Teachers fail to help children acquire the knowledge and skills inherent in art and music.

- Art and music are provided only when time permits. Art consists of coloring predrawn forms, copying an adult-made model of a product, or following other adult-prescribed directions.

- Opportunity for large-muscle activity (indoor or outdoor) is limited to once a day or less. Outdoor time is limited because it is viewed as interfering with instructional time.

- Adults are not involved during outdoor time, which is viewed as recess (a way to get children to use up excess energy) rather than an integral part of children's skill development and learning.

- Children are given fine-motor tasks that are too difficult or are expected to persist at fine-motor work for long periods of time.

- Teachers provide insufficient opportunity for children to develop fine-motor skill. Fine-motor activity is limited to handwriting practice, coloring predrawn worksheets, or similar structured lessons.

Appropriate Practices	**Inappropriate Practices**
• Children have opportunities and teachers' support to demonstrate and practice developing **self-help skills,** such as dressing, toileting, serving and feeding themselves, brushing teeth, washing hands, and helping to pick up toys. Teachers are patient when there are occasional toileting accidents, spilled food, and unfinished jobs.	• Teachers or other adults often perform routine tasks for children because it is faster and less messy. • Adults display anger or shame children for toileting accidents or spills.

Assessing children's learning and development

• Teachers use observational assessment of children's progress, examination of children's work samples, and documentation of their development and learning to plan and adapt curriculum to meet individual children's developmental or learning needs, identify children who may have a learning or developmental problem, communicate with parents, and evaluate the program's effectiveness.	• Children's progress is measured by how well they conform to rigid expectations and perform on standardized readiness tests. Test results are used to group or label children (e.g., as "unready") but are not used to provide information about children's degrees of understanding or progress. • There is no accountability for what children are doing and little focus on supporting learning and development. No systematic observations or assessments of children's progress or needs are done. When individual children appear to be having difficulty outside the typical performance range, no systematic assessment is conducted to adapt curriculum or to follow up.
• The program has a place for every child of legal entry age, regardless of the developmental level or prior learning of the child. Teachers work together to help all children develop and learn, adapting instruction to the developmental needs and levels of the individual children. Decisions that have a major impact on children are based on multiple sources of information, including that obtained from observations by teachers and parents and specialists, when such information is applicable for identification, diagnosis, and planning for children with special needs or disabilities.	• Readiness or achievement tests are used as the sole criterion for entrance to the program or to recommend that children be retained or placed in remedial classrooms. Eligible-age children are denied entry to the program on the basis of a screening test or other arbitrary determination of the child's lack of readiness. Children are denied entry or retained because they are judged not ready on the basis of inappropriate and inflexible expectations of their academic, social, or self-help abilities.

Appropriate Practices	**Inappropriate Practices**

Reciprocal relationships with parents

- Teachers work in partnership with parents, communicating regularly to build mutual understanding and ensure that children's learning and developmental needs are met. They listen to parents, seek to understand their goals and preferences for their children, and respect cultural and family differences.

- Teachers and parents work together to make decisions about how best to support children's development and learning or to handle problems or differences of opinion as they arise. Teachers solicit and incorporate parents' knowledge about their children into ongoing assessment, evaluation, and planning procedures.

- Parents are always welcome in the program, and home visits by teachers are encouraged. Opportunities for parent participation are arranged to accommodate parents' schedules. Parents have opportunities to be involved in ways that are comfortable for them, such as observing, reading to children, or sharing a skill or hobby.

- Teachers communicate with parents only about problems or conflicts. Parents view teachers as the only experts and feel isolated from their child's experiences.

- Teachers blame parents when children have difficulty, demand that parents punish children at home for infractions at school, or capitulate to parents' demands, even if these are potentially harmful.

- Teachers view parents' visits to the program as intrusive and discourage parents from visiting by saying such things as, "He'd be better behaved if you'd leave." Parent participation is so limited that parents' rare visits disrupt the classroom.

- Parent meetings or other participation opportunities occur only during the day when many employed parents are unavailable.

Program policies

- Teachers are qualified to work with preschool and kindergarten children as a result of college-level preparation in early childhood education or child development and supervised experience with this age group. Teachers engage in ongoing professional development activities. Time and opportunities are available for teachers to plan, reflect on their practices, and collaborate with colleagues.

- Teachers lack early childhood professional preparation and/or do not engage in ongoing professional development; they do not remain current in their practice by reading professional literature nor do they engage in reflection on their practice with colleagues.

- Teachers with no specialized training or supervised experience in working with 3- through 5-year-old children are viewed as qualified because they are state certified at some other age level of certification.

Appropriate Practices	**Inappropriate Practices**
• The group size and ratio of teachers to children is limited to enable individualized and age-appropriate programming. Three-year-olds are in groups of no more than 16 children with 2 adults, and 4-year-olds are in groups of no more than 20 children with 2 adults. Kindergartners do not exceed 25 with 2 adults.	• Because older children can function reasonably well in large groups, it is assumed that group size and number of adults can be the same for 3- through 5-year-olds as for elementary-grade children.
	• Although the group size and adult-child ratio meet recommended standards, adults do not take advantage of the smaller group to individualize curriculum and teaching.
• The program is administered and staffed in such a way as to ensure continuity of care and relationships among adults and children over a given day and across many months and even years. Strategies like multiage grouping or keeping a group of children with the same teachers more than one year may be used to achieve this goal.	• The group composition changes frequently during the course of a day as well as every few months. Teacher turnover, combined with constant regrouping of children, makes it impossible for children and teachers to know each other well and establish positive relationships or for children to maintain friendships with each other.
• Administrators responsible for programs serving children between 3 and 6 years of age have professional preparation or inservice training relevant to the development and learning of this age group, including training on establishing positive relationships with families.	• Administrators of programs serving children between 3 and 6 years of age may have expertise in management but no specialized preparation or inservice training relevant to the development and learning of young children.

Nothing contributes more to children's becoming eager readers than enjoying books together.

References

AAP & APHA (American Academy of Pediatrics and American Public Health Association). 1992. *Caring for our children: National health and safety performance standards—Guidelines for out-of-home child care programs.* Washington, DC: APHA.

ACYF (Administration for Children, Youth, and Families). 1987. *Easing the transition from preschool to kindergarten.* Washington, DC: U.S. Department of Health and Human Services.

Adams, G., & J. Sandfort. 1994. *First steps, promising futures: State prekindergarten initiatives in the early 1990s.* Washington, DC: Children's Defense Fund.

Anderson, D., & S. Levin. 1976. Young children's attention to *Sesame Street. Child Development* 47: 806–11.

Behrmann, M.M., & E.A. Lahm. 1994. Computer applications in early childhood special education. In *Young children: Active learners in a technological age,* eds. J. Wright & D. Shade, 105–20. Washington, DC: NAEYC.

Berk, L. 1996. *Infants and children: Prenatal through middle childhood.* 2d ed. Boston: Allyn & Bacon.

Berk, L. 1997. *Child development.* 4th ed. Boston: Allyn & Bacon.

Berk, L., & A. Winsler. 1995. *Scaffolding children's learning.* Washington, DC: NAEYC.

Bowman, B. 1994. The challenge of diversity. *Phi Delta Kappan* 76 (3): 218–24.

Brice-Heath, S. 1988. Language socialization. In *Black children and poverty: A developmental perspective,* ed. D.T. Slaughter, 29–41. San Francisco: Jossey-Bass.

Case, R., & Y. Okamoto. 1996. *The role of central conceptual structures in the development of children's thought.* Monographs of the Society of Research in Child Development, vol. 61, no. 2, serial no. 246. Chicago: University of Chicago Press.

Chomsky, N. 1968. *Language and mind.* New York: Harcourt, Brace & World.

Clements, D., & B. Nastasi. 1993. Electronic media and early childhood education. In *Handbook of research on the education of young children,* ed. B. Spodek, 251–75. New York: Macmillan.

Cocking, R.R., & C.E. Copple. 1987. Social influences on representational awareness: Plans for representing and plans as representation. In *Blueprints for thinking: The role of planning in cognitive development,* eds. S.L. Friedman, E.K. Scholnick, & R.R. Cocking, 428–65. New York: Cambridge University Press.

Copple, C., I.E. Sigel, & P. Saunders. 1984. *Educating the young thinker: Classroom strategies for cognitive growth.* Hillsdale, NJ: Erlbaum.

Dale, P. 1976. *Language development: Structure and function.* New York: Holt, Rinehart & Winston.

Day, M.C. 1975. Developmental trends in visual scanning. In *Advances in child development and behavior, Vol. 10*, ed. H.W. Reese. New York: Academic.

Edwards, C., L. Gandini, & G. Forman, eds. 1993. *The hundred languages of children: The Reggio Emilia approach to early childhood education*. Norwood, NJ: Ablex.

Flavell, J.H., P.T. Botkin, C.L. Fry, J.W. Wright, & P.E. Jarvis. 1968. *The development of role taking and communication skills in children*. New York: John Wiley & Sons.

Flege, J.E. 1981. Phonological basis of foreign accent: A hypothesis. *Teachers of English to Speakers of Other Languages Quarterly* 15 (4): 443–55.

Forman, G. 1994. Different media, different languages. In *Reflections on the Reggio Emilia approach*, eds. L. Katz & B. Cesarone, 37–46. Urbana, IL: ERIC Clearinghouse on Elementary and Early Childhood Education.

Frese, M., & J. Stewart. 1984. Skill-learning as a concept in life-span developmental psychology: An action-theoretic approach. *Human Development* 27: 145–62.

Friedman, S.L., E.K. Scholnick, & R.R. Cocking. 1987. Reflections on reflections: What planning is and how it develops. In *Blueprints for thinking: The role of planning in cognitive development*, eds. S.L. Friedman, E.K. Scholnick, & R.R. Cocking, chapter 7. Cambridge, England: Cambridge University Press.

Gallahue, D. 1993. Motor development and movement skill acquisition in early childhood education. In *Handbook of research on the education of young children*, ed. B. Spodek, 24–41. New York: Macmillan.

Garbarino, J., N. Dubrow, K. Kostelny, & C. Pardo. 1992. *Children in danger: Coping with the consequences of community violence*. San Francisco: Jossey-Bass.

Gelman, R., & E. Meck. 1983. Preschoolers' counting: Principles before skill. *Cognition* 13: 343–59.

Glicksman, K., & T. Hills. 1981. *Easing the child's transition between home, child care center and school: A guide for early childhood educators*. Trenton: New Jersey Department of Education.

Hale-Benson, J. 1986. *Black children: Their roots, culture, and learning styles*. Baltimore: Johns Hopkins University Press.

Harris, A.C. 1986. *Child development*. St. Paul, MN: West.

Hart, B., & T. Risley. 1995. *Meaningful differences in the everyday experiences of young American children*. Baltimore: Paul H. Brookes.

Hartup, W.W., & S.G. Moore. 1990. Early peer relations: Developmental significance and prognostic implications. *Early Childhood Research Quarterly* 5 (1): 1–17.

Heath, S.B. 1983. *Ways with words*. New York: Cambridge University Press.

Hohmann, M., & D. Weikart. 1995. *Educating young children: Active learning practices for preschool and child care programs*. Ypsilanti, MI: High/Scope Educational Research Foundation.

Howes, C. 1988. Relations between early child care and schooling. *Developmental Psychology* 24 (1): 53–57.

Istomina, Z.M. 1975. The development of voluntary memory in preschool-age children. *Soviet Psychology* 13 (Summer): 5–64.

Kagan, L., E. Moore, & S. Bredekamp, eds. 1995. *Reconsidering children's early development and learning: Toward common views and vocabulary*. Washington, DC: National Education Goals Panel.

Kamii, C. 1982. *Number in preschool and kindergarten*. Washington, DC: NAEYC.

Katz, L. 1995. *Talks with teachers of young children: A collection*. Norwood, NJ: Ablex.

Katz, L., & S. Chard. 1989. *Engaging children's minds: The project approach*. Norwood, NJ: Ablex.

Kendrick, A., R. Kaufmann, & K. Messenger. 1995. *Healthy young children: A manual for programs*. Washington, DC: NAEYC.

Kohlberg, L. 1976. Moral stages and moralization: The cognitive-developmental approach. In *Moral development and behavior: Theory, research, and social issues*, ed. T. Lickona, 34–55. New York: Wiley.

Ladefoged, P. 1969. *Child-adult differences in second language acquisition*. Rowley, MA: Newbury House.

Lee, A.M. 1980. Childrearing practices and motor performance of black and white children. *Research Quarterly for Exercise and Sport* 51: 494–500.

Love, J., M.E. Logue, J.V. Trudeau, & K. Thayer. 1992. *Transitions to kindergarten in American schools: Final report of the national transition study*. Washington, DC: U.S. Department of Education, Office of Policy and Planning.

Mallory, B., & R. New, eds. 1994. *Diversity and developmentally appropriate practices: Challenges for early childhood education*. New York: Teachers College Press.

Miller, P. 1982. *Amy, Wendy, and Beth: Language learning in south Baltimore*. Austin: University of Texas Press.

Miller, P.H. 1985. Metacognition and attention. In *Metacognition, cognition, and human performance, Vol. 2*, eds. D.L. Forest, M. Pressley, G.E. MacKinnon, & T.G. Waller. New York: Academic.

Mitchell, A., M. Seligson, & F. Marx. 1989. *Early childhood programs and the public schools*. Dover, MA: Auburn House.

Murphy, M.D., & A.L. Brown. 1975. Incidental learning in preschool children as a function of level of cognitive analysis. *Journal of Experimental Psychology* 19: 509–23.

NAEYC. 1996. NAEYC position statement: Responding to linguistic and cultural diversity—Recommendations for effective early childhood education. *Young Children* 51 (2): 4–12.

Nebraska and Iowa State Departments of Education. 1993. *The primary program: Growing and learning in the heartland. A joint project of Nebraska Department of Education, Iowa Department of Education, Iowa Area Education Agencies, & Head Start/State Collaboration Project*. Lincoln, NE: Author.

Nelson, K. 1978. How children represent knowledge of their world in and out of language: A preliminary report. In *Children's thinking: What develops?* ed. R.S. Siegler. Hillsdale, NJ: Erlbaum.

Pellegrini, A., & B. Boyd. 1993. The role of play in early childhood development and education: Issues in definition and function. In *Handbook of research on the education of young children*, ed. B. Spodek, 105–21. New York: Macmillan.

Pellegrini, A., & L. Galda. 1982. The effects of thematic-fantasy training on the development of children's story comprehension. *American Educational Research Journal* 19: 443–52.

Pellegrini, A., & L. Galda. 1991. Longitudinal relationships among preschoolers' symbolic play, linguistic verbs, and emergent literacy. In *Play and early literacy*, ed. J. Christie, 47–68. Albany: State University of New York Press.

Perlmutter, M., & N.A. Myers. 1979. Development of recall in 2- to 4-year-old children. *Developmental Psychology* 15: 73–83.

Piaget, J. 1952. *The origins of intelligence in children*. New York: Norton.

Pramling, I. 1991. Learning about "the shop": An approach to learning in preschool. *Early Childhood Research Quarterly* 6 (2): 151–66.

Reggio Emilia Department of Early Education. 1987. *The hundred languages of children: Narrative of the possible* (exhibit catalog). Reggio Emilia, Region of Emilia Romagna, Italy: Author. (Assessorato Scuola Infanzia e Asilo Nido, Via Guido Castello 12, 42100 Reggio Emilia, Italy.)

Sameroff, A., & S. McDonough. 1994. Educational implications of developmental transitions: Revisiting the 5- to 7-year shift. *Phi Delta Kappan* 76 (3): 188–93.

Schank, R.C., & R.P. Abelson. 1977. *Scripts, plans, goals, and understanding.* Hillsdale, NJ: Erlbaum.

Schrader, C. 1989. Written language use within the context of young children's symbolic play. *Early Childhood Research Quarterly* 4 (2): 225–44.

Schrader, C. 1990. Symbolic play as a curricular tool for early literacy development. *Early Childhood Research Quarterly* 5 (1): 79–103.

Seifert, K. 1993. Cognitive development and early childhood education. In *Handbook of research on the education of young children,* ed. B. Spodek, 9–23. New York: Macmillan.

Shantz, C.U. 1975. The development of social cognition. In *Review of child development research,* vol. 5, ed. E.M. Hetherington. Chicago: University of Chicago Press.

Shantz, C.U. 1982. Children's understanding of social rules and the social context. In *Social cognitive development in context,* ed. F.C. Serafica. New York: Guilford.

Shuy, R.W., & J. Staton. 1982. Assessing oral language ability in children. In *The language of children reared in poverty: Implications for evaluation and intervention,* eds. L. Feagans & D.C. Farran, 181–95. New York: Academic.

Siegler, R. 1983. Information processing approaches to child development. In *Handbook of child psychology Vol. 1,* ed. P. Mussen, 129–211. New York: Wiley.

Slaby, R., W.C. Roedell, D. Arezzo, & K. Hendrix. 1995. *Early violence prevention: Tools for teachers of young children.* Washington, DC: NAEYC.

Smart, M.S., & R.C. Smart. 1973. *Preschool children: Development and relationships.* New York: Macmillan.

Smilansky, S., & L. Shefatya. 1990. *Facilitating play: A medium for promoting cognitive, socioemotional, and academic development in young children.* Gaithersburg, MD: Psychosocial & Educational Publications.

Sroufe, L.A., R.G. Cooper, & G.B. DeHart. 1993. *Child development: Its nature and course.* 2d ed. New York: McGraw-Hill.

Stipek, D., D. Daniels, D. Galluzzo, & S. Milburn. 1992. Characterizing early childhood education programs for poor and middle-class children. *Early Childhood Research Quarterly* 7 (1): 1–19.

Tobin, J., D. Davidson, & D. Wu. 1989. *Preschool in three cultures: Japan, China, and the United States.* New Haven, CT: Yale University Press.

Vygotsky, L. 1978. *Mind in society.* Cambridge, MA: Harvard University Press.

Waters, H.S., & C. Andreassen. 1983. Children's use of memory strategies under instructions. In *Cognitive strategies: Developmental, educational, and treatment-related issues,* eds. M. Pressley & J.R. Levin. New York: Springer-Verlag.

Weikart, D. 1995. An observational look at early childhood settings in 15 countries. Presentation at the Annual Conference of the National Association for the Education of Young Children, Washington, D.C., 29 November.

White, S. 1965. Evidence for a hierarchical arrangement of learning processes. In *Advances in child development and behavior,* eds. L.P. Lipsett & C.S. Spiker, 187–220. New York: Academic.

White, S. 1970. Some general outlines of the matrix of developmental changes between five and seven years. *Bulletin of the Orton Society* 20: 41–57.

Whiting, B., & C. Edwards. 1988. *Children of different worlds: The formation of social behavior.* Cambridge, MA: Harvard University Press.

Wong Fillmore, L. 1992. When learning a second language means losing the first. *Early Childhood Research Quarterly* 6 (3): 323–46.

Woodhead, M. 1996. *In search of the rainbow: Pathways to quality in large-scale programmes for young disadvantaged children.* The Hague, Netherlands: Bernard van Leer Foundation.

Wright, J., & D. Shade, eds. 1994. *Young children: Active learners in a technological age.* Washington, DC: NAEYC.

Developmentally Appropriate Practice for 6- through 8-Year-Olds in the Primary Grades

The NAEYC position statement presented in Part 1 points out that teacher decision-making is necessary for developmentally appropriate practice. The purpose of Part 5 is to help teachers in this complex decisionmaking process and in applying to primary-grade education the principles of development and learning and the guidelines for practice articulated in the position statement. This section includes (1) an overview of the integrated nature of learning and development during the age range of 6 through 8; (2) a sketch of the developmental characteristics and widely held expectations of children from 6 through 8 years of age (children usually enrolled in first through third grades) and considerations for early childhood educators; (3) a discussion of individual and cultural variation; and (4) examples of teaching practices in the primary grades that are consistent or inconsistent with the guidelines for decisions about developmentally appropriate practice (see Part 1, pp. 16–22), which are derived from well-established principles of development and learning.

The trend toward critical examination of our nation's educational system has recently included concerns about the quality of education provided in elementary schools (Copple 1992; NCC 1993; Boyer 1995; Carnegie Task Force 1996). Educators and policymakers have raised concerns because "by the fourth grade, the performance of *most* children in the United States is below what it should be for the nation and is certainly below the achievement lev-

els of children in competing countries" (Carnegie Task Force 1996, viii). The failure of our schools to educate all children to their fullest potential has many causes. The Report of the Carnegie Task Force on Learning in the Primary Grades summarizes the most significant reasons why schools fail:

> They fail because of the low expectations they hold out for many students; the heavy reliance that schools place on outmoded or ineffective curricula and teaching methods; poorly prepared or insufficiently supported teachers; weak home/school linkages; the lack of adequate accountability systems; and ineffective use of resources by schools and school systems. (Carnegie Task Force 1996, ix)

As the NAEYC position statement on developmentally appropriate practice (see Part 1) states, too many schools narrow the curriculum or adopt instructional approaches that are incompatible with current knowledge about how young children learn and develop. Specifically, schools often emphasize rote learning of academic skills rather than active, experiential learning in a meaningful context. As a result, many children are being taught basic academic skills, but they are not learning to apply those skills to problems and real situations. They are not developing more complex thinking skills, such as conceptualizing and problem solving (Mullis et al. 1991; Mullis et al. 1994; Campbell et al. 1996; NEGP 1996). Other children, including disproportionate numbers of children from low-income families, are not acquiring the basic skills—the fundamentals of reading, writing, communicating, and basic conceptual understanding of mathematics, science, and other content areas—that are needed as a foundation for all later learning in school (Alexander & Entwisle 1988; NCC 1993).

Along with concerns about uneven academic progress among our nation's children are growing concerns about children's moral, social, and emotional development. Increases in aggressive, even criminal, behavior and substance abuse among younger and younger children are cause for alarm. Less dramatic but more pervasive is the concern about the general decline of civility and caring in human relationships (see Lickona 1992; Noddings 1992; Bennett 1995; Boyer 1995; Character Counts! Coalition 1996). Along with the home, church, and community, primary-grade schools and school-age care programs are among the key settings in which children's character is shaped. Therefore, the primary-grade years are an important time not only to support children's intellectual development but also to help them develop the ability to work collaboratively with peers; express tolerance, empathy, and caring for other people; function responsibly; and gain positive dispositions toward learning, such as curiosity, initiative, persistence, risk taking, and self-regulation.

The NAEYC position statement describes principles of child development and learning and guidelines for decisions about developmentally appropriate practice in programs serving children from birth through age 8. Decisions about educational practice draw on many sources of information. For decisions to be developmentally appropriate, teachers must draw on at least three important sources of knowledge. They use their knowledge of how young children learn and develop, including knowledge of the sequences and structures of content learning and skills acquisition. Teachers also make decisions in terms of what they know about the individual children and families they work with. Finally, teachers use their knowledge of the social and cultural context within which children and families live.

Decisions about curriculum are always complex because curriculum derives from many sources, including the content of the disciplines, the goals of families and the community, and the demands of society. The curriculum in preschool programs typically provides opportunities for children to acquire knowledge of content in ways that support and re-

flect children's development. As children progress into the primary grades, the emphasis on content increases, as it should. The challenge for curriculum planners and teachers is ensuring the teaching of the rich content of the primary-grade curriculum, while taking full advantage of the child's developing abilities, interests, and enthusiasm for learning.

Classrooms serving primary-age children are typically part of larger institutions and complex educational systems with many levels of administration and supervision. Classroom teachers do not make decisions in isolation; many teachers have little control over the curriculum or policies they are expected to carry out. Although ensuring developmentally appropriate practice in primary education requires the efforts of the entire group of educators who are responsible for planning and implementing curriculum—teachers, curriculum supervisors, principals, superintendents, and school boards—it remains the professional obligation of each individual educator. No professional should abdicate this responsibility, using the excuse that colleagues or supervisors have other ideas. NAEYC's position statement (pp. 16–22) and the examples of appropriate and inappropriate practices (pp. 161–79 in this section) help support the current appropriate practices of many primary-grade programs. They can guide the decisions of administrators so that developmentally appropriate practices for primary-age children become more widely accepted, supported, and used.

A note about kindergarten is necessary. The kindergarten year of schooling marks an important life transition in many ways. Historically, kindergarten was a preparatory year of education, designed primarily to support children's social and emotional adjustment to group learning. The increased number of children attending preschool and child care centers at younger ages, combined with the increased academic demands of the early years of school, has greatly transformed the role of kindergarten. In most places in America today, kindergarten is considered the beginning of formal schooling. In addition, the age at which children begin kindergarten varies from state to state. In some states, depending on the prevalence of practices like "redshirting," some parents feel compelled to hold their children out of kindergarten until they are older and can cope with its

At any grade level, children vary enormously—not only in physical growth but also in virtually every aspect of development and behavior—for both environmental and genetic reasons.

academic, emotional, and physical demands. Given that kindergarten is still a program primarily serving 5-year-olds, this volume addresses developmentally appropriate practice for kindergartners in Part 4. Nevertheless, the great individual variation among children of the same age group and the large numbers of 6-year-olds physically present in kindergarten ne-

cessitate that kindergarten practices be responsive to a broad developmental range as well as individual and cultural variation (as is true for every other grade as well). Kindergarten teachers and administrators will find in both Parts 4 and 5 of this book descriptions of child development and learning that fit the children they teach.

Development and learning in primary-age children

In making decisions about developmentally appropriate primary education, it is essential to understand the development that typically occurs during this period of life and to know how 6- through 8-year-old children learn. From this understanding, principles of appropriate practice are derived for teaching primary-age children. One of the most important constants throughout human development is that all domains of development—physical, social, emotional, and cognitive—are interrelated (see Part 1, p. 10). Development in one dimension influences and is influenced by development in other realms. When schools focus solely on the cognitive domain, ignoring or slighting other aspects of children's development, they violate this fundamental principle. Because development cannot be neatly separated into parts, failure to attend to all aspects of an individual child's development is often the root cause of a child's lack of success in school. To take a simple example, a lack of social skills leading to neglect or rejection by peers impairs a child's ability to work cooperatively in a school setting. The child is likely to be preoccupied with social anxieties that further interfere with her learning. Such situations can have long-term negative consequences for children's adjustment in school and later life (Burton 1987).

Likewise, the connection between emotion and learning is becoming increasingly clear from research on brain development and memory. While highly stressful emotional contexts interfere with human beings' learning, activities with a strong emotional dimension—simulations, role playing, and cooperative projects—can make learning more meaningful and memorable (Sylvester 1995). The line between challenging children and inducing stress in them can be difficult to determine and will vary for individuals. But research increasingly supports the need to provide intellectually challenging curriculum within the context of supportive, positive human relationships. As Sylvester points out, "Doing worksheets in school prepares a student emotionally to do worksheets in life" (1995, 77).

Recognition of the connections between and among children's social, emotional, physical, and cognitive development has led to the development of several nationally recognized, effective elementary education programs. Programs like James Comer's School Development Project (Comer 1988, 1993) and the Child Development Project (Battistich et al. 1995; Lewis, Schaps, & Watson 1996) headquartered in Oakland, California, demonstrate that children learn best when the school is a democratic, caring community with high family involvement—a community in which children feel valued and consistently receive meaningful learning experiences.

Because children's learning is integrated during the early years, the primary-grade curriculum should also be integrated. One major pressure on elementary teachers has always been the need to "cover the curriculum." Frequently, teachers have tried to fit everything in by tightly scheduling discrete time segments for each subject. This approach grows out of an adult-organized scheme rather than from the way young children learn and construct their understandings. Children do not need always to distinguish learning by subject area. In fact, current knowledge of brain development offers strong support for integrating curriculum; the human brain seeks meaningful connections when presented with new information (Caine & Caine 1994). For example, integrated curriculum in which children study topics that cross discipline areas help children more deeply understand and apply concepts (Krogh 1995). An integrated curriculum in which children use knowledge or skills from one area in another subject area can extend their knowledge of the connections across disciplines—for example, applying reading and writing skills in social studies projects or using mathematical concepts in music and physical education (Bredekamp & Rosegrant 1995).

Integration of curriculum is accomplished in several ways. The curriculum may be planned around topics of study related to learning goals. These topics relate to children's interests; for example, children may be interested in the ocean because they live near it. Oceanographic study presents opportunities to work on a variety of activities in which children do reading, writing, math, science, social studies, art, and music. Such a project or ongoing focus of study involves sustained, cooperative effort and involvement over many days and perhaps weeks.

Providing learning areas in which children plan and select their activities also helps facilitate integrated curriculum. For example, the classroom may include a well-stocked and well-equipped publishing center, complete with materials for writing, computers for word processing and graphic design, and materials for binding student-made books. In an area fostering scientific exploration and investigation, children find tools for observing and experimenting, books to which they can refer for information, and real things at various times for them to observe and study, including such living things as caterpillars to watch in the stages of transformation. In a classroom like this, children further develop their reading and writing abilities in working on investigations and projects that engage them. Such classrooms also provide opportunities for spontaneous play, with play continuing to be a very important vehicle for development and learning in all areas during the primary years.

To achieve an integrated curriculum in the primary grades, teachers must have basic knowledge of how children develop and learn. Following are brief descriptions of widely held expectations of 6- through 8-year-olds' physical, cognitive (including language and moral development), and social-emotional development.

A long-term thematic focus or project that interests children, such as an oceanographic study in a coastal community, presents a variety of opportunities for reading and research, writing of various kinds, math, science, social studies, art, and music—and thus for integrated learning.

A sketch of physical development in 6- through 8-year-olds

Children's physical growth and maturation during the primary-grade years interact with their experiences to produce changes in gross- and fine-motor development.

Growth and maturation, sensation and perception

Between 6 and 9, the rate of children's physical growth is slower than that during the previous five years of life, but development is relatively steady with occasional growth spurts. For instance, by age 8 or 9, girls sometimes experience a preadolescent growth spurt and overtake boys in size, but not in strength. During primary-school years, on the average, children grow about two to three inches and gain three to five pounds per year; however, considerable individual and racial variation exists. For instance, measurements of 8-year-olds living in different countries throughout the world reveal a nine-inch height difference between the smallest and largest children, demonstrating the varying effects of genetic and environmental factors (Berk 1996). Given that the United States is a country whose population is composed of children from many racial groups and with ancestry from many other countries, growth norms for American children vary widely.

Much of children's growth during these years occurs in the extremities (making children appear leggy) and in the face (which elongates to accommodate permanent teeth). Whether tall or short for his age, the primary-grade child is recognizable by gaps in his teeth. Again, teething becomes a social and developmental milestone.

During these years, the brain has reached almost its adult size, and, thus, head growth is slower, but the brain continues to become more efficient in its functioning. Lateralization further improves with maturation of the corpus callosum (the tissue connecting the two halves of the brain) and this speeds mental processing of information (Harris 1986).

By the primary-grade years, children have developed greater immunological resistance and often experience better health with fewer infections and illnesses than preschoolers have. Of course, envi-

Primary-grade children are inclined to compare themselves with peers, both favorably and unfavorably.

ronmental conditions, nutrition, and other individual factors affect children's health.

By about age 6, binocular vision—the ability of the eyes to work together—is usually well established, preparing the child for reading instruction and closer-focus work. Children continue some farsightedness until after age 9, still necessitating larger print.

Gross- and fine-motor development

Children's growth and greater coordination of their bodies in space contribute to their greater ability to control movements, such as running, jumping, and balancing, and to sequence a series of movement skills as they do in a somersault. Their reaction time improves, making them more competent at throwing and catching a ball and in other skills used in team sports. The primary-grade child's improved physical coordination, combined with enhanced cognitive and social understanding, enables the child to engage in games with rules and to cooperate as a member of a team. At the same time, children are highly sensitive to social comparison at this age, and it is especially difficult when they lose. For this reason, schools should minimize competition. Many children of this age also are great risk takers and may suffer injuries because their bones and muscles are still not mature. Consequently, children's participation in sports with high-injury potential, such as football and strenuous dance or gymnastics, should be minimized.

Children with physical disabilities that affect their gross-motor development often share their agemates' interest in sports. Therefore, playgrounds and outdoor equipment should be accessible for children with disabilities. Similarly, modified equipment, such as racing wheelchairs or skis, enables these children to fully participate with their peers.

The primary-age child's fine-motor development also undergoes refinement. Children become more capable of fine-motor work without the neurological fatigue that the preschooler often experiences. Children's writing and drawing skills become more controlled and precise, although considerable individual variation exists. Overall, girls are ahead of boys in fine-motor development, just as boys exceed girls in gross-motor skills requiring strength. In intricate, detailed tasks such as sewing or origami, some 7- and 8-year-old children are capable of creating products that rival work done by adults.

A sketch of cognitive development in 6- through 8-year-olds

Children in the primary grades make great strides in cognitive development. This growth affects not only their academic work and other areas of intellectual functioning but also their language and communication abilities and their moral reasoning. Brief descriptions follow, on pages 148–54, of each of these areas of development.

Early childhood educators' understanding of children's cognitive functioning during the primary grades continues to be grounded in at least three theoretical perspectives: Piaget's theory that characterizes this cognition period as one of concrete operations, Vygotsky's theory of sociocultural learning, and information-processing theories that focus on this age group's increased memory capacity and the increasing use of memory strategies and awareness of mental processes (metacognition and metamemory).

Piaget (1952; Piaget & Inhelder 1969) postulated that children's cognition undergoes a major reorganization by about age 7. From an information-processing perspective, it is gradual changes in the way children process information and the procedures they follow in solving a problem that explain the changes in thinking and reasoning at this age. In his theory, Vygotsky (1978) emphasized the changes in the expectations, demands, and structuring by adults of the social and cultural context within which children live. Rogoff and her colleagues (1975) further explicated this perspective by studying communities around the world to identify the age at which the cultural expectations of children's roles and responsibilities undergo major changes; they identified a pattern of children between ages 5 and 7 typically being given greater responsibilities for chores and more adultlike tasks. Neuroscientists explain the changing capacities at this age as the result of processes like brain lateralization; also during this period, the synapses of the brain appear to go through "pruning," a process that scientists speculate makes brain functioning more efficient (Chugani 1996; Dana Alliance on Brain Initiatives 1996).

Whatever one's theoretical perspective on why such change occurs, ample evidence exists that the thinking and reasoning powers of primary-grade children are different from those of the typical preschooler. This concrete operational thinking of primary-age children is beautifully illustrated by an interaction that a colleague Suzanne McFarland (1992) had with her two sons several years ago. Her 8-year-old son often became exasperated with his 4-year-old brother and would call him "stupid" when he failed to grasp his older brother's point of view. One day Suzanne, a professor of early childhood education who herself was feeling a little exasperated at this point, told the elder brother that his little brother was not stupid. "You're in different stages of cognitive development," she explained, playfully using the terms she would use with her college class: "He's in a stage called 'preoperational' and you're in a stage called 'concrete operational,' so he doesn't understand things the same way you do. That doesn't mean he's stupid." A few days later, the 8-year-old again became frustrated with his younger brother and, in an attempt to control his own temper, he hollered, "Mom! What stage is that I'm in again? Cement?"

Suzanne's son clearly demonstrates the characteristic thinking of this age. His question reveals his active attempt to assimilate new information and experience, and he is capable of a level of reasoning that his younger brother cannot attain. Yet his reasoning is still not mature. He is much more capable than his brother of conceptualizing and solving problems about situations, objects, or symbols, but they must have a concrete referent; thus, his connecting the abstract concept of a cognitive development stage to something real and familiar—cement. He continues to try to make sense of new experience and relate new ideas or experiences to what he already knows. Nevertheless, it will be several years before he can reason about a hypothetical situation or abstract construct such as "concrete operational thinking."

Current thinking about cognitive development has moved away from the notion of a major reorganization of thought at the beginning of this period (see Gelman & Baillargeon 1983) to the idea of a more gradual but nevertheless real and significant shift in cognitive abilities that occurs in most children by approximately age 7 (White 1965; Sameroff & McDonough 1994; Case & Okamoto 1996). Between 5 and 7 years of age, most children begin to acquire the ability to think about and solve a wide range of problems. They are more proficient and flexible in their use of mental representations. The changes that occur in children's cognition during these years equip them to perform the mental op-

erations required for reading, mathematics, and other content learning in the early grades.

This shift in cognitive ability has important implications for every area of primary-age children's development. For instance, at play, children engage in games with rules because they now can understand and consistently apply rules. Similarly, their ability to understand multiple perspectives has important consequences for the development of moral reasoning. Likewise, their language use becomes more complex, partly because they understand that the same word can have multiple meanings. In the social-emotional domain, children's newfound cognitive ability has important implications for their developing understanding of self (Harter 1990). Each of these important developments is described in more detail later in this section.

Characteristics of thought in 6- through 8-year-olds

A few major achievements of thinking that occur in children from 6 through 8 years of age are briefly described here in contrast to characteristics of preschool thinking (see Part 4).

Decentration, reversibility, and conservation. Unlike their preschool counterparts, primary-grade children increasingly become able to understand the viewpoint of others, focus on several aspects of a problem at one time, and reverse their thinking—mentally go through a series of steps and then reverse them or understand that one operation can undo another, for example, that subtraction can undo or reverse addition. These capabilities have important implications for the kinds of problems that children can solve, as dramatically shown in the conservation problems that Piaget (1952) investigated. Outward appearances still fool the preschool child. The child is likely to think that there is "more cookie" when it is broken into pieces or think there is more water when it is poured from the short/fat glass into the tall/thin one. Primary-grade children, however, are usually able to reason that nothing was added or taken away and, therefore, that the quantity is the same—that is, they "conserve" the quantity of mass or liquid.

During the primary-school years, children develop several conservation ideas and can begin using them with true understanding in measurement and math-

Primary-grade children's thinking and reasoning are markedly more mature than preschoolers'; for instance, in creating a representation they consider not only their own viewpoint but also the perspective of others who will encounter it.

Reasoning and logic. Unlike preschoolers, whose reasoning is often from the particular to the particular, primary-grade children gradually gain the ability to engage in syllogistic logic; so by age 8 or 9 most children know that if stick A is longer than stick B, and B is longer than stick C, then A is also longer than C, at least when they encounter such problems in reality rather than as hypothetical situations (Sroufe et al. 1992). Similarly, primary-grade children are better able to engage in spatial reasoning. For instance, 5- and 6-year-olds are confused about left/right directionality when facing a person. By age 7 or 8 most children can mentally reverse the directions and understand left and right from a perspective other than their own (Berk 1996).

Concept acquisition. The primary-grade child shows progress in understanding complex concepts like number and time. By age 6 or 7, children's understanding of one-to-one correspondence and number is complete. For instance, these children realize that the number of cookies (eight, for instance) does not change when the cookies are rearranged, distributed, or divided into different subsets (5 + 3, 6 + 2, and so on). Their concepts of time and distance are improving but still are not mature. Not until after age 8 are children reasonably accurate in placing events in time sequence. They can generally categorize past, current, and future events, but they are not yet able to use dates to sequence historical time—another example of their ability to reason about concrete, but not abstract, concepts (Thornton & Vukelich 1988; Barton & Levstik 1996).

ematical problem solving. In Western cultures, researchers have found that these abilities develop in some predictable order, although considerable individual variation exists. This variation is exemplified by the age ranges at which 50% of children demonstrate various kinds of conservation tasks: number (age 4 to 6), mass (age 6 to 9), length (age 4 to 9), area (age 7 to 10), and weight (age 8 to 10) (Sroufe et al. 1992).

Primary-grade children's understanding of classification and seriation enables them to grasp many concepts—in math, science, social studies, and other disciplines—that would be incomprehensible to younger children.

Classification and seriation. Children's capacity for classification—the ability to group objects by common attributes—gradually extends to the ability to use more than one attribute to classify and to understand class inclusion, that is, the capacity for an object to be a member of more than one group simultaneously. For example, 6- and 7-year-old children can usually sort blocks by color, shape, and size (as in a matrix). And by age 8, most children understand that with a group of four cats and five dogs, there are more animals than dogs. By contrast, the preschool child in this situation usually is unable to compare a part to the whole and responds that there are more dogs than animals (Inhelder & Piaget 1964).

During the primary grades, children typically master seriation, the ability to place objects in order by length, weight, or size. Sequencing requires the ability to hold two pieces of information simultaneously—noting that an object is both larger than one object and smaller than another. This seriation ability is another example of the newly acquired capacity to decenter from a single focus to more than one.

Developmental constraints. Despite these changes in approach to many cognitive tasks, primary-age children typically are still not capable of thinking and problem solving in the same way as adults do. While they can symbolically or mentally manipulate concrete concepts, it will be some time before they can mentally manipulate abstract ideas—for example, use certain mathematical algorithms, grasp dates in history, or fully comprehend the irreversibility of death. Accordingly, while children can use symbols such as words and numbers to represent objects and relations, they still need concrete reference points.

Although primary-grade children have overcome the egocentrism of preschoolers' thinking, another form of egocentrism emerges during this period. Primary-grade children can become fixed on the validity of their own hypotheses and change the facts to fit a hypothesis rather than modify the hypothesis because the facts do not support it. For example, if a 7-year-old's theory is that he is a poor soccer player, he may hold fast to this belief despite specific contrary evidence that his parents cite. This form of egocentrism can become a challenge for teachers who believe strongly in helping children develop and test their own hypotheses as part of the science and math curriculum. The teacher needs to understand this developmental tendency rather than assume that children are being obstinate or stubborn.

Information processing in 6- through 8-year-olds: Short- and long-term memory

Most information-processing theorists attribute primary-grade children's improved ability to solve problems, such as conservation and classification, to their increased capacity to store information and retrieve it from memory. During these years children show improved capacity in both short- and long-term memory, although again these capacities are not yet mature. For example, the adult capacity for short-term memory is seven chunks or bits of information (words, numbers, phrases, etc.); preschoolers can hold two or three chunks while 7-year-olds can usually retain five chunks of information. During the primary years, short-term memory also improves because attention generally becomes more focused and children are better able to ignore irrelevant information. Of course, for some children, those who are accurately diagnosed with attention deficit hyperactivity disorder (ADHD), this memory capacity does not develop naturally and may require that adults attend more carefully to the kinds of stimuli that children receive (Douglas 1983).

Once information is in short-term memory, it must be transferred to long-term memory if it is to be retained. During the school years, children become better able to employ memory strategies such as rehearsal (repeating information to remember it) and

organization (grouping information into similar categories). Children begin to apply these memory strategies more systematically (such as distinguishing vowels from consonants or remembering the multiplication tables) as the demands of school increase. The child in the stage of concrete operations is better able to retain decontextualized information, although adults can help greatly by structuring the memory tasks and guiding children to systematically use memory strategies. In this effort, teachers can activate primary-grade children's expanding ability to think about their own memory functioning—that is, their metamemory—and thus can promote children's use of memory strategies. During these years, all areas of children's metacognition improve as children can think about and reflect on their own thinking processes.

One factor that contributes to children's improved memory is their increasing body of accumulated knowledge and concepts. In other words, children's experiences and memories provide categories or structures to which they can more readily connect new experiences. As adults are aware, when we know a lot about a topic, we find new information on this topic more meaningful and easier to retain and retrieve. Information-processing theorists believe that school-age children's improved memory capacity is due largely to the fact that school-agers have accumulated more knowledge than their preschool counterparts to which to connect new information or experiences. This theoretical perspective argues that children's concrete thinking is not just the result of age-related constraints on cognition; it is also a lack of prior knowledge in the content area (see Metz 1995). As Metz points out, "Even adults' reasoning can be bound to the perceptual and concrete in spheres where they do not have the knowledge to support deeper thinking" (1995, 105–06).

Compared with adults, 6- through 8-year-old children are novices in virtually every cognition area, and their thinking and reasoning reflect this shallow level of prior knowledge. Such a perspective on children's thinking supports practices, such as integrated curriculum studies and long-term projects, that enable children to gain in-depth knowledge and understanding of a topic rather than merely to cover every topic of study quickly and shallowly. Likewise, encouraging primary-grade children to pursue interests or hobbies in depth is another strategy to support concept development. Children can develop "expertise" in any area that is of intellectual interest to them—dinosaurs, stars, rocks, state flags—and the habits of mind they develop from deep study in one area are broadly applicable to learning in other areas.

Language and communication development in 6- through 8-year-olds

Closely tied to cognitive development are changes in children's language and communication capacity. The explosion of language development during the preschool years is followed by a dramatic transition in the primary grades—the movement from mere oral self-expression to written self-expression. During these years, children's receptive vocabulary increases not just by listening but by reading, and their expressive vocabulary expands from spoken to written communication. The result is that by age 8, children's vocabularies usually double to approximately 20,000 words and by the end of elementary school increase fourfold (Berk 1996). Children learn new words at a far more rapid rate than previously—almost 20 words a day when their language and print environment is sufficiently rich in vocabulary. This exponential increase results, in part, from children's broadened perspective taking and better understanding of part/whole relationships. These abilities enable them to understand parts of words and to apply that understanding to a new word (Berk 1996). For example, *extra* can mean "out of," as in *extraordinary* or *extraterrestrial*, but such an understanding can also lead children to confuse the meanings of words and make up their own words, such as "extratime."

The greatly expanded vocabulary of primary-grade children, along with their new awareness that the same word can have multiple meanings, has implications for social interactions. The ability to take multiple points of view vastly expands the child's communication skills. Research demonstrates that engaging in conversation about their learning strengthens children's abilities to communicate, express themselves, understand, reason, and solve problems (Wells 1983; Wilkinson 1984; Nelson 1985; Chang-Wells & Wells 1993; Cobb, Wood, & Yackel 1993; Palincsar, Brown, & Campione 1993). Research also suggests that adults can help prolong and expand children's conversations. Children gain greater control of language and subsequently use it to think and to influence others' thinking.

Primary-school-age children engage in interactive, reciprocal conversations with adults and other children and more effectively use the power of verbal communication, including humor. Unlike preschoolers who tend to be limited to silliness and bathroom humor, 6- through 8-year-olds typically love the kinds of jokes, puns, tongue twisters, and riddles that reflect their new language capacities. During these years, children also use language (e.g., nicknames, teasing, or secret words) to include or exclude others from their social circle. Their speech is fluent, but they still struggle with some syntactical complexities of language, such as passive voice. Until the age of 8 or 9, children often misinterpret a sentence like "The boy was hit by the ball" as meaning that the boy hit the ball.

As clearly demonstrated in countries throughout the world, young children have great capacity to acquire bilingual and even multilingual competence. Although bilingual education unfortunately has become a politically divisive topic in the United States (Garcia & Baker 1995), research strongly supports the benefits of bilingualism in cognitive, language, and literacy development. Bilingual children perform better than monolingual speakers on measures of analytical ability, concept formation, and cognitive flexibility (Hakuta, Ferdman, & Diaz 1987). Bilingual education supports children's learning in two languages (usually English and the home language, be it Spanish, Japanese, or one of the 150 Native American languages). In contrast, abrupt submersion in an English-only environment creates a risk of "semilingualism"—inadequate proficiency in both languages that contributes greatly to school failure, especially among low-income Hispanic children (August & Garcia 1988). In well-designed bilingual education programs, children acquire the English-language competence needed to succeed in American society, but not at the expense of their home language (Wong Fillmore 1991; NAEYC 1996).

Moral development in 6- through 8-year-olds

The cognitive shift that occurs at about age 7 has important implications for children's moral development. As their reasoning improves and their ability to understand multiple perspectives increases, chil-

Primary-grade children's appreciation of jokes, puns, and tongue twisters reflects their developing language capacities.

age 7, children realize that not all rules are the same and breaking a rule is not always wrong. They are better able to consider a person's intention in deciding whether an action is right or wrong, good or bad (Piaget 1965; Irwin & Ambron 1973). Children at this age also begin to make more accurate judgments about what is true and false, but they often rigidly apply their newfound understanding of justice and fair play (Elkind 1981).

Around the time they are 6, most children begin to internalize moral rules of behavior and thus develop what we think of as "conscience." This internal monitoring of their own conduct enables them to function more independently of adult supervision and to be trusted to take on more responsibility. However, children's behavior at this age often shows that they find it difficult to live with and by their new self-monitoring and that they need adults' assistance. For instance, they may mistake accidents or chance occurrences for punishments for their misbehavior ("I lied about going to my friend's house, so she got sick"). Likewise, the child's newly developed conscience is often excessively strict. For example, children of 6 or 7 typically treat every little mistake as a major crime, deserving of terrible punishment or dire consequences. Adults can help children assess mistakes realistically and find ways of correcting them.

dren become better able to think about and reflect on rules of behavior and to understand right and wrong. The child is now aware that another person can have different thoughts than his or her own (Shantz 1975). With this advance in social understanding, the child has the basis for beginning to grasp others' intentions and allow for them.

Children beyond age 5 or 6 are also less rigid than preschoolers are in applying rules. Before this cognitive shift, the young child generally sees rules as fixed and unchangeable and considers breaking one rule as equally bad as breaking another. By about

Children of this age are very concerned with fairness. They closely observe adult infractions and inequitable actions, so adults behaving fairly is important. Before 6 or 7, children insist that fairness requires absolute equality in treatment (for instance, everyone must get the same exact amount of snack food). In the primary grades they have begun to consider merit in decisions about fairness (a special treat going to someone who worked extra hard). By 8 they are better able to empathize with other people and accept the idea of giving special consideration to those in greater need (Berk 1996).

Of course, all these developments in children's moral reasoning are not automatic, and a wide variation exists among individual children as a product of their experience and the adult guidance they receive. For instance, children from various cultural groups may differ in their reactions to specific moral situations. This is not surprising since one defining characteristic of cultural groups is agreement on the rules for social and moral behavior and the transmission of these rules to children.

Children's increased cognitive capacity makes more mature moral reasoning possible, but adult encouragement and guidance and opportunities for positive peer interaction are necessary for children to become sensitive and caring human beings. Children are more likely to show advanced moral reasoning if adults reason with them and help them to understand the rationale for the rules they follow. Sensitive adults help children develop empathy by appealing to children's respect for fairness and rules in their interactions with others or when denying their request is necessary—for example, "If I allow you to do that, I would be unfair to the others. I need to try to be fair to everyone" (Furman 1980, 1987). Of course, children's cognitive and moral development relates to their social and emotional development, a description of which follows.

Working together in small groups promotes intellectual and language development, lively engagement with content, and skills in collaborating and working with other group members.

A sketch of social and emotional development in 6- through 8-year-olds

The cognitive shift between ages 5 and 7 not only affects children's understanding of other people's perspectives but also affects their understanding of self (Harter 1990). While preschool children typically describe themselves in terms of their behavior (e.g., "I play outside a lot" or "I like cookies"), school-age children describe themselves as to traits and competencies ("I am good at math" or "I am friendly"). By around 7 or 8, children understand that they can feel two emotions at the same time (e.g., "I like Joan, but I hate the way she always hangs around"). They judge themselves in a more balanced way ("I'm good at math, but I'm not good at reading"). School-agers typically form at least three images of themselves: their perceptions of their academic, social, and physical competence. By age 8, these images combine into a generalized image of self that children can verbalize—whether they like themselves and how much (Sameroff & McDonough 1994).

During these years children's gender identification becomes very strong. Unlike preschoolers, children by age 5 or 6 clearly understand that their gender is a permanent characteristic that does not vary depending on their clothes or behavior. During the early school years, children's gender identification—their boyness or girlness—becomes connected to culturally accepted roles and expectations and more strongly influences their behavior and choice of friends.

During the primary-grade years, children's self-esteem (estimation of their self-worth, pride or shame in their competence) becomes more realistic and accurate. Preschool and kindergarten children most often overestimate their own powers and arrive at school with a delightful confidence that they will achieve (Covington 1984; Stipek 1984). They are developing and acquiring skills so rapidly that they seem to assume that what they cannot do today will be possible tomorrow (Hills 1986). As children get older, they begin to understand the limits of their own abilities and they also become more prone to social comparison. In the typical course of development, children compare themselves to others favorably and unfavorably. This information becomes part of their self-concept and can affect their motivation

for activity. For example, children learn whether they excel in science or art or soccer, and such learning influences life decisions. Unfortunately, when schools rely unduly on competition and comparison among young children, they magnify children's tendency to engage in social comparison, lessen children's optimism about their own abilities and prospects in school, and stifle motivation to learn (Hills 1986).

Experiences that shape self-concept and self-esteem are especially important during the early school years because children's self-esteem influences their behavior. And as children get older, their self-concept becomes more difficult to change. For example, if children have a negative image of themselves as learners, they generally exert less effort in school. In the social context, too, children with a negative image of themselves are likely to be more aggressive and disliked by peers, further exacerbating their low self-esteem. In depriving children of the interaction with peers—important agents of socialization in childhood—this cycle of low self-esteem and social isolation may have very negative long-term consequences. A large body of research provides powerful evidence that children who fail to develop minimal social competence and experience rejection or neglect by their peers are at significant risk of dropping out of school, becoming delinquent, and experiencing mental health problems in adulthood (Cowen et al. 1973; Asher, Renshaw, & Hymel 1982; Asher, Hymel, & Renshaw 1984; Gronlund & Holmlund 1985; Parker & Asher 1987). Research also demonstrates that adult intervention and coaching can help children develop better peer relationships (Asher & Williams 1987; Burton 1987).

Children of primary-grade age are becoming intensely interested in peers. They show marked preference for same-gender playmates and almost stereotypic rejection of the opposite sex. They now are more capable of playing cooperative, rule-regulated games and of sticking to the rules. Establishing productive, positive social and working relationships with others close to their age gives children the foundation for developing a sense of social competence.

During the early school years, children usually develop their first truly reciprocal friendships. Preschoolers typically define friendship as doing things together, whereas primary-grade children's friendships are marked by genuine give and take, negotiation of differences, shared experiences, and mutual trust. School structures or practices that arbitrarily divide children from their friends can undermine their capacity to develop this important social skill. Without opportunity and support for maintaining relationships, children continually revisit the initial stages of friendship and do not learn how to sustain friendships over time.

The ability to work and interact effectively with peers is only one dimension of the major social-emotional developmental task of the early school years—the development of a sense of mastery or competence. Erikson (1963) describes this major developmental challenge as the child's struggle between developing a sense of "industry" or feelings of inferiority. To develop this sense of competence or industry, primary-age children need to acquire the knowledge and skills recognized as important by their culture. In the United States today, foremost among those competencies are reading, writing, and computing numerically. Toward the goal of mastery, school-age children are willing to practice skills, persisting for longer than they would have done as preschoolers. When children do not succeed in acquiring the competence needed to function in the world, they develop a sense of inferiority or inadequacy that may seriously inhibit their future performance.

For primary-age children, the urge to master the skills of esteemed adults and older children is as powerful as the urge to stand and walk is for 1-year-olds. For primary classrooms, the challenge is to tap children's strong motivation for mastery, to give them the opportunities and support they need to develop skills, and at the same time to remember that primary-grade children all too easily can feel that they have failed (at math, reading, etc.) and become discouraged. When children are pressured to acquire skills too far beyond their ability or judged competitively—receiving low grades on their work or hearing constant correction—their motivation to learn as well as their self-esteem may be impaired. A major cause of negative self-image for children this age is not succeeding in school—for instance, failing to learn to read "on schedule" or being assigned to the lowest-ability math group. In short, children develop a solid basis for self-esteem when adults help them develop efficacy in the valued skills of the culture, especially literacy and numeracy (Weissbourd 1996).

Considerations for early childhood educators

Recognition of the kinds of development that typically occur during the primary years leads to several considerations for practice. For example, although primary-age children gain greater control over their bodies and can sit and attend for longer time periods, they are far from mature physically and need to be active. Long periods of sitting fatigue primary-grade children more than running, jumping, or bicycling does. Physical action is essential for 6- through 8-year-olds to refine their developing skills, such as batting a ball, skipping rope, or balancing on a beam. Expressing their newly acquired physical power and control also enhances their self-confidence.

Physical activity is vital for children's cognitive growth as well. When presented with an abstract concept, primary-grade children still need physical actions to help them grasp the idea, much as adults need vivid examples and illustrations to grasp unfamiliar concepts. In comparison to adults, however, primary-age children are more dependent on first-hand experiences; therefore, an important principle of practice for primary-age children is that they should be engaged in active rather than passive activities (Katz & Chard 1989). For example, children should have opportunities to manipulate real objects and learn through direct experiences rather than be expected to sit and listen for extended time periods. Teachers need to understand, however, that manipulating objects does not automatically improve children's understanding; skilled teaching also is required. Nor should educators be too literal about the importance of hands-on activity. The "concrete objects" that are manipulated can be figures on a computer screen, for example, just as effectively as they can be Cuisinaire rods (Clements & McMillen 1996; see also Wright & Shade 1994).

In knowing how primary-age children think and learn, teachers are more likely to plan curriculum with concrete materials and experiences for children to investigate and think about and opportunities for interaction and communication with other children and adults. Similarly, the content of the curriculum should be relevant, engaging, and meaningful to the children themselves. The purpose of such content is not, as some people assume, to make school more fun but to support children's ability to connect new

In the early grades children begin to enjoy learning about people, places, and phenomena beyond their own immediate experience, and they are able to use charts, maps, models, and other representations that are too abstract for younger children.

learning to prior knowledge, which also has the effect of expanding their memory and reasoning capacity (Bredekamp & Rosegrant 1995). In short, if educators want children to think, we need to give them something to think about. If we want them to remember, we need to make new information and tasks as meaningful as possible and connect these in some way to prior learning. Because young children construct their own understanding of concepts from their experiences, they need many challenging opportunities to use and develop the thinking skills they bring with them and to identify and solve problems that interest them (Kamii 1985).

Knowledge of key aspects of social, emotional, and moral development in the primary-grade years leads teachers to use positive approaches to help children learn appropriate behavior. Role-playing problem situations and involving children in establishing and enforcing the few basic rules necessary for congenial group living are more effective than punishing, criticizing, or continually comparing chil-

dren. Teachers recognize the importance of developing positive peer group relationships and provide opportunities and support for cooperative small-group projects that provide rich content for conversation. Teachers also facilitate discussion among children by making comments and soliciting children's opinions and ideas. Beyond the obvious benefits of positive peer relationships to each child, such collaborative work also has value for children's cognitive and language development and their ability to take on and solve problems (Forman, Minick, & Stone 1993).

During the early school years, children are not only learning knowledge and skills, but they also are acquiring dispositions toward learning and school that could last a lifetime (Gottfried 1983; Katz 1985; Elkind 1987; Katz & Chard 1989). Dispositions, such as curiosity, humor, or helpfulness, are enduring habits of mind and action or tendencies to respond to events or situations (Katz & Chard 1989). Longitudinal research indicates that educators need to design curriculum and teaching methods that enable children to acquire not only knowledge and skills but also the disposition or inclination to use these. Evidence exists that overemphasis on mastery of narrowly defined reading and arithmetic skills and excessive drill and practice of already mastered skills threaten children's dispositions to use the skills they have acquired (Walberg 1984; Dweck 1986; Schweinhart, Weikart, & Larner 1986; Katz & Chard 1989). During the primary grades, it is essential for children to acquire the mechanics of reading, but it is also important for them to develop the desire to read. Similarly, it is as important for children to want to apply math to solve problems as it is for them to know their "math facts."

Despite their increased independence and developing conscience, 6-, 7-, and 8-year-old children still need supervision and the support of trusted adults. As a result, teachers should not expect children of this age group to supervise themselves in school or after school for extended time periods. Teachers and parents can provide opportunities for children to assume responsibility but should not expect primary-age children to display adult levels of self-control.

Responding to individual and cultural variation

Knowledge of widely held expectations of 6- through 8-year-olds is only one dimension of knowledge to consider in making decisions about developmentally appropriate practice in the primary grades. Equally important is knowledge about the specific children in a classroom and knowledge of the social and cultural context. Although fairly stable and predictable sequences of human development appear to exist, a major premise of developmentally appropriate practice is that each child is unique and has an individual pattern and timing of growth. Each child also has individual personality characteristics, learning styles, experiences, and a particular family background. As children get older, their range of experience broadens, as does their individual variability. Developmentally appropriate schools set high standards for children's learning but are flexible in their expectations about when and how children gain certain competencies.

During the early school years, children are acquiring attitudes and approaches toward learning and work—such as persistence, resourcefulness, and initiative—that may last a lifetime.

Recognition of individual differences dictates using a variety of teaching methods (Durkin 1980, 1987, 1990; Katz & Chard 1989). Because children's backgrounds, experiences, socialization, and learning styles are so different, any method is likely to succeed with some children and fail with others. Howard Gardner's (1983, 1991) work on multiple intelligences further supports the need for schools to provide many ways for children to approach learning tasks and expand their thinking. The principle of practice is that the younger the children and the more diverse their backgrounds, the wider the variety of teaching methods and materials required (Gardner 1983; Durkin 1987; Katz & Chard 1989).

Children's sense of self-worth derives from their experiences within the family and community and from their ability to master the skills expected within the social context in which they live and grow. Children develop and learn within a cultural context, coming to understand the world, what is appropriate behavior, and how to express their developmental accomplishments. Children experience easier transitions when the skills, abilities, and understandings they construct in the family and community are congruent with the expectations of the school. However, if children's developmental accomplishments go unrecognized, their adjustment to school may be very difficult. For example, a child may have developed a high level of communicative competence in his home language, but if that language is not English, the teacher may fail to recognize the child's language competence. Teachers need to recognize that cultural variety is the American norm and that familiar cultural forms most easily demonstrate children's abilities (Hale-Benson 1986; Bowman 1994; Hale 1994).

When children enter school, their self-esteem comes to include perceptions of their families by teachers and others at school. When children sense that teachers respect and value their families, this supports their own sense of self-esteem and competence. Fully knowing children and responding to their individuality are possible only if parents are integral partners in the educational process. This happens only when teachers and parents communicate frequently and respectfully and parents feel welcome in the school at all times. If children's diversity is rejected or, worse, treated as a deficit, their healthy development and capacity to learn face serious threat, a risk Sameroff and McDonough eloquently describe:

The timing and quality of this [5- to 7-year cognitive] shift is influenced by characteristics of the child, the home environment, the cultural context, and previous experiences with group learning. When the resulting heterogeneity of children's characteristics and capacities is met by a uniformity of teacher expectations and behavior, many children become cognitive and social casualties. If we wish to change these outcomes, then the elementary school must become more attuned to the individuality that each child brings to the classroom. (1994, 193)

*　　*　　*

An obvious limitation here and in any text is the impossibility of conveying the rich diversity and individuality of the children who occupy any one classroom on any given day. This section next returns to some of the young children introduced in Part 4 (see pp. 119–20)—now in their primary-grade years. Revisiting these children's lives illustrates the phenomenon of continuity and change in human development, the ways they remain the same and ways they are different. The integrated nature of development and learning and the growing impact of school experience on every aspect of children's development are evident again.

These are only snapshots of four young children at this specific point in their development, but each of their stories reveals several important dimensions of development and learning during the early years of school. In each child, one sees the powerful influence of physical, cognitive, and social-emotional changes on their developing self. The effect of social comparison and the peer group on self-esteem is apparent. One sees the children's strong need for mastery and for meeting the demands of the sociocultural context— especially to acquire fundamental competence in literacy and numeracy. The pervasive influence of school and community expectations is also evident.

During the primary grades, children typically become more realistic and less optimistic in judgments about their own competence. This tendency is apparent even in these brief descriptions. All of these children are doing well; none has become a casualty of schooling, yet many opportunities have been missed to support their development and learning to their fullest potential. One wants more for them. All of them deserve to experience a primary-grade school that includes more examples of the developmentally appropriate practices described on pages 161 through 179.

Nicole and Andres in First Grade

Nicole enters first grade already able to read, having "broken the code" in kindergarten. By the end of the year she is reading chapter books at home, but language arts worksheets at school bore her. Her creative responses to the required task are not always appreciated by her teacher. Nicole's mathematics understanding exceeds that of the other children and the curriculum demands of first grade. Fortunately, her class does science experiments that intellectually intrigue and interest her. She also does very well in games like Concentration; she can even articulate the memory strategies she uses to win every time. Nicole's fine-motor skills are good; she especially enjoys writing in her journal and sewing, although sewing sometimes tries her patience. As in preschool, her gross-motor skills are still behind those of others her age; she dislikes physical education and outdoor play because she cannot jump rope like the other girls do.

First grade is a challenge for Andres. He continues to be reticent about performing a skill in public before he has mastered it. This tendency, always a part of his personality, is intensified by his growing awareness of social comparison and the fact that he is in a multiage class where older children can read and he cannot. He starts to feel he is stupid. Although his teacher reports that he is making good progress in reading, Andres says he does not like school.

The teacher assigns homework every night, and Andres feels fatigued by the fine-motor requirements of the tasks. His gross-motor development remains advanced, and he is very skilled at dribbling a soccer ball and playing basketball. When one coach yells at him for a missed play in the community instructional league, however, Andres refuses to go back to soccer. His favorite part of school is after school, which is when he and his several close friends play ball.

Adam and Lourdes in Third Grade

Adam will always be among the youngest in his class, but this appears to have had no negative effects as he enters third grade—except that he still has not lost a tooth and he longs to be like the other kids. He is still very responsible and socially mature. Adam is involved in team sports, playing on community teams and listening and following his coaches' directions as carefully as he does those of his teachers. He sees himself as a caring, loving person and is not even embarrassed when his 3-year-old cousin comes up to the bench during a game and hugs him. Adam still loves working on the computer at home and at school; his favorite programs are those that involve him in writing stories or learning about historical events. Adam says his favorite U.S. presidents are Washington and Lincoln, and he hopes to meet them some day in heaven.

By third grade, Lourdes scores at the top of her class on assessments of reading comprehension but at the bottom on capitalization and punctuation. Her teacher says that she just does not attend to detail. Math is a struggle because Lourdes does not understand place value. She still is impulsive and has a great deal of difficulty speaking in turn and staying in her seat for even relatively short time periods. On the other hand, her artwork shows enormous detail and intricacy. Her music teacher is frustrated because Lourdes shows great potential as a musician—as a singer and violinist—but she neglects practice. In sports she excels; she is the star of her soccer team and a budding gymnast.

In a conversation with Lourdes's mother about Gardner's theory of multiple intelligences, her teacher indicates that Lourdes's great strengths lie in musical and bodily-kinesthetic approaches to understanding the world rather than in the linguistic and logical-mathematical approaches that the school emphasizes. The teacher explains that there is little opportunity in school for Lourdes to exercise her strengths, because the children need to stay in their seats.

Examples of Appropriate and Inappropriate Practices
for 6- through 8-Year-Olds

The following examples, which are by no means exhaustive, contrast appropriate, excellent practice in primary-grade education with inappropriate, less effective practice. The aim is not to issue a prescriptive set of practices but to encourage educators to reflect on their practice. Part 1 states 12 principles of learning and development from which are derived the guidelines for decisions about developmentally appropriate practice (see pp. 16–22) and the examples in this chart. Because people construct an understanding of a concept by considering both positive and negative examples, the chart includes not only practices that are viewed as developmentally appropriate but also practices that are seen as inappropriate or highly questionable for children of this age. Of the practices identified as inappropriate, some are harmful to children; others merely waste children's time.

There are many reasons for the persistence of inappropriate practices of the kinds described here. Some teachers are poorly prepared or out-of-date with the professional knowledge base. Class sizes are too big—30 to 35 or more—making it difficult for teachers to know children and their families well and to individualize instruction. Children's emotional and physical needs are not being met, and the school and community lack the resources or services to assist them. The mandated curriculum is incoherent, fragmented, or unrealistic. The learning environment is unsafe or has insufficient supplies of books and other learning materials. Administrative policies require outdated methods and structures. Any of these factors or all of them together could be the root cause for observed practices such as those described as inappropriate in this chart.

The examples are designed to apply to the school day, but many also pertain to school-age child care that is provided before and after school hours. A fuller description of appropriate and inappropriate practices in school-age care is available in *Developmentally Appropriate Practice in School-Age Child Care Programs* (American Association of Family and Consumer Sciences 1993) and in other publications (National School-Age Care Alliance 1995; Koralek, Newman, & Colker 1995; and Koralek, Colker, & Dodge 1995).

Appropriate Practices	**Inappropriate Practices**

Creating a caring community of learners

Promoting a positive climate for learning

• Teachers ensure that primary-grade classrooms function as caring communities of learners in which all children and adults feel accepted and respected. Children learn personal responsibility, how to develop constructive relationships with other people, and respect for individual and cultural differences as well as important skills and knowledge to enable them to function in society.	• No efforts are made to build a sense of the group as a community. To maintain classroom order, teachers continually separate children from friends and discourage conversation. Some children who lack social skills are isolated or rejected by peers and receive no assistance from teachers in developing positive relationships within the classroom. • Teachers emphasize the need for children to do their own work independently at all times and do not provide opportunities for them to work together on cooperative projects or activities.

Appropriate Practices	**Inappropriate Practices**

Creating a caring community of learners (cont'd)

	Appropriate Practices	Inappropriate Practices
Promoting a positive climate for learning (cont'd)	• Teachers have high (challenging but achievable) expectations and standards for every child's learning and development. To foster children's self-confidence, persistence, and other positive dispositions as learners, teachers adjust the rate and pace of the curriculum as well as the content so that all children engage in learning experiences in which they can succeed most of the time and yet are challenged to work on the edge of their developing capabilities.	• Teachers have low expectations of the children's learning abilities or potential. Minimal competence is expected, and this is communicated to the children.
	• Teachers know each child well. As they plan learning experiences and work with children, they take into account individuals' differing abilities, developmental levels, and approaches to learning. Responsiveness to individual children is evident in the classroom environment (where children's unique products and work are collected and displayed), curriculum, and teaching practices. Teachers make sure that every child has opportunities to actively participate and make contributions.	• Teachers use the same lesson and methods for all children ("teach to the mean") without regard to differences in children's prior experience, how individual children learn best, how much and what kinds of structure they need, and other individual characteristics.
		• Children with special needs are constantly pulled out of the classroom to receive services elsewhere in the building, fragmenting the child's day, preventing teachers from getting to know these children, and undermining the security of their place in the group.
Building a democratic community	• Teachers use a variety of strategies to help build a sense of the group as a democratic community. For example, class meetings occur regularly and children participate in group decisionmaking. Group action is decided through a consensus-building process (such as setting classroom rules or agreeing on a project to undertake). Teachers provide opportunities to explore the concepts of voting and majority/minority, such as voting on the name of the class pet. Children may work on group activities, such as a schoolwide recycling project.	• Teachers' behaviors and techniques undermine a sense of community; for example, children most often work alone or in competition with others. Teachers do not help children learn strategies for problem solving and conflict resolution.
		• Children are rarely allowed to choose a partner to work with or sit by; the development of friendships is not considered an important curriculum objective.
	• Shared schoolwide curriculum goals include the development of character and promotion of ethical behaviors, such as trustworthiness, respect, responsibility, fairness, caring, and citizenship. Character education goals are developed within the school community and reflect the contributions of parents, teachers, and children.	• Character education is not taught or is only a brief unit of study from a prepackaged curriculum and without involvement of parents and representatives of the school community.

Appropriate Practices	Inappropriate Practices
• Teachers bring each child's home culture and language into the shared culture of the school so that children feel accepted and gain a sense of belonging. The unique contributions of each child's family and cultural group are recognized and valued by others. Children learn to appreciate and respect similarities and differences among people. Through literature and social studies content, including historical and current events, teachers help children understand American cultural values—tolerance, equality, and personal freedom—and the impact of biases in society on groups of people.	• Children's cultural and linguistic backgrounds and other individual differences are devalued or ignored. Some children do not see their race, language, family, or cultural background reflected in the classroom, making it difficult for them to feel part of the group.

• Differences among people are stressed to such an extent that some children feel excluded. |
| • Teachers use a variety of ways of flexibly grouping children to promote learning and social-emotional development. Whole-group meetings or discussion times give children an opportunity to build a sense of community and shared purpose and to take part in group problem solving. Children often work in small, flexible, cooperative groups on short- and long-term projects. Children have daily opportunities to learn with others through conversation during work or play. Teachers acknowledge and use children's diverse interests and ability levels. Mixed-ability groups are available, as are those designed for specific children with similar interests or needs. | • Teachers routinely group children or set up competing teams by age or gender or in other ways that may diminish children's sense of being part of a whole group.

• Teachers work with the whole group most of the time or track children into homogeneous groups according to ability level, which children clearly identify as the "smart group" and the "dumb group."

• Teachers give children feedback about their performance or abilities in public ways that embarrass or humiliate children who fail to meet group expectations (such as posting test scores on timed tests of math facts). |
| • Children with disabilities or special learning needs are included as members of the class socially and intellectually as well as physically. Necessary supports are provided both to teachers and children to ensure that children's individual needs are met. School personnel take care not to isolate children with disabilities in a segregated classroom or not to pull them out of the classroom frequently. Promoting continuity of children's educational experiences and feelings of belonging to the group is given high priority. | • Children with disabilities or special learning needs are nominally assigned to a class, but most of their instruction occurs with special teachers elsewhere in the building. These children have only a vague sense of what is happening in their classroom, and the classroom teacher is unfamiliar with their educational program because she assumes they are getting intensive treatment elsewhere.

• Children with moderate to severe disabilities are placed in a classroom without sufficient supports from specialists or teaching assistants to ensure that their needs are met. Teachers and peers may see their presence as disruptive and a nuisance. |

163

Appropriate Practices	**Inappropriate Practices**

Creating a caring community of learners (cont'd)

Building a democratic community (cont'd)

- Administrators work with teachers to create a school climate that promotes an attitude of "we're all in this together" to ensure that every child succeeds. Teachers and children work across as well as within grade levels to build a sense of shared purpose and develop positive character traits in children (like caring, empathy, and responsibility). For instance, younger children may have a buddy from an upper grade who reads to them on a regular basis.

- Administrators employ a highly competitive, hierarchical management style that leads teachers to blame other teachers for "sending" them unprepared children. Inflexibility of school schedules and structures discourages collegiality among teachers and inhibits opportunities for teachers to work with and learn from each other.

Teaching to enhance development and learning

Environment and schedule

- Teachers plan the curriculum, time schedule, and environment so that children can learn through active involvement in various learning experiences with each other, with adults, and with a variety of materials. The classroom organization includes comfortable work areas where children can interact and work together, a library area for reading silently or sharing a book with a friend, and places for working on construction projects, writing, playing math or language games, and exploring science.

- Teachers give insufficient time to preparing the classroom environment and to planning for groups and individuals. Children have little or no opportunity to work on projects or activities of their own choosing or to use the materials creatively. Project work is rare and/or is only used as a reward for the most able or best-behaved students.

- Teachers provide a safe environment and age-appropriate supervision that allow for children's increasing responsibility. For instance, children learn to move throughout the building independently, but teachers know where they are and what they are doing. Teachers anticipate and prevent situations in which children might be injured or hurt. Teachers support children's risk-taking behavior within safe boundaries (such as using tools, playing sports with proper equipment, or doing jobs and errands in the building).

- Teachers are inattentive in supervision and preventable injuries occur often, or teachers fail to intervene when some children are too aggressive and hurt others.

- Concern for health and safety leads teachers to severely restrict children's risk-taking behavior, thus failing to help children develop a sense of appropriate confidence and judgment and personal responsibility for their own health and safety.

Appropriate Practices	**Inappropriate Practices**
• Teachers provide a variety of materials and activities that are concrete, real, and relevant to children's lives. Objects for children to manipulate and experiment with, such as construction materials, games, computers, art media, and scientific equipment, are readily available. Tables or flexible arrangements of desks enable children to work alone or in small groups. Individual work does not preclude conversations and occasional assistance from others. A variety of work places and spaces is provided and used flexibly.	• Available materials are limited primarily to textbooks, workbooks, and pencils. Children are assigned a place for the entire year and are rarely moved. Few manipulative objects or hands-on materials are available to assist children in constructing their understanding of math and science concepts, such as multiplication, floating and sinking, gears and levers, or the relationship between form and function.
• Teachers organize the daily schedule to allow for alternating periods of physical activity and quiet time. They allocate ample time for children to get deeply engaged in investigation of problems or creation of products (writing, constructing models). Teachers give children advance notice of transitions and, when possible, allow them to complete what they are working on.	• The organization of the time schedule is rigid and arbitrary, with discrete and often insufficient periods of time devoted to each subject area of study. Transitions are too frequent and disruptive, often interrupting children's work and wasting time that could better be used for learning.

Teaching strategies

• Teachers use a variety of strategies for ensuring each child's progress in accomplishing the expected, age-appropriate learning objectives. Teachers are aware of the continuum of learning in each curriculum area (such as literacy, mathematics, science, and social studies) and adapt instruction for individual children who are having difficulty as well as for those who are capable of more advanced levels of competence.	• Teachers are unaware of the continuum of learning in various disciplines. They do not pick up cues that children are confused and cannot adapt when children's learning is ahead of or behind predetermined expectations and benchmarks. Little adaptation is made for children who fail to make progress in learning. Teachers do not feel accountable to help all children succeed.
• To help children learn and develop, teachers use a variety of active, intellectually engaging strategies, including posing problems or discrepancies, asking thought-provoking questions, adding complexity to tasks, and engaging in reciprocal discussion in which they take children's ideas seriously. Teachers also model, demonstrate, and explain, and provide the information, coaching, direct instruction, and other assistance that a child needs to progress.	• Instructional strategies involve limited individual teacher-child interaction. Teachers lecture to the whole group and assign paper-and-pencil practice exercises or worksheets to be completed by children working silently and individually at their desks. Teachers introduce new content or skills to children through worksheets, with little prior explanation, discussion, or connection to previous learning. When speaking to individual children, teachers are usually just repeating directions rather than engaging children in substantive conversation or discussion.

165

Appropriate Practices	Inappropriate Practices

Teaching to enhance development and learning (cont'd)

Teaching strategies (cont'd)

• Teachers use grouping as a deliberate teaching strategy and make it a key part of their planning. Classroom groups vary in size and composition depending on the activity and children's needs. Children have opportunities to work in small heterogeneous groups as well as homogenous groups for various purposes. Children also have opportunities to create their own informal groupings. The composition of these groups is flexible and temporary, changing with the learning experience.	• Teachers do not help children make good use of time to work independently (such as at writing or sustained silent reading) or on group projects. Although children who have difficulty working independently do the same thing repeatedly or become disruptive, teachers fail to intervene. Rather than assisting children in developing self-regulation and decisionmaking skills, teachers ignore uninvolved children or punish disruptive children.
• Teachers and children together select and develop sustained, in-depth project work to be carried out by small groups of children who report back to the larger group. Teachers consider ways to pursue vital curriculum goals through these activities, which typically grow out of or expand on children's interests. To extend children's ideas and challenge their thinking, teachers encourage involvement in collaborative learning and group problem solving that require children to share their own perspectives, listen to the views of others, and negotiate shared goals and strategies.	• Teachers do not use projects as a means of engaging children in meaningful work directed to the integration of curriculum goals and objectives. Rather, projects are seen as "filler" for occupying or entertaining children. Teachers adopt a passive role as children work on projects.
	• Children have opportunities to work in small groups, but activities are unsystematic, disorganized, or fragmented. Any type of "hands-on" activity is assumed to be valuable, even if unconnected to curriculum goals, meaningful content, or children's needs and interests.
• Teachers guide children in evaluating their own work and participating in determining where improvement is needed. They assist children in figuring out how to improve their work. Some work is corrected in small groups in which teachers and children give feedback and children edit their own or each others' work. Errors are viewed as opportunities for learning. Teachers analyze children's errors and use the information to plan instruction.	• Teachers correct children's work, but the results are not used to inform curriculum and teaching decisions; children are informed of their weaknesses but are not helped to do better. During most work times, children are expected to work silently and alone on worksheets or other seat work. Children rarely receive encouragment or even permission to help each other in their work.

Appropriate Practices

- By observing and interacting with individuals and small groups during learning experiences, teachers maximize their understanding of children's current capabilities and what each child is capable of doing with scaffolding or other assistance from an adult or peer. To help children acquire new skills or understandings, teachers select instructional strategies, taking into consideration the intellectual demands of the learning task in relation to the participating learners. For example, the teacher first allows the children to explore materials being introduced, next demonstrates a new technique, and then gives structure or cues, such as steps to include in solving the problem. For a more advanced group, the teacher gives only the problem and the resources to solve it.

- Teachers provide many opportunities for children to plan, anticipate, reflect on, and revisit their own learning experiences. They engage children in discussion and representation activities (such as writing, drawing, or constructing models) to help children refine their own concepts and thinking and help themselves understand children's thinking. Teachers use children's own hypotheses about how the world works to engage them in problem solving and experimentation. They share their observations of the learning process and outcomes with the children and use the information gained to inform subsequent instructional decisions.

Inappropriate Practices

- Because children do much seat work or independent work on problems in which teachers only monitor right or wrong answers, teachers have little idea about the processes of children's problem solving or specific areas of difficulty and competence. As a result, teachers do not know how to help children who do not understand or how to further challenge children who get the problem right. Teachers do not intervene when some children get frustrated and fail to learn key concepts and skills or when others are bored and progress far more slowly than they could.

- Teachers are uninvolved in children's projects, play, or other learning experiences, providing minimal guidance or support. Teachers are passive, failing to take action when necessary, assuming that children will develop intellectual and social skills (e.g., negotiation, problem-solving, and conflict-resolution) on their own without adult assistance.

- Feeling pressured to cover the curriculum and believing that returning to the same topic is a waste of time, teachers assume that if they have presented information or provided an experience once, children should have learned the content.

- Expecting children to respond correctly with one right answer most of the time, teachers view children's naive or partial hypotheses as simply wrong answers rather than clues to their thinking or measures of the effectiveness of instructional strategies. Not realizing how much learning young children are capable of, teachers do not engage them in dialogues in which adults show they take children's ideas seriously.

Appropriate Practices

Inappropriate Practices

Teaching to enhance development and learning (cont'd)

Motivation and guidance

- Teachers draw on primary-grade children's eagerness to make sense of the world and to acquire competence by engaging them in interesting and challenging learning experiences. Teachers encourage children to set high but achievable goals for themselves and to tackle challenging problems and tasks. For example, when children impose low thresholds for their own performance ("I can't write a story. I can only write four sentences"), teachers lead them to raise their sights and reach a higher standard ("I'm curious to know what happens next in this story. Tell me about it and I'll help you write it down if you need me to").

- Teachers promote initiative, prosocial behavior, perseverance, task orientation, and self-regulation by providing many engaging activities, encouraging individual choices, allowing ample time for children to complete work, and ensuring numerous opportunities for one-to-one time with the teacher or with close friends.

- Teachers provide many daily opportunities for children to develop social skills, such as helping, cooperating, negotiating, and talking through interpersonal problems with those involved. Teachers facilitate the development of social skills, considered a central part of the curriculum. They intervene promptly when children engage in antisocial behavior and provide timely coaching in development of social skills for those children neglected or rejected by peers.

- A preponderance of experiences that are uninteresting and unchallenging or too difficult and frustrating undermines children's intrinsic motivation to learn. To obtain children's participation in such activities or to get children to complete assignments, teachers typically rely on external rewards (such as stickers, gold stars, candy or privileges, or a grade on each piece of work) or punishments (detention or no recess time).

- Teachers lecture about the importance of appropriate social behavior and use punishment, public humiliation, or deprivations (such as no recess) to enforce rules. They do not have time for private conversations with children, and only the most able students finish their work in time to pursue special interests or interact with other children.

- Children have few opportunities to practice social skills and develop positive peer relationships in the classroom because they are always seated and doing the silent, individual work assigned or are involved in teacher-directed group work. Social interaction occurs almost entirely on the playground, where adults rarely interact with children other than to admonish them to behave.

- Teachers believe that if they ignore unacceptable behavior it will decrease, so they fail to take action when children are not progressing in social skills. For example, children who are persistently taunted or teased by classmates are told to ignore the taunts or "work it out yourselves."

Appropriate Practices

- Teachers promote children's development of respect for others, conscience, and self-control through positive guidance techniques: involving children in establishing clear and reasonable rules for social living and conflict resolution; enforcing clear, consistent consequences for unacceptable, harmful behavior; redirecting children to an acceptable activity; and meeting with an individual child having problems or with the child and parents together. Teachers keep misbehavior in perspective, recognizing that every infraction does not warrant attention and identifying those that can be used as learning opportunities.

Inappropriate Practices

- Teachers do not involve children in setting clear limits and standards of acceptable social behavior. Teachers place themselves in an adversarial role with children, spending considerable time threatening children for lack of impulse control and punishing infractions.

- Teachers do not hold children accountable to acceptable standards of behavior and ignore unacceptable behavior, leaving some children to become bullies and others, victims. Lack of clear limits on unacceptable behavior and disproportionate reliance on children to solve all their own social problems leave the classroom without order and the teacher without authority.

Constructing appropriate curriculum

Integrated curriculum

- The curriculum is designed to develop children's knowledge and skills in all content areas (language and literacy, mathematics, science, social studies, health, physical education, art, and music) and to help children establish a foundation for lifelong learning. Teachers know the content they teach, are familiar with national and local standards for curriculum content, and design curriculum to help children achieve standards for learning, while also supporting their healthy development in all areas (cognitive, social, emotional, and physical).

- The curriculum is organized and integrated so that children acquire deeper understanding of key concepts, skills, and tools of inquiry of each subject area, are able to apply their knowledge in different areas, and also understand the connections between and across disciplines. At times a discipline area, such as reading, math, or science, is the focus of study, but teachers help children see how the skills or concepts addressed relate to learning in other areas. Specialists in art, music, physical education, and other areas work with regular classroom teachers to ensure curriculum integration.

- The curriculum is designed mainly to help children do well on standardized multiple-choice tests that are used for accountability purposes. Narrowly focusing on the acquisition of discrete skills, the curriculum lacks interest and intellectual challenge.

- Teachers have low expectations and water down the curriculum either to avoid pushing children or because they underestimate children's capabilities (for instance, limiting children to one-digit addition when they are capable of understanding larger numbers).

- Curriculum is always divided into separate subjects and a fixed amount of time is allotted for each. Teachers rarely take advantage of the natural opportunities for integration, such as having children write and draw about what they observe in a science experiment.

- Teachers devote so much time to reading and math that other key areas, such as social studies, science, and health, are neglected or included only if time permits. Art, music, and physical education are taught only once a week and rarely integrated into the regular curriculum. Specialists who teach these subjects operate independently of the classroom teachers.

Appropriate Practices	**Inappropriate Practices**

Constructing appropriate curriculum (cont'd)

Integrated curriculum (cont'd)

- The content of the curriculum is integrated, so learning often occurs through engaging activities that reflect current interests of children. Field trips and visits from community resource people are planned to enable children to do direct investigation and first-hand research. For example, in a social studies project involving first-graders in operating a store, children gain a rudimentary understanding of economic principles such as supply and demand and develop math skills related to use of money, pricing, and making change. Such projects offer opportunities for children to plan and predict; share their hypotheses and knowledge; draw, write about, and otherwise represent their understanding; conduct research in resource books; work cooperatively; gain information and skills relevant to subject matter disciplines in context; and acquire a sense of competence.

- Teachers are more focused on carrying out adult-oriented themes (like holiday celebrations) than on incorporating key concepts and skills from the subject-matter disciplines into learning experiences that build on what the children are ready to learn.

- Projects, field trips, play, and outdoor time are seen as embellishments and are offered only if time permits or as reward for good behavior.

The continuum of development and learning

- The curriculum is designed to help children acquire important skills like literacy and numeracy and to learn the key concepts and tools of inquiry of discipline areas in ways that are meaningful and accessible for their developmental level. For example, in social studies 6-year-olds explore local history by taking oral histories of community elders, or 8-year-olds read biographies of American historical figures, but neither age group is expected to place historical events in chronological order by dates.

- Teachers are knowledgeable about the continuum of development and learning for primary-grade children in each content area, and they adapt instruction for children who are ahead of or behind the age-appropriate expectations. For example, while teachers expect that most children will learn to read by the end of first grade, they also understand that some children will continue to need direct instruction in beginning reading skills in second grade and that a few children will need intensive, individualized instruction and literacy experiences to learn to read by age 8 or 9.

- Curriculum expectations are not well matched to most children's developmental level, either exceeding or underestimating children's cognitive capacity. For example, the curriculum requires first-graders to understand such abstract concepts as *north*, *south*, *east*, and *west* or it omits mapping skills as completely beyond this age group. Teachers fail to recognize the continuum of learning in discipline areas for this age group.

- The curriculum lacks intellectual integrity and depth. Content too often is trivial, unimportant, and unworthy of children's attention. Various skills are seen as having to be learned one at a time in rigid, linear progression. For example, teachers expect children to master all phonetic distinctions before exposing them to meaningful text, or they assume that children must perform addition with accuracy before real-life problems calling for addition can be introduced.

170

	Appropriate Practices	**Inappropriate Practices**
Coherent, effective curriculum	• Teachers plan and implement a coherent curriculum to help children achieve important developmental and learning goals, drawing on their knowledge of content areas, the likely interests of children this age, and the community context. For example, 7- and 8-year-old children are usually interested in accumulating collections of objects (such as stamps, coins, and bottle caps). Teachers use this interest to engage children in learning such math skills as number and hierarchical classification. In a fishing community teachers might engage children in related classification tasks (such as with fishing lures, boats, and species). Teachers also recognize that learning experiences are more effective when the curriculum is responsive to children's interests and ideas as these emerge. For example, children's interest in buried treasure, after several of them read a book on the topic, is the catalyst for introducing a series of experiences on mapping and reading maps.	• Teachers rigidly follow a prescribed curriculum plan (sometimes commercially prepared or adopted across an entire district or school) without attention to individual children's interests and needs or the specific and changing community context.
		• There is little or no accountability for children's achieving a core set of skills. Teachers do not adequately plan experiences and thus the curriculum is fragmented.
	• Teachers plan curriculum that is responsive to the specific context of children's experiences. Culturally diverse and nonsexist activities and materials are provided to support individual children's development of self-identity, to help children construct understanding of new concepts by building on prior knowledge and creating shared meaning, and to enrich the lives of all children with respectful acceptance and appreciation of differences and similarities. Books and other learning materials reflect the great diversity of the community, country, and world.	• Multicultural curriculum reflects a "tourist approach" in which artifacts or other particulars of various cultures are presented as foreign, exotic, or marginal.
		• Children's language, family or cultural background, and other individual differences are ignored, devalued, or treated as deviations from the "normal" majority culture.

| **Appropriate Practices** | **Inappropriate Practices** |

Constructing appropriate curriculum (cont'd)

Curriculum content

• The goals of the **language and literacy** program are for children to expand their ability to communicate through speaking, listening, reading, and writing and to develop the ability and disposition to acquire knowledge through reading. Technical skills or subskills, such as those related to phonics, word recognition, capitalization, and punctuation, are taught in ways that are meaningful to children. Teachers support the development of children's spelling ability from temporary "invented" spelling toward the goal of conventional spelling, with minimal reliance on teacher-prescribed spelling lists.

Teachers provide generous amounts of time and a variety of interesting activities for children to develop language, writing, spelling, and reading abilities. Children have numerous opportunities to read or hear high-quality children's literature and nonfiction for pleasure and information; discuss readings; draw, dictate, and write about their experiences; plan and implement projects involving research at suitable levels of difficulty; jointly create with teachers lists of steps to follow in accomplishing a project; interview various people to obtain information for projects; make books (e.g., riddle books, "what if" books, books about pets); listen to recordings or view films of children's books; and use the school library and classroom reading areas regularly. Teachers also teach literacy skills when children are working on science, social studies, and other content areas.

• Reading is taught only as the acquisition of discrete skills and subskills. Teachers teach reading primarily as a separate subject and do not capitalize on the possibilities for furthering children's progress in reading when teaching other subjects. Language, writing, and spelling instruction relies heavily on workbooks. Children are rarely given the opportunity to revise their work, so they are unable to acquire a sense of the writing process. Children's writing efforts are rejected or downgraded if correct spelling and standard English are not used.

• The focus of the reading program is the basal reader, used primarily in reading groups and with accompanying workbooks and worksheets. Even capable readers must complete the same worksheets and the basal reader, although they have skills and interests in reading far more advanced material. Less able readers are given very limited exposure to interesting text. Through the groupings teachers use, they make it clear which children are in the slowest reading group.

• With a lack of specified goals for the language and literacy program and standards for achievement, teachers make little effort to further children's progress in reading and writing, and children fail to acquire fundamental literacy skills.

• Curriculum approaches are adopted without being well understood by teachers. For example, teachers who fail to understand the purpose of "invented spelling" may refuse a child's request for the conventional spelling of a word, not recognizing that the educational use of invented spelling is to expand children's construction of letter/sound relationships and enable beginning writers to proceed without constant teacher help and correction.

Appropriate Practices

- The **mathematics** program is designed to help children acquire and apply understanding of mathematics concepts and skills. Teachers plan for children to learn mathematical concepts through solving meaningful problems. Math skills and problem solving are the focus of instruction and are also fostered through spontaneous play, projects, and situations of daily living. A variety of math manipulatives and games is provided and used to aid concept development and application of mathematics. Noncompetitive, oral "math-stumper" and number games are played for practice. Math activities are integrated with other relevant projects, such as those in science and social studies.

- A **social studies** topic is identified as the focus of in-depth work for an extended period of time. Key knowledge and concepts in the various related social studies domains (history, geography, economics, civics) are learned through a variety of projects and activities involving use of library resources, visits to sites and interviews of visitors, discussions, relevant use of language and writing and reading skills, and opportunities for developing social skills, such as planning and working in committees. The classroom is treated as a laboratory of social relations where children learn rules of social responsibility and respect for individual differences through structured experiences directed toward those goals. Relevant art, music, dance, drama, games, and other activities are integrated in social studies.

Inappropriate Practices

- Math is taught only as a set of facts and skills to memorize, and many children have insufficient time or opportunity to develop understanding of mathematical concepts or the ability to apply math to problems of various kinds. Children have few opportunities for hands-on activities or small-group problem-solving projects in which they need to use math. Only children who finish their math seat work get the chance to use the few math manipulatives and games in the classroom. Teachers frequently give and grade timed tests on number facts.

- In trying to integrate curriculum, teachers assume that they teach math "in everything," and no systematic focus or engaged time is spent on helping children acquire the continuum of math skills and understanding. Teachers assume that the availability of math manipulatives alone is sufficient for children to construct mathematical skills and concepts. Opportunities to focus on mathematics are few because children are distracted by many other activities. Children who do not have an affinity for math make little progress in mathematical concepts and skills.

- Social studies instruction is included sporadically. Social studies projects, often related to holidays, consist of completing brief activities from the social studies textbook or reading a commercially developed weekly newspaper and doing the accompanying seat work.

- Social studies curriculum content is too abstract and far removed from children's experience (such as geographic concepts like latitude) or underestimates children's capacity and never goes beyond a constricted range of very familiar experiences (such as limiting study to "our families" or "community helpers"). There is little recognition that children's firsthand experiences now go beyond their immediate physical environments (through communication with faraway people and places via technology or travel) and that by the primary grades the curriculum should expand children's experiences and learning.

173

Appropriate Practices	**Inappropriate Practices**

Constructing appropriate curriculum (cont'd)

Curriculum content (cont'd)

- **Science** is a major part of the curriculum, building on children's natural interest in the world and offering rich opportunities for fostering development of thinking skills. Science projects are experimental and exploratory and encourage every child's active engagement in the scientific process. The science program takes advantage of local outdoor environments for children to explore and study. Through science investigations, resource books, and field trips, children learn to plan; dictate and/or write their plans; apply thinking skills such as predicting, hypothesizing, observing, experimenting, and verifying; and utilize many key science concepts and processes related to these experiences.

- A variety of **health and safety** projects (for example, in nutrition, dental health, exercise, personal hygiene, prevention of substance abuse) are designed to help children learn important concepts about health and safety, integrate their learning into daily habits, and incorporate health practices and routines into their daily lives at home and at school.

- **Art, music, drama, dance,** and other fine arts are the explicit focus of children's study at times. On other occasions when relevant, the fine arts are integrated in other areas of the curriculum, such as social studies or mathematics. Children are encouraged to express themselves physically and aesthetically, represent ideas and feelings, and acquire fundamental concepts and skills in the fine arts. Classroom teachers work with specialists in the arts to help children explore and experiment with various art media and music forms. The school demonstrates that all children's artistic creations are valued by displaying children's works of art, providing regular opportunities for performances, and developing children's appreciation for the arts.

- Discovery science may be the goal but hands-on activities do not reflect the key concepts of the discipline and do not promote children's understanding of key concepts. Hands-on experiments or demonstrations leave children with shallow understanding of the observed phenomenon rather than provide opportunities for serious questioning and hypothesis testing.

- Science is rarely taught and then only from a single textbook. Children complete related worksheets on science topics. Science consists of memorizing facts or watching teacher demonstrations. Field trips related to science occur rarely or not at all. The science area may have a few plants, seashells, or pine cones, but these items remain there for many months, essentially ignored by the children and the teacher.

- Health instruction is limited to a health lesson scheduled once a week or a unit on health completed once a year. Teachers teach health as a list of prohibited behaviors rather than help children acquire understanding and concepts related to health and safety.

- Art, music, drama, and dance opportunities and materials are available, but children are not supported in moving beyond the exploration level. No attempt is made to support the acquisition of fundamental skills and processes in these curriculum areas.

- Art and music are taught as separate subjects once a week or less often. Specialists do not coordinate closely with classroom teachers. Adults expect children to follow specific directions, resulting in similar products that conform to adult representations. Group-copied crafts substitute for individual artistic expression. The talents of only a few children as artists or musicians, usually those who have received private instruction, are displayed in exhibits or performances.

Appropriate Practices	**Inappropriate Practices**

Appropriate Practices

- **Physical education** is an integral part of the curriculum. Children have opportunities to actively participate in motor-development activities, games, sports, recreation, or dance. Children develop and refine motor skills in planned movement activity both indoors and outdoors. Specialists communicate with classroom teachers about children's physical development. Safe play equipment, such as balls and bats, jump ropes, hoops, balance beams, ladders, and climbing structures, that interests this age group and promotes their skill development is available. Adults assist children in acquiring and refining physical skills.

- Outdoor activity is planned and provided daily so that children can learn about outdoor environments, experience unstructured time, get fresh air, and play and express themselves freely and loudly. Safe, age-appropriate equipment and play spaces are available for children to play games and sports. Places are also available for quiet reflection or nature study. Teachers support children's engagement in physical activity.

- Playground equipment and design conform to nationally recognized standards for protection of children's health and safety and are regularly monitored and maintained by adults.

Inappropriate Practices

- During physical education periods, children spend more time receiving instructions, watching, or waiting their turn than participating. Physical education emphasizes competition, with teams picked in ways that make some children feel inadequate or unpopular. Adults fail to provide systematic support and coaching to help every child acquire movement skills; as a result, some children progress and others, who do not have opportunities for motor-skill development at home, may be left behind.

- During physical education or recess, children are required to participate in sports for which they are not yet physically mature, such as having 6- or 7-year-olds play baseball or basketball without any accommodations for their size. Adults yell at children to pay attention, catch the ball, or perform skills that children clearly are not capable of.

- Outdoor time is limited because it is viewed as interfering with instructional time or, if provided, is viewed strictly as recess (a way for children to use up excess energy). With minimal supervision by adults (who use this time for personal breaks), outdoor time becomes a free-for-all with aggressive behavior going uncontrolled.

- Teachers make outdoor activity available daily but do nothing to make this time valuable for children in developing fundamental motor and social skills.

- Playground equipment and space do not meet health and safety standards and are not maintained or monitored regularly.

Assessing children's learning and development

Appropriate Practices

- Teachers assess each child's learning progress primarily through written records of observation and evaluation of work samples collected systematically at regular intervals. Results of assessment are used to improve and individualize instruction. Teachers involve children in evaluating and revising their own work, helping them to understand and learn from their errors. Parents also participate in assessment of children's learning progress.

Inappropriate Practices

- Children are tested regularly on each subject, and teachers "teach to the test" to ensure higher scores.

- Teachers claim to place great emphasis on children developing at their own rate and pace, but they fail to see the need for adaptation in content, processes, or strategies when children do not make expected progress.

175

Appropriate Practices	**Inappropriate Practices**

Assessing children's learning and development (cont'd)

• Teachers and parents share useful, specific feedback about individual children's learning and developmental strengths and needs. Children's progress is shared with parents in the form of narrative comments following an outline of topics and in language that parents understand. A child's progress is reported in comparison to his or her own previous performance, and parents are given general information about how the child compares to age-related expectations. Letter or numerical grades are considered inadequate reflections of children's ongoing learning.	• Teachers report children's progress to parents only in letter or numerical grades. Parents do not get clear information about children's capabilities and areas of difficulty. Emphasis is on how well the child compares to others in the same grade and to standardized national averages.
• Teachers solicit parents' knowledge about children's learning and developmental progress and incorporate this information into ongoing assessment and evaluation strategies.	• Parental perceptions and observations of children's intellectual, social, and motor development are not considered in the assessment process or for the determination of instructional goals.
• Children make continuous learning progress. Because they advance through sequential curriculum at different paces, children can progress in all areas as they acquire competence. Children who fall behind receive individualized support, such as tutoring, personal instruction, focused time on areas of difficulty, and other strategies to accelerate learning progress. Efforts are made to avoid grade retention of children who fail to make expected progress, because retention generally does not improve achievement and harmfully alters children's attitude toward school.	• Children repeat a grade or are placed in a special "transition" grade if they have not mastered the expected reading and math skills. It is assumed that their performance will improve with repetition or as they mature. Many placement decisions are based on children's ability to sit still and complete paperwork, follow directions, and read at or near grade level.
	• Social promotion (children advancing in grade level but not necessarily in learning) is used as the alternative to retention, without adapting teaching strategies or trying other approaches and interventions (individualized instruction or more time) for children who are not making adequate progress.

Establishing reciprocal relationships with parents

• Teachers and administrators view parents as partners in the educational process. Teachers have time for periodic conferences with each child's parents; conferences may include the teacher, parents, and the child. Parents' visits to school are welcomed at all times, and home visits by teachers are encouraged and supported. Opportunities for parent participation are arranged to accommodate parents' schedules. Goals and celebrations of learning are shared with all who are involved.	• The administration does not give teachers adequate time for work with parents. Subtle messages convey that schools are for teachers and children, not parents. Parent meetings or other participation opportunities occur only during the day when many employed parents are unavailable. Teachers view parents' role as supporting but not participating in determining the school's agenda.

Appropriate Practices	**Inappropriate Practices**
• Educators and parents share decisions about children's education. Teachers listen to parents and seek to understand their goals for their children. Teachers work with parents to resolve problems or differences of opinion as they arise and are respectful of cultural and family differences.	• School personnel do not involve parents in decisions about how best to handle children's problems or support their learning. They see parents in a negative light, complaining that they have not raised their children well or blaming children's poor school performance on the home environment.
	• Teachers make only formal contacts with parents through report cards and one yearly conference.
• Members of each child's family are encouraged to participate in the classroom in ways that they feel comfortable. For example, family members may take part in classroom activities (sharing a cultural event or language, telling or reading a story, tutoring, making learning materials, or playing games), contribute to activities related to but not occurring within the classroom (designing or sewing costumes, working in the school library), or participate in decisionmaking.	• Schedules are so tight that parents are seen as one more frustration to teachers who need to "cover the curriculum." A policy for parent participation exists, but it receives little time or effort.

Policies

Staffing, grouping, and environment

• Class size and ratio of adults to children are carefully regulated to allow active involvement of children and planning time for teachers. Teachers have time to plan and prepare group work that integrates learning and skills in many subject areas and relates to children's interests, plan for and work with individual children having special needs or interests, plan and work with parents, and coordinate with other teachers, teams of specialists, and administrators involved in each child's school experience. Optimum group size for classes of 6-, 7-, or 8-year-olds is 15 to 18 children with one adult, or up to 25 with a second adult.	• Classrooms consist of more than 25 children, which keeps teachers from individualizing instruction. Teachers have very little time to encourage and maintain parent involvement or to coordinate with other teachers or specialists.
• Six- through 8-year-old children are assigned a primary teacher and remain in relatively small groups of 15 to 25 because so much of their learning and development is integrated and cannot be divided into separate subjects each taught by a different teacher. In planning the curriculum and learning experiences, the classroom teacher works with any specialists who supplement the regular program (e.g., in physical education) and colleagues who have special expertise in an area.	• Departmentalized settings with groups of 80 or more children and a team of teachers are common. Teachers teach their special areas of interest in isolation of one another. Children move from one subject area to another, eliminating the possibility for integration of curriculum. Teachers do not have enough time to get to know each child and establish relationships with children and their families.

Appropriate Practices	**Inappropriate Practices**

Policies (cont'd)

Staffing, grouping, and environment (cont'd)

- Adults assist children in making smooth transitions from one program or group to another throughout the day. Teachers provide program continuity, maintain ongoing communication, prepare children for the transition, involve parents, and minimize the number of transitions necessary.

- Teachers assist children in making smooth transitions from one grade level or group (in a multiage setting) to another by providing program continuity, maintaining communication, preparing children, and involving parents and colleagues.

- The school environment is safe, comfortable, and aesthetically pleasing, with adequate heating/cooling and sufficient space so that children are not overly crowded.

- A child's day is fragmented among many different groups and programs, with little attempt by adults to communicate or coordinate successful transitions.

- Great disparity in the expectations, teaching strategies, or academic demands from one grade to the next (such as from kindergarten to first grade) creates excessive stress and discontinuity for children. Lack of communication or planning between the personnel responsible for children's education at various levels exacerbates the difficulty of transitions for children.

- Teachers and children become isolated in an age group, with no opportunity for interaction with others in different grade levels.

- The school environment is unhealthy and/or unsafe. Limited space for learning opportunities contributes to frustration, conflict, and unhealthy conditions.

Staff qualifications and development

- Teachers are qualified to work with 6- through 8-year-olds through early childhood education degree programs or elementary education degree programs with a concentrated course of study in early childhood education. These studies include supervised field experience with the primary-school age group and required course work in child development and learning, integrated curriculum and instructional strategies, and communication with families.

- Through ongoing professional development opportunities, teachers are able to remain knowledgeable and current with respect to best practices and innovations. They have time to become familiar with and adapt new curriculum resources. Opportunities are available for teachers to plan, reflect on their practices, collaborate with colleagues, and work with parents.

- Elementary or secondary teachers with no specialized training or field experience in working with 6- through 8-year-olds are considered qualified because they are state certified, despite the grade level for which their course work and teaching experience prepared them.

- Teachers may participate in continuing professional development to maintain certification, but courses are often unrelated to the primary-school-age group. Professional development opportunities for teachers are fragmented or irrelevant to their work.

Appropriate Practices	**Inappropriate Practices**
• Administrators responsible for programs serving primary-age children have professional preparation or inservice training relevant to development and learning of this age group, and the training includes how to establish positive relationships with families.	• Administrators of primary-school-age programs have expertise in management but no specialized preparation or inservice training relevant to the education and development of young children. Administrators do not attend or seek out relevant professional development opportunities.

Teachers observe children in the classroom, examine samples of their work, and document their learning and development in order to shape the curriculum and plan for each child's individual needs.

References

Alexander, K., & D. Entwisle. 1988. *Achievement in the first 2 years of school: Patterns and processes.* Monographs of the Society for Research in Child Development, vol. 53, no. 1, serial no. 218. Chicago: University of Chicago Press.

American Association of Family and Consumer Sciences. 1993. *Developmentally appropriate practice in school-age child care programs.* 2d ed. Alexandria, VA: Author.

Asher, S.R., & G.A. Williams. 1987. Helping children without friends in home and school contexts. In *Children's social development: Information for teachers and parents.* Urbana, IL: ERIC Clearinghouse on Elementary and Early Childhood Education.

Asher, S., S. Hymel, & P. Renshaw. 1984. Loneliness in children. *Child Development* 55: 1456–64.

Asher, S., P. Renshaw, & S. Hymel. 1982. Peer relations and the development of social skills. In *The young child: Reviews of research,* vol. 3, eds. S. Moore & C. Cooper, 137–58. Washington, DC: NAEYC.

August, D., & E. Garcia. 1988. *Language minority education in the United States.* Springfield, IL: Thomas.

Barton, K.C., & L.S. Levstik. 1996. "Back when God was around and everything": Elementary children's understanding of historical time. *American Educational Research Journal* 33 (2): 419–54.

Battistich, V., D. Solomon, D. Kim, M. Watson, & E. Schaps. 1995. Schools as communities, poverty levels of student populations, and students' attitudes, motives, and performance: A multilevel analysis. *American Educational Research Journal* 32 (3): 627–58.

Bennett, W. 1995. *The book of virtues: A treasury of great moral stories.* New York: Simon & Schuster.

Berk, L. 1996. *Infants and children: Prenatal through middle childhood.* 2d ed. Boston: Allyn & Bacon.

Bowman, B. 1994. The challenge of diversity. *Phi Delta Kappan* 76 (3): 218–25.

Boyer, E. 1995. *The basic school: A community of learners.* Princeton, NJ: Carnegie Foundation for the Advancement of Teaching.

Bredekamp, S., & T. Rosegrant. 1995. Transforming curriculum organization. In *Reaching potentials: Transforming early childhood curriculum and assessment, volume 2,* eds. S. Bredekamp & T. Rosegrant, 167–76. Washington, DC: NAEYC.

Burton, C.B. 1987. Children's peer relationships. In *Children's social development: Information for teachers and parents.* Urbana, IL: ERIC Clearinghouse on Elementary and Early Childhood Education.

Caine, R., & G. Caine. 1994. *Making connections: Teaching and the human brain.* Alexandria, VA: Association for Supervision and Curriculum Development.

Campbell, J.R., P.L. Donahue, C.M. Reese, & G.W. Phillips. 1996. *NAEP 1994 reading report card for the nation and the states. Findings from the National Assessment of Education Progress and Trial State Assessment.* Washington, DC: National Center for Education Statistics, Office of Educational Research and Improvement, U.S. Department of Education.

Carnegie Task Force on Learning in the Primary Grades. 1996. *Years of promise: A comprehensive learning strategy for America's children.* New York: Carnegie Corporation of New York.

Case, R., & Y. Okamoto. 1996. *The role of central conceptual structures in the development of children's thought.* Monographs of the Society for Research in Child Development, vol. 61, no. 2, serial no. 246. Chicago: University of Chicago Press.

Chang-Wells, G., & G. Wells. 1993. Dynamics of discourse: Literacy and the construction of knowledge. In *Contexts for learning: Sociocultural dynamics in children's development,* eds. E.A. Forman, N. Minick, & C.A. Stone, 58–90. New York: Oxford University Press.

Character Counts! Coalition. 1996. *Character counts: Important facts.* Marina del Rey, CA: Josephson Institute of Ethics.

Chugani, H.T. 1996. Neuroimaging of developmental non-linearity and developmental pathologies. In *Developmental neuroimaging: Mapping the development of brain and behavior,* eds. R.W. Thatcher, G.R. Lyon, J. Rumsey, & N. Krasnegor. San Diego: Academic.

Clements, D., & S. McMillen. 1996. Rethinking "concrete" manipulatives. *Teaching Children Mathematics* (January): 270–79.

Cobb, P., T. Wood, & E. Yackel. 1993. Discourse, mathematical thinking, and classroom practice. In *Contexts for learning: Sociocultural dynamics in children's development,* eds. E.A. Forman, N. Minick, & C.A. Stone, 91–119. New York: Oxford University Press.

Comer, J. 1988. Educating poor minority children. *Scientific American* 259: 42–48.

Comer, J. 1993. *School power: Implications of an intervention project.* New York: Free Press.

Copple, C. 1992. *Starting right: Reforming education in the early grades (prekindergarten through grade 3).* New York: Carnegie Corporation of New York.

Covington, M.V. 1984. The motive for self-worth. In *Research on motivation in education: Vol. 1. Student motivation,* eds. R. Ames & C. Ames, 78–113. New York: Academic.

Cowen, E., A. Pederson, M. Babigian, L. Izzo, & M. Trost. 1973. Long-term follow-up of early detected vulnerable children. *Journal of Consulting and Clinical Psychology* 41: 438–46.

Dana Alliance on Brain Initiatives. 1996. *Delivering results: A progress report on brain research.* Washington, DC: Author.

Douglas, V. 1983. Attentional and cognitive problems. In *Developmental neuropsychiatry,* ed. M. Rutter, 280–329. New York: Guilford.

Durkin, D. 1980. *Teaching young children to read.* Boston: Allyn & Bacon.

Durkin, D. 1987. A classroom-observation study of reading instruction in kindergarten. *Early Childhood Research Quarterly* 2 (3): 275–300.

Durkin, D. 1990. Reading instruction in kindergarten: A look at some issues through the lens of new basal reader materials. *Early Childhood Research Quarterly* 5 (3): 299–316.

Dweck, C. 1986. Motivational processes affecting learning. *American Psychologist* 41: 1040–48.

Elkind, D. 1981. *Children and adolescents: Interpretive essays on Jean Piaget.* New York: Oxford University Press.

Elkind, D. 1987. *Miseducation: Preschoolers at risk.* New York: Knopf.

Erikson, E. 1963. *Childhood and society.* New York: Norton.

Forman, E.A., N. Minick, & C.A. Stone. 1993. *Contexts for learning: Sociocultural dynamics in children's development.* New York: Oxford University Press.

Furman, E. 1980. Early latency: Normal and pathological aspects. In *The course of life: Vol. 2. Latency, adolescence and youth,* eds. S. Greenspan & G. Pollock. Washington, DC: National Institute of Mental Health, U.S. Department of Health & Human Services.

Furman, E. 1987. The teacher's guide to helping young children grow. Madison, CT: International Universities Press.

Garcia, E., & C. Baker, eds. 1995. *Policy and practice in bilingual education: Extending the foundation.* Bristol, PA: Multilingual Matters.

Gardner, H. 1983. *Frames of mind.* New York: Basic.

Gardner, H. 1991. *The unschooled mind: How children think and how schools should teach.* New York: Basic.

Gelman, R., & R. Baillargeon. 1983. A review of some Piagetian concepts. In *Handbook of child psychology,* vol. 3, ed. P.H. Mussen, 167–230. New York: Wiley.

Gottfried, A. 1983. Intrinsic motivation in young children. *Young Children* 39 (1): 64–73.

Gronlund, N., & W. Holmlund. 1985. The value of elementary school sociometric status scores for predicting pupils' adjustment in high school. *Educational Administration and Supervision* 44: 225–60.

Hakuta, K., B. Ferdman, & R. Diaz. 1987. Bilingualism and cognitive development: Three perspectives. In *Advances in applied psycholinguistics: Reading, writing, and language learning, Vol. 2*, ed. S. Rosenberg, 284–319. New York: Cambridge University Press.

Hale, J. 1994. *Unbank the fire: Visions for the education of African-American children.* Baltimore: Johns Hopkins University Press.

Hale-Benson, J. 1986. *Black children: Their roots, cultures, and learning styles.* Baltimore: Johns Hopkins University Press.

Harris, A.C. 1986. *Child development.* St. Paul, MN: West.

Harter, S. 1990. Causes, correlates, and the functional role of global self-worth: A life-span perspective. In *Perceptions of competence and incompetence across the life span*, eds. J. Kolligan & R. Sternberg. New Haven, CT: Yale University Press.

Hills, T. 1986. *Classroom motivation: Helping students want to learn and achieve in school.* Trenton: New Jersey Department of Education.

Inhelder, B., & J. Piaget. 1964. *The early growth of logic in the child.* London: Routledge & Kegan Paul.

Irwin, D.M., & S.R. Ambron. 1973. Moral judgment and role-taking in children ages three to seven. Paper presented at the biennial meeting of the Society for Research in Child Development, Philadelphia.

Kamii, C. 1985. Leading primary education toward excellence: Beyond worksheets and drill. *Young Children* 40 (6): 3–9.

Katz, L. 1985. Dispositions in early childhood education. *ERIC/EECE Bulletin* 18 (2): 1, 3.

Katz, L., & S. Chard. 1989. *Engaging children's minds: The project approach.* Norwood, NJ: Ablex.

Koralek, D.G., L.J. Colker, & D.T. Dodge. 1995. *The what, why, and how of high-quality early childhood education: A guide for on-site supervision.* Rev. ed. Washington, DC: NAEYC.

Koralek, D.G., R.L. Newman, & L.J. Colker, eds. 1995. *Caring for children in school-age programs.* Vols. 1 & 2. Washington, DC: Teaching Strategies.

Krogh, S. 1995. *The integrated early childhood curriculum.* New York: McGraw-Hill.

Lewis, C., E. Schaps, & M. Watson. 1996. The caring classroom's academic edge. *Educational Leadership* 54 (1): 16–21.

Lickona, T. 1992. *Educating for character: How our schools can teach respect and responsibility.* New York: Bantam.

McFarland, S. 1992. Personal communication, July.

Metz, K. 1995. Reassessment of developmental constraints on children's science instruction. *Review of Educational Research* 65 (2): 93–127.

Mullis, I., J. Dossey, M. Foertsch, L. Jones, & C. Gentile. 1991. *Trends in academic progress.* Washington, DC: National Center for Education Statistics, U.S. Department of Education.

Mullis, I., J. Dossey, J. Campbell, C. Gentile, C. O'Sullivan, & A. Latham. 1994. *NAEP 1992 trends in academic progress.* Washington, DC: National Center for Education Statistics, U.S. Department of Education.

NAEYC. 1996. NAEYC position statement: Responding to linguistic and cultural diversity—Recommendations for effective early childhood education. *Young Children* 51 (2): 4–12.

National School-Age Care Alliance. 1995. *Pilot standards for quality school-age child care.* Indianapolis: Author.

NCC (National Commission on Children). 1993. *Increasing educational attainment.* Washington, DC: Author.

NEGP (National Education Goals Panel). 1996. *Profile of 1994–95. State assessment systems and reported results.* Washington, DC: Author.

Nelson, K. 1985. *Making sense: The acquisition of shared meaning.* New York: Academic.

Noddings, N. 1992. *The challenge to care in schools: An alternative approach to education.* New York: Teachers College Press.

Palincsar, A.S., A.L. Brown, & J.C. Campione. 1993. First-grade dialogues for knowledge acquisition and use. In *Contexts for learning: Sociocultural dynamics in children's development*, eds. E.A. Forman, N. Minick, & C.A.Stone, 43–57. New York: Oxford University Press.

Parker, J., & S. Asher. 1987. Predicting later outcomes from peer rejection: Studies of school drop out, delinquency, and adult psychopathology. *Psychology Bulletin* 102 (3): 357–89.

Piaget, J. 1952. *The child's conception of number.* London: Routledge & Kegan Paul.

Piaget, J. [1932] 1965. *The moral judgement of the child.* New York: Free Press.

Piaget, J., & B. Inhelder. 1969. *The psychology of the child.* New York: Basic.

Rogoff, B., M. Sellers, S. Pirotta, N. Fox, & S. White. 1975. Age of assignment of roles and responsibilities to children. *Human Development* 18: 353–69.

Sameroff, A., & S. McDonough. 1994. Educational implications of developmental transitions: Revisiting the 5- to 7-year shift. *Phi Delta Kappan* 76 (3): 188–93.

Schweinhart, L., D. Weikart, & M. Larner. 1986. Consequences of three preschool curriculum models through age 15. *Early Childhood Research Quarterly* 1 (1): 15–46.

Shantz, C.U. 1975. The development of social cognition. In *Review of child development research*, vol. 5, ed. E.M. Hetherington, 257–353. Chicago: University of Chicago Press.

Sroufe, L.A., R.G. Cooper, & G.B. DeHart. 1992. *Child development: Its nature and course.* New York: Knopf.

Stipek, D. 1984. The development of achievement motivation. In *Research on motivation in education: Vol. 1. Student motivation*, eds. R. Ames & C. Ames, 145–74. New York: Academic.

Sylvester, R. 1995. *A celebration of neurons: An educator's guide to the human brain.* Alexandria, VA: Association for Supervision and Curriculum Development.

Thornton, S., & R. Vukelich. 1988. Effects of children's understanding of time concepts on historical understanding. *Theory and Research in Social Education* 16: 69–82.

Vygotsky, L. 1978. *Mind in society: The development of higher pschological processes.* Cambridge, MA: Harvard University Press.

Walberg, H. 1984. Improving the productivity of America's schools. *Educational Leadership* 41 (8): 19–30.

Weissbourd, R. 1996. The feel-good trap. *The New Republic* 19 & 26 August: 12–14.

Wells, G. 1983. Talking with children: The complementary roles of parents and teachers. In *Early childhood development and education*, eds. M. Donaldson, R. Grieve, & C. Pratt, 127–50. New York: Guilford.

White, S. 1965. Evidence for a hierarchical arrangement of learning processes. In *Advances in child development and behavior*, eds. L.P. Lipsitt & C.S. Spiker, 187–220. New York: Academic.

Wilkinson, L. 1984. Research currents: Peer group talk in elementary school. *Language Arts* 61 (2): 164–69.

Wong Fillmore, L. 1991. When learning a second language means losing the first. *Early Childhood Research Quarterly* 6 (3): 323–46.

Wright, J., & D. Shade, eds. 1994. *Young children: Active learners in a technological age.* Washington, DC: NAEYC.

Index

Information about NAEYC

NAEYC is . . .

a membership-supported organization of people committed to fostering the growth and development of children from birth through age 8. Membership is open to all who share a desire to serve and act on behalf of the needs and rights of young children.

NAEYC provides . . .

educational services and resources to adults who work with and for children, including

- *Young Children,* the journal for early childhood educators
- **Books, posters, brochures,** and **videos** to expand your knowledge and commitment to young children, with topics including infants, curriculum, research, discipline, teacher education, and parent involvement
- An **Annual Conference** that brings people together from all over the country to share their expertise and advocate on behalf of children and families
- **Week of the Young Child** celebrations sponsored by NAEYC Affiliate Groups across the nation to call public attention to the needs and rights of children and families
- **Insurance plans** for individuals and programs
- **Public affairs** information and access to information available through NAEYC resources and communication systems for knowledgeable advocacy efforts at all levels of government and through the media
- The **National Academy of Early Childhood Programs,** a voluntary accreditation system for high-quality programs for children
- The **National Institute for Early Childhood Professional Development,** which offers resources and services to improve professional preparation and development of early childhood educators
- **Young Children International** to promote international communication and information exchanges

For free information about membership, publications, or other NAEYC services, visit the **NAEYC** Website at http://www.naeyc.org

National Association for the Education of Young Children
1509 16th Street, NW
Washington, DC 20036-1426
202-232-8777 or 800-424-2460